Committees and Commissions in India
1980

Concepts in Communication
Informatics & Librarianship-56

General Editor : **S.P. Agrawal**

Committees and Commissions in India 1980

Volume 18

PART B

A Concept's Project

Compiled by a team of professionals
under the guidance of
VIRENDRA KUMAR

CONCEPT PUBLISHING COMPANY, NEW DELHI 110059

ISBN 81-7022-511-6 (Vol. 18, Part B)

First Published 1994

Published and Printed by
Ashok Kumar Mittal
Concept Publishing Company
A/15-16, Commercial Block, Mohan Garden
NEW DELHI 110059 (India)

Lasertypeset by
Printing Express
H-13, Bali Nagar
NEW DELHI 110015

CONTENTS

PART A

PART B

11

STUDY GROUP ON INSAT TELEVISION UTILIZATION FOR EDUCATION AND DEVELOPMENT, 1980 — REPORT[1]

Chairman Shri S. Sathyam
Members Dr. T.N. Dhar; Prof. C. Srinivasan, Shri P.V. Krishnamoorthy.
M. Secy. Miss S. Rahman.

Appointment

In July 1979, Ministry of Education took steps to develop a plan of operation for the liberalisation of television and other facilities that would become available with the launching of the first Indian satellite then expected in mid-1981. In view of the experience and involvement of the Space Application Centre, Ahmedabad in different aspects of television, it was decided to elicit their cooperation in preparing a basic document for consideration and discussion. It was expected that the document would provide, among other things, an outline of the institutional, human, technical and financial resource available, and those that could be developed in the country, and were necessary for a national system of utilisation of television for education. In response to the Ministry's request, the Space Application Centre prepared a background paper entitled *INSAT Utilisation for Education and development*. The paper provided a brief description of the INSAT capabilities, the ground segment requirements for TV, the possible hardware required for utilisation of the satellite for developmental communication, and an approach to developing a design for the purpose.

On January 30, 1980 a meeting was convened by the Ministry of Education to discuss the background paper and all connected issues in-

1. New Delhi, Ministry of Education and Culture, 1981, 70 p.

volved in the development of a national plan of operation for the utilisation of radio and television facilities that would become available with the launching of satellite. The meeting was held under the chairmanship of Education Secretary and attended by representatives of the Space Application Centre, Ministry of Information and Broadcasting, Doordarshan, All India Radio, Planning Commission, National Council of Educational Research and Training, Directorate of Adult Education, University Grants Commission and the Ministry of Education.

At the meeting, it was agreed that an allout effort should be made to take the fullest advantage of the radio and television facilities and for that purpose detailed plans should be prepared. To this end it was decided that urgent steps should be taken to involve all user Ministries in the preparation of a software plan for INSAT utilisation. The meeting for the purpose was to be convened by the Ministry of Education as the largest user Ministry or the Ministry of I&B as the nodal Ministry of Broadcasting. It was also decided that the Ministry of Education as an important user Ministry would have its own group for preparing plans for the educational component.

Immediately thereafter, on February 2, 1980, the Ministry of Information and Broadcasting set up a Working Group to draw up a detailed software plan for utilisation of INSAT through the medium of television. The Working Group consisted of representatives of all user Ministries (Agriculture, Education, Health and Rural Reconstruction), Planning Commission, Space Application Centre, Doordarshan and Department of Electronics, under the Chairmanship of Secretary, Ministry of Information and Broadcasting. The Working Group was assisted by four Sub-Groups namely:

(i) for identification of programmes, priorities, areas of application and time frame,
(ii) on manpower planning,
(iii) on training aspects, and
(iv) on deployment of Community TV sets.

The Report of the Working Group was completed in September, 1980.

On the question of responsibility for producing programmes, the Working Group recommended that the concerned Ministries and their associated agencies should develop programme production, capability and take upon themselves specific responsibility for producing programmes. After due consideration, the Ministry of Education took the decision that the educational authorities will take the responsibility for the production of programmes intended for their specific uses. The decision was conveyed to the Working Group.

The Ministry of Education also indicated to the Working Group that the major educational objective for setallite television would be to promote alternative approaches to education for children, youth and adults. The thrust of the specific programmes would be to emphasize direct teaching, moving away from curriculum-oriented approach and aim at reduction of load in the class room, and improve the quality of programmes through training of manpower.

The Ministry of Education set up a Study Group to plan the educational component of INSAT television utilization keeping in view these two major decisions in May 1980.

Terms of Reference

(i) To define the role of television in education and its application in the priority areas;

(ii) To prepare software plans for geographical areas and languages to be covered initially;

(iii) To identify instructions which have potential for ETV production and their needs (equipment, manpower, training, etc.);

(iv) To plan for utilisation of television in terms of training of teachers/instructors, provision of support materials, provision, custody and maintenance of sets;

(v) To determine the structure at the national and State levels and the mechanism for coordination;

(vi) To work out the financial implications, specifically the contribution of the Centre and the States; and

(vii) To prepare a software plan with reference to existing TV facilities and pre-test the programmes on experimental basis in preparation of INSAT.

Contents

Preface; Background; Study Group; Framework for Programmes; Production Infrastructure; Manpower for Production Centre; Directorate of Educational Television and Planning and Monitoring Cell;

Costs; Training; Further Action; Acknowledgements; Annexures from 1 to 12.

Recommendations

DIRECTORATE OF EDUCATIONAL TELEVISION AND PLANNING AND MONITORING CELL

In the context of INSAT programme, the responsibilities of the Ministry of Education will vastly increase both qualitatively and quantitatively.

5.2 On the software side, the work will involve conceptualisation, planning and execution in liaison with the State Governments, of a daily programme-output of about 40 minutes duration per centre.

5.3 On the hardware side, ten television production centres will have to be planned, installed, tested and commissioned after the equipments have been procured, indigenously and by import. Arrangements for the maintenance of these production centres will have to be made. The installation of these centres will also involve civil works which may be contracted out but will need to be supervised.

5.4 A suitable infrastructure will be required for research and evaluation which will have to be centrally organised.

5.5 Additionally, work related to budgetting, policy formulation, coordination and control will also have to be handled as a part of this project.

5.6 These enormous responsibilities can be, shouldered only by a full fledged Directorate of Educational Television, which will function as a technical wing working outside the Ministry, possibly as an attached or subordinate office. This technical wing will consist of experts and administrators from various disciplines such as education, administration, engineering, programme production, research and evaluation. Also, the Ministry of Education will have a Planning and Monitoring Cell which would be responsible for the policy formulation and implementation of the programme.

5.7 It would be relevant to mention that this will be an on-going programme. After INSAT-I presently scheduled to be in space in January, 1982 there will be INSAT-II and INSAT-III. The infrastructure will also be useful for taking advantage of the terrestrial expansion of television which is going a pace.

An expenditure of about Rs. 68.2 lakhs has been estimated for a five-year period for this infrastructure as follows:

1980-81	4.2	lakhs
1981-82	16.0	lakhs
1982-83	16.0	lakhs
1983-84	16.0	lakhs
1984-85	16.0	lakhs
Total	68.2	lakhs

Since the satellite will be operative by about March 1982, it is essential that the Cell in the Ministry and the Directorate of Educational Television should be set up with the utmost expedition.

COSTS

6.1 The total cost of one production centre including building, hardware, installation, manpower and production costs is Rs. 159 lakhs approximately. The cost for ten centres will thus be Rs. 1590 lakhs or Rs. 15.9 crores.

6.2 The cost of one Film Processing and Sound Transfer Unit is about Rs. 35 lakhs. The expenditure on the Directorate of Educational Television and the Planning and monitoring Cell in the Ministry of Education is estimated at Rs. 68.20 lakhs for the Plan period.

6.3 The total budget requirement for the Sixth Plan Period (1980-85) is Rs. 18.11 crores approximately (Annexure XI).

6.4 This should be considered a very modest investment in terms of our target that each centre should produce daily two 20-minute programme capsules for an average of 200 days a year.

TRAINING

7.1 Educational television is a new area for which training courses are not readily available. The task was not only to identify areas of training and devise their contents, but also to develop approaches to training which would be relevant within the context of a developing society, more so within the framework of the philosophy of INSAT. As a result of the detailed discussions a number of important considerations and recommendations emerged.

Some Considerations

7.2 Training programme deserves the highest importance. While training in any area is important it is particularly so in the case of educational television which is a complex process involving team work consisting of persons with different skills and abilities. Also, since this is a new area where expertise and regular training facilities are not readily available, the planning for training and its conduct require urgent and careful attention.

7.3 All persons involved in different areas of production, evaluation and utilisation should have an understanding of the developmental objectives of the INSAT programme and its programme philosophy. It is, therefore, necessary that all trainees for different areas should be exposed to a common course aimed at providing general orientation on educational television and its place in development. The contents of such a course would include the concept and perspective of development, basic technology of television and concept and role of education.

7.4 Though we have a number of persons who have basic skills in graphics and preparation of visual aids they are not, by and large, oriented for use in television since television is new area. Precisely for this reason institutions providing training facilities in these areas have not yet modified their curricula to the requirements of television. As a result, persons possessing skills in these different fields are presently working in their own narrow spheres of specialisation and have not been exposed to the inter-relationship and inter-dependence of these skills in the television production process. They are also not aware of the potential of their skills for communication through TV programmes. There is thus a need for developing new approaches to training in different areas which have a relevance for television.

7.5 It is generally accepted that a practical base is desirable and improves the quality of training. However, in the case of training for educational television the practical training is absolutely indispensable without which the training almost losses its meaning. The availability of hardware facilities is thus an important factor for all training programmes. In particular, for courses in ETV scriptwriting and ETV production the number of trainees that can be admitted is strictly dependent on the hardware and manpower facilities available at the training centres. Training centres should therefore be properly equipped in relation to the numbers to be trained and the pace at which training is required.

7.6 Proper selection of personnel for training in different areas is particularly important, since training facilities are scarce. Care must be taken to avoid wastage of limited resources and to ensure their optimum use for rapidly building up the programme.

7.7 It is equally important to test the aptitude of the trainees. In the area of locating writers for television and film, two methods have evolved. The Centre for Educational Technology organises two week orientation-*cum*-selection workshops where potential trainees are exposed to the methods and techniques of television and called upon to write scripts for television. On the basis of this exposure and the work done by the trainees a final selection is made. On the other hand the Films Division and Doordarshan invite samples of scripts from intending candidates and examine them for expression, imagination and ability to write. In other fields the skill and experience in specific areas should form the basis of selection.

7.8 Since younger persons have greater resilience, the age of the trainees should preferably be below 35 years.

7.9 A coordinated approach in training is desirable. While skilled personnel in different specific areas are required, it is necessary that personnel in each specific area also have some knowledge of an exposure to other areas in order to develop a coordinated approach. Also, training in some areas will serve as a base for training in other areas. For example, trainees in ETC production should preferably be drawn from those already trained in ETV scriptwriting.

7.10 Evaluation must be an essential element of all training courses as the effectiveness, relevance and improvement of programmes will depend upon the ability of the personnel involved to obtain feedback on their contribution. Therefore new approaches to evaluation and workable methods will have to be developed.

7.11 The requirement of training in different skills and for the large numbers needed is not likely to be available immediately in existing institutions. Approach to training should therefore be collaborative so that excellence available in different institutions can be pooled. The training programmes will therefore require careful planning and management. It would be desirable to record lectures, demonstration and experimental efforts for subsequent used and widescale dissemination. Such a collaborative and managerial approach should make it possible to increase the intake in certain programmes.

Training Areas and Courses

7.12 The need for training different types of personnel involved in the production of educational television programmes was appreciated. However, the course content was worked out in detail only in the following priority areas:

1. General Orientation
2. ETV Script Writing
3. Visual Inputs for ETV
4. ETV Production
5. ETV Presentation
6. Utilisation of ETV Programmes

The contents of these courses are at Annexure XII.

7.13 Training material for different aspects of ETV is not readily available. The few institutions that are imparting training are in the process of evolving course materials which need to be modified in the light of experience. The course materials which have been prepared may be developed in detail in workshops into proper training manuals.

7.14 In view of the fact that resources are limited and a large number of personnel need to be trained in different areas within a short period of time, it is necessary to plan the courses carefully. As stated earlier, the lectures, demonstrations and experimental efforts could be recorded for subsequent modification if necessary and for wider use.

7.15 Training in the operation of hardware, e.g., Camera, Audio-mixer, vision-mixer, etc., is at present not available in many institutions. Specific courses in the maintenance of such equipment also do not exist. The IITs, Polytechnics, etc., should examine the possibility of modifying existing courses to meet the requirements of ETV or consider the introduction of new courses specifically for ETV.

Institutional Support

7.16 A large number educational institutions will have to involve themselves in organising training programmes of different kinds if the educational technology programme is to take root in the educational system of the country. The Group noted that the Report of the Ministry of Education's Working Group on Educational Technology had identified specific roles for a number of institutions, including universities.

The Group endorses those recommendations.

7.17 Some specific programmes were further suggested for the following institutions:

(i) *Teacher Training Institutions*

All teacher training institutions in the country may take cognizance of the decisions taken in the context of the INSAT programme with a view to making appropriate adjustments in their in-service and pre-service training programmes. The Report of the Study Group should be made available as a basic document for the purpose.

(ii) *Art Colleges*

The Art colleges may include in their graphic art courses, the requirements of communication through TV. The possibility of short orientation courses may also be considered for personnel already engaged in these areas in state educational institutions.

(iii) *Polytechnics, Indian Institutes of Technology*

These institutions may examine the possibility of introducing courses relating to maintenance and repair of equipment required for ETV production and reception.

(iv) *Technical Teacher Training Institutes*

It was noted that some TTTIs are already providing training in scriptwriting and other TTTIs may wish to develop this capability as well.

(v) *Institutes of Mass Communication and Research, University Departments of Sociology and Education*

These institutions may consider undertaking research in the impact of educational technology programmes in general and INSAT in particular. They may train students in developing appropriate methodology for such work.

(vi) *Universities*

Universities may be urged to establish mass communication centres and also undertake experimentation in the production and use of television for development.

7.18 So far as the electronic engineering aspect of hardware is concerned the training courses provided by IITs and Polytechnics were adequate. However, for training in the operation of production equipment additional facilities will have to be created in institutions like the FTII, Pune; IFT, Madras and SJ Polytechnic, Bangalore.

FURTHER ACTION

8.1 For the implementation of the INSAT programme efforts will have to be made on several fronts at national and State levels. To coordinate and monitor the implementation of the programme the Planning and Monitoring Cell should be set up immediately.

8.2 For all work connected with the establishment of the production centres, e.g., procurement of equipment, overseeing construction, modification of buildings, installation of equipment, the Directorate of Education Television should be set up immediately.

8.3 The NCERT should be galvanised for work assigned to it especially in training and production.

8.4 The production centres should be set up/strengthened at the earliest possible. The States should identify the site, prepare building plans, identify personnel for the centre and arrange for their training.

8.5 The primary responsibility for programming will be of the educational authority. But it may enlist a cross sectional participation in programming through a system of contract in addition to its own production.

8.6 All available production resources should be mobilised in a national effort. An advertisement could be issued to obtain information about and attract organisations who would be willing to assist in the implementation of the INSAT programme in accordance with requirements.

8.7 A National Workshop should be organised to determine programme focii thrusts under identified themes. The results of this Workshop should be widely disseminated and the National Workshop should be followed by State level Workshops so as to place the work of development of guidelines within a nationally agreed framework on a continuing basis. Training for script writers should be based on the material evolved out of these Workshops.

8.8 Workshops should be organised to develop further the course content in identified areas in the form of training manuals.

8.9 An agency/agencies should be specied for identifying and obtaining suitable films and audio-visual material for use in the INSAT programmes. These materials could either be obtained from within India or procured under Cultural Exchange Programmes.

8.10 The Report should widely disseminated among media and educational personnel. Their comments and reactions should be obtained and discussed at national seminars. The recommendations of these seminars should be incorporated in the Report.

WORKING GROUP ON THE DEVELOPMENT OF SCHEDULED CASTES 1980-1985, 1980 — REPORT[1]

Chairman Shri P.S. Krishnan

Members Shri K.K. Srivastava; Miss K. Dutt; Shri V.K. Dixit; Shri G.S. Vidyarthy; Shri P.D. Srivastava; Shri J.A. Kalyana Krishnan; Miss P.S. Sairntala; Shri C.N.S. Nair; Shri A.M. Kurup; Shri R. Srinivasan; Shri Bharat Sahay; Shri Shiromani Sharma; Shri A. Rama Rao; Dr. Ranjit Sen; Shri V.R. Iyer; Shri M. Shringaravelu; Shri Parmatam Singh; Shri P.S. Habib Mohammed; Shri B.N. Raman; Shri K.S. Singh; Dr. B.D. Sharma; Shri P.C. Hota; Shri Seetharam Das

Special Invitees Secretary, Social Welfare Department, Gujarat; Shri S.K. Jain, Haryana; Secretary Welfare Department, Himachal Pradesh; Secretary, Social Welfare Department, Karnataka; Secretary Rural Development Department, Trivandrum; Shri S.S. Iate, Maharashtra, Secretary, Welfare of Scheduled Castes Department Punjab; Shri J.C. Pant, Lucknow; Secretary, Scheduled Castes Welfare Department, West Bengal.

Appointment

A Working Group for the formulation of the strategy and priorities for the development of the Scheduled Tribes, Scheduled Castes and Weaker Sections of the Society 1980-85 was constituted by the Planning Commission vide their letter No. PC/BC/11-9(GEN) 20 dated 8th July, 1980.

The Working Group held its first meeting on 29th July, 1980, under

1. New Delhi, Ministry of Home Affairs, 1981, 155 p.

the Chairmanship of Shri B.G. Deshmukh, Additional Secretary, Ministry of Home Affairs, and it was decided *inter alia* to constitute a Sub-Working Group for the development of the Scheduled Castes.

Terms of Reference

(a) To review the approach, strategy and priorities in respect of protection and developmental programmes for Scheduled Tribes/Scheduled Castes and weaker sections;

(b) To review the administrative arrangements States and Central Ministries in respect of these categories;

(c) To formulate concrete proposals for 1980–85 in the context of a ten-year perspective and suggest the phasing of development programmes, indicating financial, physical, legislative and other aspects; and

(d) To review the administrative arrangements for implementation of programmes in States and Centre and suggest measures for improvement.

Contents

Profile of the Scheduled Castes; Flows of Benefits and Outlays to the Scheduled Castes from Previous Plan; Approach to the Development of the Scheduled Castes; Economic Development; Educational Development; Planning for Social Services and Minimum Needs; Human Resources Development; Important Instruments and Mechanisms for the Development of the Scheduled Castes; Institutional Finance; Role of the Scheduled Castes/Backward Class Sector; Arrangements for Implementation, Monitoring and Evaluation; Personnel Policy; Conclusion; Summary of Recommendations; Annexures from 1 to 10.

Recommendations

3.12 (i) The important element of a guiding philosophy for the development of the Scheduled Castes should be that when the adult members of family are willing to work with their pairs of hands for a specified and reasonable number of hours every day they ought to be in a position to get a fair return sufficient to meet the basic needs of the family, maintain a reasonable level of nutrition and health for all members of the family, and to release their children from having to earn for the family's subsistence and thereby make it economically possible to go to school.

(ii) The approach to the development of the Scheduled Castes should comprehensively cover their economic educational and social development and fulfilment of minimum needs and human resources development.

(iii) The core should be their rapid economic development as the base for a permanent solution of the situation of the Scheduled Castes.

(iv) Simultaneously, their educational development and social services covering various essential amenities should be specifically and adequately programmed and provided for commensurate with their needs.

(v) At the same time, the Scheduled Castes should be enabled to acquire the capability of organising themselves in an effective and constructive manner to take developmental initiatives and manage their own development as the essence of human resources development.

(vi) What the development of the Scheduled Castes mainly requires is, based on clear-cut comprehensive objectives and a functionally integrated strategy, the creation of leakage proof delivery systems, in order to channelise to them their fair share of the benefits of the general infrastructure and developmental opportunities existing in the areas of their residence, and composite developmental programmes with all linkages and inputs, in terms of their various occupational categories.

(vii) At the same time their development also requires some infrastructural investment of a local and directly relevant nature.

(viii) The approach should contain measures for securing for the Scheduled Castes, full access to the modern secondary and Tertiary Sector including the public services.

(ix) The approach should contain measures for the protection of and prevention of erosion of their existing command over their land based and other resources.

(x) The approach should contain measures for the expansion of their land resource base and other resource base.

(xi) The approach should contain measures for enabling Scheduled Castes in traditional professions to consolidate and advance their position in them.

(xii) The objectives and programme thrusts adumbrated in the framework of the Sixth Five Year Plan of 1980–85, in order to be successfully fulfilled, should concentrate on the Scheduled Castes.

(xiii) The development, especially, the economic development of the Scheduled Castes, should be clearly and unambiguously recognised as being at the core of the approach to development in the Central as well as State Plans as a whole.

(xiv) In plan formulation at the Central as well as State levels it should be recognised that the economic development of the Scheduled Castes and enabling them to cross the poverty line is the core and substance of the assault on poverty, underemployment and unemployment in the country.

(xv) New resources, capable of being channelled in small, viable unit-sizes within the reach of the poor as well as large unit sizes beyond them, should be exclusively and totally pre-empted in favour of the poor, with the major share for the Scheduled Castes, and jealously guarded against intrusion by others by means of the conscious operation of all Government and other public agencies and financial institutions in this direction.

(xvi) While the development programme is in progress, the task of the effective protection of the Scheduled Castes, in the immediate context, from atrocities and of the elimination of discriminatory practices and the total enforcement of their civil rights without any abridgement should received continuous attention.

3.23 The development plans for the Scheduled Castes in the Central as well as State sectors, should be based on the general objectives listed in para 3.13 and the specific objectives along the lines detailed in paras 3.15 to 3.21 setting out in concrete terms, the physical goals in each sector, the outlays required, and how these outlays are to be effectively utilised to achieve the physical goals.

3.27 (i) The three important instruments for Scheduled Castes development, namely, Special Component Plans of the States as well as Central ministries, Special Central Assistance for the Special Component Plans of the States, Scheduled Castes Development Corporations in the States and Central Assistance therefore must be made effective and fully utilised.

(ii) The crucial inputs of institutional finance and of quantitatively and qualitatively adequate machines required for the successful implementation of the various programmes and for their concurrent and continuous monitoring and evaluation and timely correctives, should be provided.

(iii) The Sixth Plan in the States as well as in the Central Sector should be so formulated as to provide mescapably and in an inbuilt manner for the integration of the developmental programmes in all sectors with the focus on the Scheduled Castes families and with a clear recognition of the needs of the Scheduled Castes in terms of the various general and specific objectives.

3.45 (i) it should include the effort in every sector by every department and agency.

(ii) it should be based on the developmental needs of the Scheduled Castes.

(iii) The target group approach, taking into account the occupational categories, in which there are large numbers of Scheduled Castes, must be adopted. The important categories of the Scheduled Castes, that must be at the focus of development programmes are:

(a) Landless agricultural labourers.
(b) Cultivators.
(c) Traditional Artisans

1. Leather Workers.
2. Weavers.
3. Other artisans.

(d) Fishermen
(e) Essential Health Service Workers

1. Civil Sanitation.
2. Traditional Dais.

(f) Urban unorganised labour
(g) The educated.

Each State should undertake a detailed exercise to identify the specific target groups in each area of the State, and specific listing of the Scheduled Castes families in each category and in every village, with suitable phasing. Without waiting for this exercise and surveys therefore to be completed, the States should formulate and go ahead with the implementation of meaningful programmes for the Scheduled Castes in each of the major target groups, on the basis of available information, which is adequate for commencing planning and implementation without loss of time on the high priority task of Scheduled Castes development.

(iv) The programmes for development should be composite and integrated and must incorporate all necessary linkages right from the Plan formulation stage, with the Scheduled Castes family as the focal point;

(v) Adequate coverage must be ensured in the economic developmental programmes, commensurate with the objectives.

(vi) The responsibility for drawing up composite schemes should rest with the Department which is primarily concerned with each developmental programme. Thus for a programme such as Dairying the Annual Husbandry Department or the Dairy Development Department should be put in overall charge with the role of integrating all concerned and relevant agencies so that a total approach is brought in.

(vii) Minimum needs and social services to Scheduled Castes localities/Basties must be fully brought into the Special Component Plan.

(viii) The programmes in the Special Component Plan should include steps for the development of capability and internal organisation among the participants, *inter alia* by promoting a cadre of non-formal extension-cum-managerial workers from among the participants themselves.

3.49 The Special Component Plans should fully tap all types of Apex Institutions and Corporations and through them secure for the Scheduled Castes their due share of the benefits flowing from them and from their subordinate bodies/affiliates/branches.

3.51 Power, Major Irrigation and other such socalled non-divisible sectors should be suitably tapped so as to extend their benefits to the Scheduled Caste in magnitudes large enough in relation to their needs and help build up optimal Special Component Plans.

3.52 (i) Every Central Ministry/Department must be formulate a Special Component Plan for the Schedule Castes in their respective sectors, in magnitudes commensurate with the developmental needs of the Scheduled Castes and so as to help effectively catalyse and help the efforts of the States.

(ii) In these Special Component Plans the Central Ministries/Departments should–

(a) earmark allocations from existing Central scheme.

(b) modify existing schemes and re-orient them where necessary to suit the problems and situation of the Scheduled Castes.

(c) based on the needs of Scheduled Castes, take up new Central and Centrally sponsored Schemes.

(iii) adequate outlays should be made in the Sixth Plan to accommodate and adequately provide for the new schemes for the Scheduled Castes formulated by the Central Ministries/ Departments, as well as modifications/re-orientation/ expansion of their existing schemes made in order to meet the developmental needs of the Scheduled Castes.

4.8 (1) Implementation of ceiling laws at each stage up to the delivery of undistributed and peaceful possession of the lands should be expedited.

(2) All lands owned by the Central or State Government or any other public authority or institution which are not required for any public purpose, and Bhoodan and Gramdan lands should be distributed among the landless poor agricultural labourers with due priority for the Scheduled Castes, as specified later, with undisturbed and peaceful possession.

(3) Lands belonging to the Central and State Governments or Public institutions, which cannot, on grounds of clear public purpose, be permanently distributed, should be let out on lease or licence for as long a term as possible to landless poor people with due priority to the Scheduled Castes as explained later.

(4) Long lease of temple lands, wherever they exist, should be given to landless poor agricultural labourers with high priority to Scheduled Castes, as specified later, while protecting the temple services.

(5) In the distribution of lands, Scheduled Castes should receive due priority, in either of the following two ways which different State Governments may follow according to local conditions:

(a) The percentage of the surplus lands allotted to the Scheduled Castes may be fixed at a level equal to their percentage among the agricultural labourers of the State plus at least an additional 10 per cent margin in recognition of extraordinary social disadvantage imposed on the Scheduled Castes through the centuries, the great handicap it places in the way of the socio-economic advancement of the Scheduled Castes, and the major role of the

Scheduled Castes have to play, under severely adverse circumstances, in completely removing the stigma of untouchability from Indian society. Where this works out to less than 50 per cent it should be subject to a minimum of 50 per cent in the State as a whole,

OR

(b) All available surplus land may be first given to Scheduled Castes (and Scheduled Tribes) and only after fully meeting their requirements, should allotments be made to landless poor members who are not Scheduled Castes (or Scheduled Tribes). This should be subject to a minimum of 50 per cent in the State as a whole, where this works out to be less than 50 per cent.

(c) In the case of temple lands, the minimum percentage of Scheduled Castes allottees should be at least 75 per cent in each case and in the State as a whole.

(6) The above task should be completed by 1981-82, at least half of it in 1980-81.

(7) The State/District machinery should actively detect cases of obstruction to the Scheduled Caste allottees/lessees/licensees taking possession of the lands and intervene firmly and quickly without the loss of even one cultivation season for them. Similar steps should be taken in the case of trespass after possession.

(8) Simultaneously with distribution of lands under any of the above categories to the Scheduled Castes, they should also be given a complete package of all necessary assistance, such as irrigation facilities wherever possible, plough bullocks, agricultural implements, and production inputs, without the loss of a single cultivation season. To the extent this assistance is provided as loan, not only should credit be made available smoothly and promptly and at a low rate of interest, but a moratorium on servicing and amortisation of the debt until production can reach an efficient level, should be provided.

(9) The formula for the distribution of the Central Pool of Plan assistance among the State should have as one of its major components, the progress in the implementation of these measures of transfer of land resources to the Scheduled Castes and the development of these lands, apart from the progress of other measures for the development of the Scheduled Castes.

(10) The land records should be brought up-to-date by including the names of the members of the Scheduled Castes who have been

given land by the Government. The land records should also include the names of the members of the Scheduled Castes who have purchased land or who have been gifted land by individuals or private organisations.

4.13 (1) The landless agricultural labourers should be provided with sources of independent livelihood like animal husbandry programmes. The highest priority in all such family-oriented schemes taken up under these programmes, including Operation Flood-II and related programmes should be accorded to this category.

(2) The Special Component Plans of the States and also the Central Plans of the Ministry of Agriculture and Rural Re-construction must earmark and channelise and adequate share for the Scheduled Castes amongst the agricultural labourers in any area plus an additional 10 per cent at least on account of their special handicaps.

(3) Care must be taken to see that Composite programmes of animal husbandry and dairy including Operation Flood-II, large enough to generate incremental incomes adequate to enable them clearly to cross the poverty line, are devised and effectively implemented.

(4) A systematic approach should be adopted of identifying the number of Scheduled Castes living each area; of specifically picking out villages and families to be covered; of ensuring the provisions of a total viable package; of ensuring the provision of infrastructure support of health service, marketing fodder, feed, etc., and of taking into account the preferences and aptitudes of the participant families.

(5) There are special live-stock production in several districts, which have been identified as suitable for and as having potential for piggery, poultry, sheep-rearing, along with growth centres and markets. The Scheduled Castes agricultural labourers must be enabled to draw their full and appropriate share from these programmes.

4.15 The Scheduled Caste agricultural labourers with artisan background should be enabled to get maximum employment and income from cottage and village industries.

4.17 (i) The Scheduled Caste landless agricultural labourers must be encouraged to develop new skil to have an access to new opportunities.

(ii) A specific exercise by each sectoral department/ agency is necessary to identify the opportunities and the potential in each area for schemes in the cottage and village Industries Sector, and small trade and business.

(iii) Linkages with programmes like TRYSEM and training at ITIs must be established and coverage of a large number of Scheduled Caste agricultural labourers ensured.

(iv) Corresponding outlays and schemes should be brought into the Special Component Plans of the States and the concerned Central Ministries.

4.20 (i) Minimum wages for agricultural labourers should be strictly enforced and the implementing machinery adequately strengthened in quantity and quality.

(ii) The National Rural Employment Programmes of labour mobilization, rural works programmes and integrated rural development should be planned so as to provide alternative and additional employment opportunities to the agricultural labourers throughout the year or for as large part of the year as possible, necessarily including the agricultural seasons so that the agricultural labourers bargaining position, at present homelessly adverse to them may be tilted in their favour and they may be able to bargain for statutory minimum wages and fair wages and their income may be maximised. Such measures should be taken in a planned manner with priority for chronically low-agricultural-wage, high unemployment and underemployment areas and areas where atrocities and social discrimination against Scheduled Castes are prevalent.

(iii) The problems of labourers engaged in construction works like buildings, roads, etc., should be properly studied for securing them minimum wages; eliminating middleman-layers of contractors; improving their working and living conditions; and ensuring employment throughout the year. They may also be provided with credit facilities for acquiring income generating assets and even consumption loans for subsistence during off seasons when there is no work for them.

(iv) Central funds should be made available generously for this programme.

4.22 Consumption credit, which is in the nature of working capital, for inevitable social obligations and health purposes, be provided to landless agricultural labourers and especially to the Scheduled Castes, as part of, and along with, credit for development purpose.

4.26 (i) The recommendations of the Sub-Committee on Bonded Labour of the Central Standing Committee on Rural Unorganised Labour be expeditiously and thoroughly implemented.

(ii) The schemes for the proper rehabilitation of the bonded labourers should be drawn up and formulated in such a way that they may not fall back upon the land owners or money-lenders and they are enabled to acquire suitable income generating assets and skills.

(iii) The Centrally Sponsored Scheme for the rehabilitation of Bonded Labour should be made open-ended.

(iv) The funds under the Scheme should be available not only for individual benefits but also for common purposes, common institutions, management and organisation and local, directly relevant information, as there are essential for the success of the individual oriented programmes.

4.30 (i) All share-croppers should be recorded by 1981-82, at least half of them in 1980-81 in all the States and rights as envisaged in the legislations made available to them.

(ii) The following legal rights should be vested in them :

(a) Right of occupancy and prevention of eviction or dispossession.
(b) Right to fair and incentive share of the produce or its value.
(c) Right of purchase of ownership on easy terms.

(iii) The State should be alert actively intervene to ensure that these rights are fully enforced and are not allowed to be abridged in practice.

(iv) The definition of personal cultivation should be amended so as to make absentee land-ownership illegal, facilitating the transfer of land in favour of actual tillers.

(v) Even where the Scheduled Caste cultivators are owners of their lands, the Revenue records do not always reflect this. This obviously hampers developmental efforts. Some States have taken special drives to bring the record of right up to date. This however, needs to be done in a concerted and effective manner according to a specific time schedule and this must at any rate be completed within the first two years of the Sixth Plan at least half of it in 1980-81.

4.33 (i) Special provisions should be made in the land laws of the States to regulate transfer of land and to ensure continued possession of land belonging to or allotted to members of the Scheduled Castes in such a way that their meagre land resource-base is not eroded. Those should, inter alia provide for the following:

(a) Cultivation of any land belonging to or allotted by Government or other competent authority to members of the Scheduled

Castes, by any non-Scheduled Caste persons or his people shall be taken as conclusive evidence of illegal acceptance of transfer by the latter.

(b) Confiscation of the land and property of such illegal alienees since they deprive the Scheduled Castes of their lands.

(c) Immediate eviction of the illegal alienees and restoration of lands to the Scheduled Castes.

(d) Creation of a machinery in States which can attend to the prompt detection of such cases, restoration as above, and confiscation of the property of the illegal alicnees.

(ii) The State should become a necessary party in all cases of illegal alienation and trespass and in cases of obstruction to the taking of possession of the lands by the Scheduled Castes.

(iii) Special summary procedure should be prescribed under the law for dealing with the cases in which one of the parties is a member of the Scheduled Castes.

(iv) It is particularly necessary that in categories of public services which are connected with land and land records, mainly village level functionaries referred to as Patwaris, etc., and survey officials the rules of reservation be fully and quickly enforced and a special recruitment be launched to built up the proportion of Scheduled Castes to a high level. Such a step will help build up the confidence of the Scheduled Caste cultivators, enable them to recognise their rights and to try to secure them.

4.38 (i) A systematic listing of all the land-holdings of the Scheduled Castes should be taken up and should be completed by 1981-82 at least half of it in 1980-81. So as to get a precise and full picture of the magnitude of the target group of Scheduled Caste cultivators in each State and in each area, is essential.

(ii) A comprehensive programme for the total development of Scheduled Caste land-holdings must be launched, initially based on readily available information and later based on more precise and fuller data to be quickly gathered now. There must be adequate provisions for ensuring coverage of all Scheduled Caste cultivators in the Special Component Plans being prepared by State Governments in the next 10 years, at least half of them in the Sixth Plan period, with commensurate proportions in each year of the Plan.

(iii) The various economic programmes should be reviewed with a view to adapting them to enable the members of Scheduled

Castes to become eligible for these programmes and partake of their benefits to the desired extent.

(iv) The quantum of subsidy should be suitably revised in all the programmes keeping in view the sub-marginal quality of the lands and weak economic conditions of the cultivators of the Scheduled Castes.

(v) The condition of a minimum holding size for irrigation well should be removed and all those members of Scheduled Castes who want to have a well should be provided one on priority basis, by meeting viability considerations in the manner detailed by us above.

(vi) A separate chapter in all Integrated Rural Development projects should deal with the development of Scheduled Castes, especially highlighting the adaptation of programmes; relaxation of norms and terms and conditions arrangements for the flow and accrual of benefits and taking up review periodically and at any rate not less than once a year.

(vii) There should be a programme to cover all the holdings of Scheduled Caste land-holders, most of whom are marginal farmers, with irrigation wells to the fullest possible extent.

(viii) Groundwater Irrigation units, which should be self-contained, including specialists from the fields of geology, hydrology, drilling, etc., should be created to provide organisational support for quickly identifying and exploiting the groundwater resources. These units should be adequate in number to exploit the entire groundwater potential in areas where there is a fair amount of land-holding by Scheduled Castes in a time-bound programme of three years. Such units should be provided with sufficient physical and financial resources including drills, etc.

(ix) Similarly, in respect of surface water irrigation, it should be ensured that the Scheduled Caste land-holdings in the command areas are fully covered through channels and necessary physical and financial resources are made available for this.

(x) An integrated project for development of land held by Scheduled Castes, whether by inheritance or private acquisition or distribution of ceiling surplus lands or by allotment of public lands not required for a public purpose or by long-term lease of temple land, etc., should be formulated so that the grant of land and its development are simultaneous, apart from quick development of lands in the holding of Scheduled Castes through means other than by governmental or institutional distribution or re-distributions.

4.40 (i) Research in farm and crop technology should specifically try to meet the needs of the Scheduled Caste cultivators and should try to tackle each problem faced by them. Location specific technology appropriate to the cultivators of the Scheduled Castes alone relevant for them.

(ii) A programme for undertaking such research in the innumerable research stations and activities in the Districts and the villages and in the State level and national level research organisations like one ICAR must be specifically taken up and specific directions in this regard should form part of the Sixth Plan.

4.42 The task of comprehensive development of the Scheduled Caste cultivator must be specifically made the responsibility of the Department of Agriculture which should coordinate with the Planning Commission for implementation of this programme in the Sixth Plan. Close coordination with the Area Development Programmes such as IRDP, CADA SFDA, etc., must also be ensured. Similar arrangements is the States should also be ensured.

4.44 (i) In order to release the Scheduled Caste cultivators from the vicious circle of poverty, economic exploitation and economic dependence upon others, a package of schemes in the subsidiary activities in the animal husbandry sector such as milch animal sheep units, goat units, piggery, poultry, etc., should be made available to them, ensuring linkage and gap filling inputs as set out in case of agricultural labourers.

(ii) In such programmes, they should be accorded the next highest priority, after Scheduled Caste agricultural labourers.

4.46 The Scheduled Caste cultivators should be enabled to diversify into other occupations depending upon the opportunities available in the area. This may include small business and trade, cottage industry, etc.

4.50 (i) Comprehensive programmes should be prepared for those occupational groups in which a large number of participants are members of the Scheduled Caste. Such programmes should cover all phases including processing, manufacture and sale. These programmes should have the primary producers and traditional artisans at the centre and should have as their objective, maximising of the share of the Primary producers and traditional artisans in the proceeds of the sale of the products.

(ii) It should be ensured that traditional artisans are not displaced by the modern sector and by the new techniques arising from advances in science and technology. Instead, they should be enabled to derive specific benefits from research and development, which should reduce laboriousness without displacing labour, remove health hazards and drudgery, reduce costs and improve quality and market value of the product.

(iii) In order to ensure that the middlemen-layers are eliminated, raw materials required by the traditional artisans should be earmarked for them to meet their full requirements. This should be one first charge on the suppliers of these raw materials.

(iv) Similarly, also there should be reservation in the market for the products made by the traditional artisans. All Government agencies and other organisations which receive the support and assistance of Government, whether at the State or at the Centre, should be required to buy from the traditional artisan sector all items which they need and which are produced by the traditional artisans; purchase of such items should be made from the modern sector only when the entire production (of those items) of the traditional artisans is fully and satisfactorily covered.

(v) Central and State-level corporations should provide them all necessary linkages from raw material to the market, thus eliminating the middlemen-layers and making available to the artisans their fair share of the net market price of their product. This should be the primary responsibility of public sector bodies.

4.59 (i) A definite and precise programme, covering all aspects of leather production namely flaying, tanning manufacturing of footwear and other products needs to be drawn up with the focus on the primary leather workers.

(ii) In every State, clusters of concentration of leather workers should be identified, the pattern of the existing trade understood and projects taken up and included in the Special Component Plan.

(iii) On the marketing side, valuable support to the leather workers should be extended by the Ministry of Supply, Ministries incharge of public sector organisations and corresponding State Departments by taking a policy decision that all governmental and public sector purchases, whether it be for internal use or for export purposes should be made directly from the producers, without any scope for middlemen, and on the basis of reasonable costs, particularly allowing for fair return to the leather workers.

(iv) The Ministry of Commerce must reorient the export

policy from the point of view of the primary leather workers. Sufficient raw materials at reasonable cost should be left with the producers of footwear and other leather goods in the country in order to meet the internal demand. Also supply for the export market should be so organised that the full benefit of the high margins of the international market becomes available to the primary leather workers in the country engaged in flaying and tanning, etc.

(v) The Ministry of Industrial Development in consultation with the Ministry of Commerce, Ministry of Rural Reconstruction and the Ministry of Home Affairs and State having large numbers of leather workers should on high priority undertake the formulation of the policy for the leather industry, with focus on the needs and interests of the leather workers engaged in each stage of the production cycle.

(vi) Steps to improve the working and living conditions of the leather workers should be taken and provided for in the Special Component Plans in appropriate sectors.

4.66 (i) A comprehensive programme for weavers taking into account all aspects spanning the supply of yarn and other raw material, modernisation of looms, improvements in middlemen-layers should be drawn up. Wherever 'necessary, subsidies may be built into the programme.

(ii) The overall responsibility for the drawing of comprehensive programmes for weavers should the borne by the Ministry of Commerce and the Development Commissioner, Handlooms. The specific roles of the State Governments, the KVIC. The State Handloom Corporations, the National Textile Corporation, the Spinning Mills, etc., must be clearly set out in a time-bound programme.

(iii) The Central Ministries, State Governments and public sector organisations which purchase textile goods, must help the handloom weavers on the market, front, by purchasing textile goods only from handloom weavers, without any middleman in between.

(iv) Intensive projects for development of handloom weavers with all necessary inputs and linkages should be taken up in States/tracts where Scheduled Castes are a majority of the weavers.

(v) In other States/tracts Scheduled Caste weavers should be enabled to become members of weavers co-operatives and other organisations and secure their due share of benefits from those cooperative and organisations in full.

(vi) Houses-cum-work places for the weavers should be further extended and made an integral part of the handloom development programme.

4.71 (i) A comprehensive programme for handicrafts artisans, spanning arrangements for the supply of raw materials, technology inputs and training, common facility centres, marketing, etc., needs to be taken up. The Ministry of Commerce and the All India Handicrafts Board and similarly the Ministry of Rural Reconstruction and KVIC should be primarily responsible for drawing up and coordinating the implementation of this efforts covering at least 50 per cent of the producers, in this Plan period.

(ii) At least 50 per cent of the new entrants into the training centres organised by all India Handicrafts Board as well as State organisations should be from the Scheduled Castes.

(iii) The young people in the training centres and in the production system should be provided facilities for non-formal education based on a syllabus relevant to their economic and other development. Since it seems to be an unavoidable compulsion of some of the handicrafts that the skills have to be acquired at an early age, the young people in the training centres and in the production system should be provided non-formal education with directly relevant syllabus.

4.74 A comprehensive programme for fishermen be started in areas and States with large concentrations of Scheduled Castes fishermen. This should cover the entire production and marketing cycle leaving no scope for middlemen and should also include arrangements for credit simultaneously wiping off their private debts. It should be ensured that at least 50 per cent of Scheduled Caste fishermen cross the poverty line in the Sixth Plan period and an appropriate proportion thereof every year.

4.81 (i) Immediate legislation banning the construction of houses with dry latrines requiring scavenging services must be enacted. Provisions of alternative arrangements like water sealed closets should be a necessary pre-condition for grant of any permit for construction of houses or other building. This should be done by all States by 1-1-1981.

(ii) All municipalities and other civic bodies and other organisations should take a decision to retire all scavengers who have attained the age of 45 years and to pay them their full pay as pension. This would apply, apart from the municipalities to organisations such as the railways, public sector undertakings, etc.

(iii) These retired scavengers should simultaneously be assisted to move into some other profession or employment/self-employment so that they are not left idle at an age when they are still energetic and capable of doing physical work. Wherever, training is necessary for this purpose, should be provided.

(iv) Since it is generally the practice to introduce children into the scavenging profession, an immediate and total programme of bringing all children of the scavenging families into schools with hostels must be introduced. This must come in right from the pre-primary stages from age five, so that the children of the scavenging families are not allowed to become accustomed to this kind of work. The entire cost of education, mess, etc., should be borne by the Government.

(v) The programme of opening hostels for the children of the scavengers must be taken immediately and the cost should be shared equally by the Central Government and the States. Suitable provisions must also be made in the Sixth Plan and relevant Annual Plans.

(vi) Simultaneously, a specific time-bound and comprehensive programme for providing alternative employment to the scavengers who are not pensioned off must be taken up on top priority. This will require coordination at different levels and between different regulatory and development departments. The primary responsibility for providing alternative employment to scavengers must be with the Department of Urban Development in the States and in the Ministry of Works and Housing at the Centre. Many of them could be accommodated in the concerned civic bodies and other organisations themselves on non-scavenging jobs. A specific committee including representatives from the Departments of Industries, Institutional Finance, Scheduled Castes Development Corporations, Animal Husbandry, Transport, Civil Supplies, etc., should also be formed to coordinate and oversee the progress of this programme.

4.83 (i) All dry latrines in the country should be converted into water-borne latrines by 31-3-1982.

(ii) Suitable legislative enactments should be made to empower the municipalities/urban development authorities to convert the dry-latrines into water-borne ones, wherever the house owner fails to do so; in such cases the cost of such conversion should be recoverable from the house owner by the municipalities/urban development authorities.

(iii) Every house owner should be enabled to choose for himself the design for a water-borne latrine which finds most convenient and suitable. In order to make this possible it will be necessary to:

(a) Pool in different designs developed by various agencies in the country and given them wide publicity and circulation.
(b) In every municipal area our of these designs those which are particularly acceptable should be selected.
(c) The manufacture of water-borne latrines on the basis of the few selected designs should be taken up in and around each municipality. Assistance and support to enable such production to get started should also be given and coordinated in a conscious and clear manner.

(iv) Some of the individual house owners may require institutional finance for the conversion of their dry latrines. Since this is an environmental improvement of which they are the direct beneficiaries, it is their responsibility to seek and obtain whatever loss they may require for this purpose from Financial Institutions which provide assistance for such purposes. The Department of Urban Development/Municipal Administration in the States and the Ministry of Works and Housing at the Centre may, with the Cooperation of Banking Department, render whatever help is possible in this regard by persuading Institutions such as the HUDCO, LIC, GIC, Commercial Banks, etc., to provide such loans when applied for.

(v) In case the Municipalities/Urban Development Authorities have, inevitably, to take up the task of conversion where the house-owners do not come forward, they will require financial support. Any expenditure on this score which is to be borne by the Municipalities/Urban Development Authorities should be borne equally by the Centre and the States until it is recovered from the house-owners.

(vi) In some localities where the poor live, there may be no possibility of water-sealed closet in each individual houses. In such areas, the Municipal bodies should set up common public facilities at suitable points. This is part of overall responsibility of the Municipal bodies to keep their civic areas clean. However, in the context of rapid programme for the elimination of scavenging in the country, this part of the activity of the Municipal bodies will have to be stopped up to fit into the time schedule.

(vii) The programme to conversion of dry latrines into water sealed closets has the advantage that it does not require the huge expenditure of an elaborate sewerage system immediately. However, in congested areas there may be need for a sewerage system to be established. The Municipal bodies should establish such limited sewerage systems so as to go ahead hand in hand, with the time-table for the conversion of dry latrines.

(viii) The works and outlays necessary for relieving the Scheduled Castes from the work of scavenging and for relieving the country of the stigma arising from the fact the some of our countrymen are being used for such work, should be given the topmost and overriding priority in the urban sector. All funds required for this purpose should be provided on an adequate and open ended basis with equal sharing by the Government of India and the States.

There is justification for giving to the people in the scavenging occupation in municipal bodies, railways, etc., salaries equal to that of Class III employees and to provide them good housing colonies in good localities and other improvement in their working and living conditions. However, we have desisted from making these recommendations in view of our far more fundamental and far-reaching recommendations for putting an end to this occupation itself immediately, while providing for the adjustment or rehabilitation of the present scavengers without any discrimination of their present income.

4.87 (i) The existing isolation between the modern mother and child care system and the traditional system of service dais should be removed so that the benefit of the former can reach the lowest strata of society through the traditional network.

(ii) The service of *dais* should be 'Municipalised' under the aegis of the Panchayats, each *dai* being paid a minimum fee of Rs. 25 for each delivery performed by her. The expenditure of this service of the panchayat should be fully reimbursed by the State, being suitably shared between the Government of India in the Ministry of Health and the State Government. The total expenditure on these schemes would come to roughly Rs. 25 crores per annum. This will also be a programme of economic assistance for Scheduled Caste *dais*.

(iii) All *dais* within the jurisdiction of a primary sub-centre should undergo intensive/refresher training periodically. They should also be provided a few scientific instruments and first-aid medicines for pre-natal and post-natal services.

4.92 (i) The entire spectrum of flaying and tanning activity should be appropriately organised by the KVIC.

(ii) The field level support for this purpose should be provided by the State Boards and the concerned State Departments.

(iii) The Bharat Leather Corporation and the State Leather

Corporations should directly and substantially contribute to the development and welfare of the flayers and tanners.

(iv) A quick study should be made of the practices adopted by the flayers and tanners and the flow of the products and returns.

(v) Suitable schemes should be prepared to maximise the returns of the flayers and tanners eliminating the middlemen layers. For its success, national level, state level, district level, block level and village level, efforts should be closely coordinated and integrated.

(vi) Carcass utilisation units should be set up for the economic use of all carcass products.

(vii) The economic focus of this should be the flayers.

(viii) The Indian Veterinary Institute and the Central Leather Research Institute should study the traditional practices of flaying and work out a package of transfer of technology to individual flayers and tanners.

(ix) The transfer of technology should be effected in close collaboration with the KVIC and BLC the State Khadi and Village Industries Board, the State Leather Corporations and the concerned State Department.

(x) A time bound programme should be prepared for pressionalising this occupation on the lines suggested above in this Plan period and adequate provision should be made in the plans of the Central Ministry concerned and the State Departments.

4.94 (i) The task in respect of urban organised labour such as rickshaw pulling, cart pulling, carrying head loads, constructions work, *bidi*-making, petty workers in the hotels, etc., should be to improve their income in their various occupations, make them owners of their means of livelihood, remove the squalor and hardships and hazards connected with their work, upgrade their skills, improve their living and working conditions and make available to them opportunities of other and better occupations through the concerted efforts of State Department, Development Corporations, Banks and Co-operatives, Municipal bodies and other public institutions.

(ii) In respect of Schemes suitable for them, Banks and other institutions should deny credit and other assistance for the relating affluent for such Schemes in the same or even larger unit sizes.

(iii) Full enrolment and retention of their children in educational institutions should be ensured.

4.99 (i) Concerted efforts should be made to improve the conditions of rickshaw pullers so long as they follow this occupation.

(ii) The ownership of the rickshaws, should be transferred by law to them. They should be given financial assistance including 50 per cent subsidy towards the cost of the rickshaw.

(iii) The legislation must also provide that none can own a rickshaw who does not himself physically ply it. The above legislation should be carefully worded so that it does not prevent the genuine rickshaw puller from plying the rickshaw on the ground that he is not owner, but only prevents the non-pullers from being owners.

(iv) Rest-shelters for rickshaw pullers at different points in the town and cities which are frequently touched by rickshaws should be constructed. All facilities for rest including beds and baths, should be provided with these shelters. A canteen selling nutritive foods on subsidised prices should be attached to these shelters.

(v) The owner-rickshaw pullers should be educated about the absolute need for at least a brief rest during the middle of the day so that they may use these shelters.

(vi) Research and development projects should be undertaken to bring technological improvements which will reduce the physical strain of this occupation.

4.102 (i) The cart-pullers should be made owners of the carts through legislative means and credit and non-pullers prevented from ownership.

(ii) Whenever municipalities engage carts for removing urban refuse, they should directly engage owner cart pullers, instead of leasing out or auctioning out to non-pulling contractors.

(iii) Research and development should be directed towards bringing about technological improvements to reduce the physical strain of cart pulling.

4.104 (i) In the case of head load workers, the rates for head load should be statutorily fixed.

(ii) research and development should bring out means by which loads can be physically transported with less strain.

4.106 (i) Innovative arrangements should be devised for establishing linkages between the system of collection of *bidi* leaves, the system of making bidis and the system of marketing the bidis, eliminating middlemen layers at all points.

(ii) Monopoly of collecting *bidi* leaves should be given to cooperatives of the Scheduled Tribes and as many of them as possible should be enabled to make *bidis* there itself. The balance of the *bidi* leaves, that will be left, should be supplied direct to *bidi* workers or their cooperatives.

(iii) For marketing purposes, their *bidis* can be linked with a reputed organisation enjoying a good brand name.

4.109 (i) The construction labourers should be helped to cooperatives and take building contract directly. Public building and construction contracts should necessarily be given to their cooperatives. They should be provided the required equipments and mechanical aids and working capital.

(ii) Measures for their development should include an insurance scheme as part of the procedures for grant of building permits.

(iii) Every builder should be required to pay to the municipal authorities for the insurance of the construction workers. The amount so collected should be used by the municipality for taking an insurance policy for the construction workers.

(iv) In the alternative, the builder should be required to take an insurance policy for the workers engaged and the production of the insurance documents should be made a necessary condition to be satisfied before a building permit is issued.

4.131 (i) While strengthening the position of the Scheduled Castes in their present occupations, simultaneously the educated sector must also receive planned attention in view of its scope for upward mobility for the community and other multiple advantages as detailed.

(ii) In view of the fact that the Government policies of Scholarships and reservations have proceeded in the right direction and have helped large numbers of members of the Scheduled Castes in deserving categories to achieve upward mobility, but have not yet succeeded in placing them on equal footing with the rest of the Society, at this stage a concerted drive at the pre-primary and primary level and secondary levels to bring into the fold of education the children of the very large numbers of Scheduled Castes agricultural labour and traditional artisan families, who do not get enrolled or drop out early, should be undertaken, through measures recommended in the Chapter on the Educational Development of the Scheduled Castes also as to bring in a lot of concealed talent to the post-matric level and expand and enrich the ranks of the educated and enable the Scheduled Castes to rise to a level of complete causality with other sections of society, in a reasonable time span.

(iii) The mismatch between educational streaming and guidance on the one hand and employment and self employment opportunities on the other, revealed by the anomaly of large numbers of the Scheduled Castes educated remaining unemployed and large numbers of reserved posts remaining unfilled for want of suitable candidates, should be removed.

(iv) For the purpose of removing this mismatch the following measures should be taken all along the front:

(a) Reserved jobs going a begging should be identified.
(b) Educated unemployed members of the Scheduled Castes who have got qualifications nearest to the requirements of these jobs should be picked up and given necessary supplementary education or training to enable them to fill these posts.
(c) Various avenues of employment and self-employment which can be placed at their disposal should be identified.
(d) In respect of such avenues of employment in the public services, a special recruitment of members of the Scheduled Castes should be undertaken, such as special recruitment of members of Scheduled Castes of different educational levels from matric upwards, at different levels of the police force, and posts in various Departments and organisations specially relevant to the economic and other development of the Scheduled Castes, such as those of teachers, cooperative and bank employees survey and revenue employees, village officers, nurses, agricultural and veterinary extension service personnel marketing service personnel, etc.
(e) Each State Government and State Organisation as well as each Central Ministry and Central Sector organisation should identify avenues of employment as suggested above and take up special recruitment to bring up the proportion of the Scheduled Castes in actual position to the level at least proportionate to their population percentage.
(f) Wherever candidates fully possessing the prescribed qualifications are not available, those possessing qualifications nearest thereto should be taken up for supplementary education and training to make them eligible for those posts.

(iv) Data shows that there is no reasonable ground for the non-Scheduled Castes to feel that the policy of reservation has conferred disproportionate benefits on the Scheduled Castes. These data should be widely publicised by the Personnel Department and by the Corresponding State Departments in order to eliminate scope for misleading and mischievous propaganda against the reservation policy.

(v) As data shows that there is still a considerable leeway before the Scheduled Castes reach actual representation in the State, Central and Public Sector services in equal proportion to their percentage in the population, the objective should be to complete the leeway in the Sixth Plan period, i.e., by 1984-85.

(vi) For this purpose, the following practical steps have to be taken in order to bringing up the reservation of the Scheduled Castes quickly to the full proportionate level in the Central Services, Central Public Sector Services, State Services and State Public Sector Services.

(a) The categories of services in each Ministry and Department and other public bodies in which the representation of the Scheduled Castes is below the par level, should identified and a positive programme of recruitment of Scheduled Castes in them should be undertaken.

(b) One of the Special measures for this purpose should be to include direct recruitment at various levels where direct recruitment is not now provided for.

(c) Another special measure should be to provide for a higher percentage of intake than the percentages at present prescribed for recruitment at various levels.

(d) A further measure that should be undertaken is to pick up, from the Employment Exchange, candidates who possess qualifications nearest to those required for these posts and give them supplementary education and training to make them eligible for these posts.

(e) Ministries, Departments and other organisations should be required not to reject candidates who have the minimum prescribed qualifications on the ground of there gettingless than the prescribed marks in selection tests examination and interviews. If the number of successful candidates is below the prescribed percentage they should also take in the rest of the 'failed' candidates to the extent required to meet the required percentage should be taken in as probationers, and given the necessary training/orientation to enable them to come up to the prescribed level of competence, after which they should be absorbed in the regular service.

(vii) The clause 'Consistently with the maintenance of efficiency of administration' should be deleted from Article 335 of the Constitution.

(viii) As the Scheduled Caste members of the Services approach the zone of consideration for promotion special training and orientation should be provided by the Ministries, Departments and Public Organisations.

(ix) The Ministries, Departments and other public organisations should make advance identification of job opportunities in their respective organisations. Qualified candidates or candidates possessing qualifications nearest to those prescribed should be identified either from the rolls of the Employment Exchanges or, in the case of shortage categories, candidates from among the students of appropriate educational institutions at suitable levels should be selected. Candidates from both streams should be put through appropriate courses of education or training or suitably guided and trained with the guarantee of absorption against such pre-identified posts. This should be undertaken by them in collaboration with the Education Ministry/Department and the Ministry/Department incharge of the Scheduled Castes.

(x) The employers in the public services and the public sector both at the Centre, State and other levels should themselves take the initiative to reach out and fulfil the letter and spirit of the Constitutional provisions for the advancement of the Scheduled Castes.

(xi) In the public services, there are some/loose ends in areas like the Banking and Educational fields which should be tied up.

(xii) The Department of Banking in the Ministry of Finance, the Ministry of Education and the University Grants Commission should assume a leadership role in bringing up the representation of the Scheduled Castes to the full par level in these fields along the lines suggested above and other lines they can devise.

(xiii) The other concerned Ministries should closely oversee and ensure educate progress in their respective jurisdictions.

(xiv) The Bureau of Public Enterprises should assume the supervisory role in respect of public sector units within its purview.

(xv) The Department of Personnel should also assume the overall responsibility of coordinating and overseeing this aspect in the State as well as the Centre and in the Public Sector, both at the Central level and the State level.

(xvi) In order to achieve the objective of quickly and effectively building up, the representation of the Scheduled Castes in public Service and public sector services suitable members of the Scheduled Castes should be given a place in the Governing Bodies of various institutions where there is scope for intake of Scheduled Castes.

(xvii) Accordingly reservations should be made for the Scheduled Caste in the various institutions and bodies listed out in para 4.120.

(xviii) Inclusion of Scheduled Caste representatives in all Departmental Promotion Committee, Selection Committees and Recruitment Boards should be made compulsory.

(xix) The members of the Scheduled Castes in such Boards, Governing Bodies, elective posts, etc., should be given necessary orientation courses, information and facilities in order to enable them to effectively play their role in channelising to the Scheduled Castes their due share of the benefits of development as well as employment within the respective spheres of these organisations, bodies and committees.

(xx) At present, at the Central Level, the policy of reservation is based on executive directions only. Some of the States have gone ahead and passed legislative enactments for this purpose. The Government of India should not lag behind and should provide such statutory backing. Similarly, the other state Governments should also do so.

(xxi) The Government of India in the Department of Personnel should prepare a package of guidelines relating to reservation in services, training of candidates, etc., along the above lines and take active initiative to get it implemented. Simultaneously, they should advice the State Government to follow the guidelines leaving the State Government free to improve upon them wherever possible.

(xxii) The formula for allocation of Plan resources should provide an attractive incentive for State Governments which follow these guidelines or improve upon them.

(xxiii) The educated unemployed members of the Scheduled Castes another be appointed in large numbers in the retail outlets for the sale by the Departments of Public Agencies such as the Milk Supply Schemes or the Dairy Corporations, etc., as this is an important area of the public services, relevant to the national struggle against untouchability.

(xxiv) The Private Sector should come forward shoulder the responsibility for giving the members of the Scheduled Castes their due position in the economic life.

(xxv) The Government both at the Central and the State levels should devise suitable measures for ensuring that the private sector does not any longer shoulder its responsibility in this regard. Acceptance of a suitable employment policy to be evolved jointly by the Ministry of Industrial Development and the Department of Banking in consultation with the Department of Personnel and the Ministry of Home Affairs, should be made a pre-condition for all advances and facilities to the Private Sector for business, trade and industry. The mechanism of licensing can and should also be legitimately used for this purpose.

(xxvi) The rules of purchase by the D.G.S.D., by the State Purchase Departments, and the Central and the State Public Sector should suitably oriented at this end.

(xxvii) There should be adequate earmarking for educated members of the Scheduled Castes in all avenues of self-employment. While the focus will have to be on the small and tiny sector, the medium sector should also be thrown open to the Scheduled Castes by introducing preferences and earmarking by the concerned institutions.

(xxviii) Public sector corporations should be required to earmark for the Scheduled Castes a proportion of the number of the unemployed assisted by them and of the benefits extended to them. They should also liberalise their schemes of assistances in view of the greater handicaps faced by the Scheduled Castes.

(xxix) An appropriate share of benefits should be earmarked for the members of the Scheduled Castes by various promotional departments of the Centre and the States which provide for training and other promotional activities.

(xxx) Every department, corporation and other public sector agency should devise self-employment schemes with suitably liberalised terms in its area of activity, so that a reasonable proportion of not less than their percentage of proportion should go to the members of the Scheduled Castes, who are capable of undertaking such schemes.

(xxxi) Contracts for looking after cycle stands, etc., should be given by the Municipal Bodies to the educated unemployed on viable terms and a proportion of it should be given to the educated members of the Scheduled Castes.

(xxxii) Reservation in services as well as in education and in the matter of scholarships and other facilities should be provided, as for the Scheduled Castes, to the children of marriages, where either of the spouses belongs to the Scheduled Castes, irrespective of whether it is the father or the mother.

(xxxiii) This should be provided to them under a head called

'Reservation for the caste-less', 'Educational facilities for the casteless', etc.

(xxxiv) Government should not unwillingly play into the hands of anti-integrationist evil social pressures by classifying these casteless children of anti-caste marriages as Scheduled Castes for the purpose of providing these reservations and other facilities, but should classify them as casteless.

(xxxv) The percentage of reservation for these categories needs be only very small at present, and should be gradually increased as Society progresses towards normalcy in this regard, until society is enriched by a very large number of such children and the need for this category of reservation disappears.

(xxxvi) The entire governmental machinery, especially the educational institutions should consciously operate to boost the morale of these children as a model for the future society of our dreams.

(xxxvii) In the case of spouses, themselves where the husband belongs to the Scheduled Castes and the wife does not, the non-Scheduled Caste wife should be given the same facilities of reservation, etc., in employment as well as in education as for the Scheduled Castes, but under a separate category of the 'casteless'.

(xxxviii) In the case of such spouses, where the husband does not belong to the Scheduled Castes, the non-Scheduled Caste husband should be given only the highest priority in the category to which he will be ordinarily entitled but for the marriage. Even this facility should be allowed only so long as there is no separation or divorce. In the event of such separation or divorce, any extra benefits derived by such husband should be withdrawn with retrospective effect.

5.7 (i) The general objective should be that the lag in the educational level of the Scheduled Castes at various stages of education is removed and they are brought on par with other communities in the Sixth Plan with a view to attaining the goal of equality of education.

(ii) The following are some of the important steps of elaboration of this objective that should taken:

(a) Spelling out of the number of individuals of Scheduled Castes to be enabled to complete education at different educational levels (including adult-level functional education).
(b) Analysis of each of the impediments like compulsion of Scheduled Castes agricultural labour families traditional artisan

families and other similarly placed categories to press into service their children even to earn more subsistence income.

(c) Arising therefrom, identification of the programmatic, financial, institutional, organisational and other inputs required for overcoming the impediments as in (ii) above and achieving the targets as in (i) above.

(d) break-up of the numbers at (i) above in terms of the Plan periods and each year thereof.

(e) Time and action schedule for each programme/scheme.

(f) The responsibilities for achieving the objectives being with the Education Department, identification of other related Departments and arrangements for their integration and coordination in implementation.

5.8 (i) To compensate for the loss of income on account of sending their children to schools who are compelled by the socio-economic system to work and earn for their families' subsistence income, provision of opportunity cost to the families of the Scheduled Castes should be made especially in respect of girls, children of families in occupational categories such as agricultural labourers, leather workers and other artisans, fishermen, civic sanitation workers ("sweepers and scavengers"), marginal farmers including share-croppers, and other labourers in the unorganised sectors, since without this basic remedy to the desperate situation any plan or programme to fulfil the nationality accepted policy regarding the educational development of the Scheduled Castes can never succeed in the foreseeable future.

(ii) Strengthening of incentive programmes such as free text books, free uniforms, mid-day meals, and board and lodging facilities, etc.

(iii) Award of scholarships/stipends at pre-matric level for Scheduled Caste boys of relevant categories and for Scheduled Caste girls. The existing rates of scholarships should be increased in the light of the rise in the cost of living and the scheme should be made open-ended.

(iv) In order to improve the performance of Scheduled Caste children in schools and colleges, special and remedial coaching should be provided for the Scheduled Caste children especially in science and mathematics at prematric and post-matric levels.

(v) Provision of necessary equipments to the Scheduled Castes students pursuing science, engineering, medicine and other courses.

(vi) Provision of Book Banks in all the educational institutions.

(vii) Provision of hostels on a massive scale. These should be provided not only at the centres of post-matric education but also at centres of secondary level education, where secondary level institutions are not within accessible distance.

(viii) Inclusion of a new Central Sector Scheme of merit scholarships for the best among the Scheduled Caste children in the following categories:

(i) Landless agricultural labourers.
(ii) Marginal farmers.
(iii) Leather workers.
(iv) Other artisan groups.
(v) Fishermen.
(vi) Urban unorganised labour like rickshaw-pullers, cart-pullers, etc.

(ix) The Central Government in the Ministry of Education should give Assistance to the States for providing the facilities for the Scheduled Caste children in an effective manner, under a Centrally Sponsored Scheme, which the Plan should accommodate in the full quantum required to achieve the objective.

(x) There is multiplicity of agencies dealing with the educational programmes for Scheduled Castes in the various States and U.Ts. While in some States these schemes are administered by the Social or Harijan Welfare Department, in other States these Schemes are implemented by the Education Department. It is, therefore, suggested that there should be only one Department implementing and monitoring all the programmes for the educational development of Scheduled Castes. The logical department for this purpose is the Ministry of Education and Culture at the Centre and Departments of Education at the State level. It should be their responsibility to ensure proper implementation of various programmes for the educational development of Scheduled Castes.

5.10 (i) The implementing machinery at the district level and block level should be strengthened adequately;

(ii) There should be at least one senior officer in the departments concerned at the State level for planning and evaluation of the programmes for the Scheduled Castes;

(iii) there should be separate monitoring and evaluation unit in the Central Ministry of Education.

5.12 (i) There should be planned channelisation of Scheduled Castes into different courses linked with job opportunities, in consultation with major employers to the fullest extent possible.

(ii) Similarly, there should be planned channelisation of Scheduled Caste students in the appropriate courses based on viable self-employment opportunities and personal aptitude.

(iii) In the case of general courses which, by themselves, cannot provide job opportunities, there should be additional training programmes linked with job opportunities. This should also be extended to educated Scheduled Caste boys and girls, remaining unemployed.

5.14 The rate of scholarships for all technical and professional courses at all levels including Industrial Training Institutes should be revised so as to cover the entire cost of the resident scholars.

5.16 For all professional and technical courses spread over four to five years, a preparatory year should be added for Scheduled Caste students admitted on the basis of relaxed standards. This year should be treated as a part of the course for the purpose of scholarships and stipend. The scheme under process in this regard in the Ministry of Education should be expedited and accommodated in the Education sector of the Plan.

5.18 (i) The rate of post-Matric scholarships should be enhanced to a level commensurate with the existing cost. This and other essential improvements to the scheme to be brought about in the light of the recommendations of the High Level Committee should be fully accommodated in the Plan.

(ii) In the interest of social integration, Scheduled Caste women should be accommodated in general hostels at least to the extent of the proportion of reservation for Scheduled Castes in the relevant educational institutions or 25 per cent whichever is more and correspondingly the rate of scholarships in those cases ought to be equated to the full cost of such hostels.

5.20 (i) Special recruitment of teachers should be undertaken from among the Scheduled Castes bringing up the actual representation of the Scheduled Castes in the teaching profession to a level at last equal to the proportion of Scheduled Castes in the State's population to start with and subsequently equal to the level of the proportion of the Scheduled Caste illiterate population among the State's illiterate population.

(ii) Wherever adequate numbers of teachers among the Scheduled Castes are not available for this purpose, suitable unemployed Scheduled Caste candidates with the minimum necessary general qualification should be selected for undergoing the necessary training and absorbed immediately thereafter.

(iii) New educational institutions that may be set up hereafter should be located in the Scheduled Castes bustee/locality but open for students of all communities.

5.23 (i) The proportion of number of Scheduled Castes among the adult educates both at the input point as well as the output point should be 60 per cent.

(ii) Among the Scheduled Castes, two-thirds should be women.

(iii) The actual number of Scheduled Castes who should be brought into the adult education on scheme should be determined on the basis of the numbers required in order to remove the illiteracy gap between the Scheduled Caste and the non-Scheduled Caste and Scheduled Tribe population in the Sixth Plan period.

(iv) At least 60 per cent of the new adult education centres should be set up in the residential localities of the Scheduled Castes.

(v) Teachers in these centres should be drawn from among the Scheduled Castes.

(vi) The content of the adult education programme should be based on what the Scheduled Castes in the occupational categories attending each centre need in order to understand their plight and exploitation, the causes and remedies therefore, and the means of securing their due share of economic and other development benefits and to protect their economic and other interests.

(vii) Similar measures should also be taken with regard to other non-formal educational programmes and centres.

6.5 (a) If drinking water is available in the village but the Scheduled Castes are not being allowed in fact to draw water from this source, action should be taken to ensure that the Scheduled Castes are actually enabled to do so, without any discrimination or disability.

(b) Where it is logistically not impossible to do so, every new source of drinking water in a village should be located in the Scheduled Castes habitation, open to all communities. This will have also a social integration impact.

(c) Where a village does not have any drinking water source and it is logistically not convenient to locate new source in the Scheduled Caste habitation of the village, the State Government may ensure that the Scheduled Castes also are enabled without any discrimination or disability, to draw water from this source located in the non-Scheduled Castes areas.

(d) If the State Government arc in practice not able to ensure that the Scheduled Castes draw water from a source located in another part of the village, where either an existing source is available or a new source is provided, another drinking water source should be located in the Harijan area of the village.

(e) Where only one drinking water source can be provided for a village it should be located in the scheduled Castes habitation.

(f) In the case of piped water supply, a fair proportion of the water-stands and hand-pumps should be located in the Scheduled Caste habitations. In such senses the ratio of water-stands and hand-pumps per unit population should not be less for the Scheduled Castes than for the others.

(g) A specific and clear exercise has to be undertaken by each State/U.T. to assess the position of the Scheduled Castes with regard to the availability of drinking water. For this purpose the following facts must immediately be gathered:

(i) Number of villages in the State.
(ii) Number of villages with facilities for drinking water.
(iii) Number of Scheduled Castes localities with drinking water facilities.
(iv) The list of villages which have a drinking water source, but where the Harijan locality is without drinking water.

With these data in hand the precise programme for providing drinking water to the Scheduled Castes must immediately be drawn up.

(h) It stands to reason, from the position of deprivation of social discrimination against the Scheduled Castes that the bulk of plan programmes and outlays for drinking water supply, both in the State Sector and Central Sector, should come into the Special Component Plan except to the extent provided in the Tribal Sub-Plans which pertain to the other distinct deprived category namely Scheduled Tribes.

(i) A list of 'Problem Villages' has been prepared without taking into account the social problem experienced by the Harijan Bastis. Therefore, all Harijan Bastis of 'Non-problem Villages' where Scheduled Castes do not experience full and equal access to the drinking water sources in the village, should be included in the list of

'Problem Villages'. Similarly, in the list of 'Problem Villages', the Harijan Bastis, where Scheduled Castes will not be able to experience full and equal access to drinking water should be separately included in the list of 'Problem Villages', so that in such cases either a common source may be located in the Scheduled Caste Basti or a separate source may be located in the Basti.

6.11 (i) A strategy for a massive programme of house building for rural poor including members of the Scheduled Castes should be evolved to improve the housing conditions according to a phased programme.

(ii) This programme should be based on local designs, local material and local skills. The contractor should not be allowed to come into the picture.

(iii) The State would give assistance for enabling the landless persons to construct their own houses with their own labour thus capitalising it in the process. The N.R.E.P. can be great help in this.

(iv) This programme should be taken up on a cluster basis, so as to bring about social cohesion and optimal services.

(v) No Housing Cooperatives should be registered unless they have 15 per cent of the members from the Scheduled Castes communities. In order to enable the Scheduled Castes to become effectively members of these Cooperatives and avail of the benefits, the prices of 15 per cent of the plots for the Scheduled Castes should be depressed. If in spite of this, Scheduled Caste individuals do not come forward, these plots should be kept vacant unit such time as they do.

(vi) Scheduled Castes should be adequately represented in all Boards of management, etc. of organisations such as Housing Societies, Housing Boards, etc. Credit flows for housing to the Scheduled Castes should also be earmarked from institutions such as LIC, HUDCO, etc.

(vii) While the massive housing programme is in progress according to its time schedule, simultaneously as a short term measure, an operation "House sites for all houseless poor" should be undertaken to provide house sites for all houseless poor persons with emphasis on Scheduled Castes, and implemented through teams of officers, moving from village to village and solving the problem in its totality within two years.

(viii) Wherever members of the Scheduled Castes and other houseless poor are in occupation of Government land and other public land and such occupation is unobjectionable, ownership rights should be conferred on them immediately.

(ix) All vacant land in the main village sites should be allocated to such persons including Scheduled Castes.

(x) In addition, suitable public land adjoining the village site should be earmarked, or private land acquired, and developed plots allotted to houseless poor persons who are not in occupation of any unobjectionable land already.

(xi) Members of the Scheduled Castes living in private land should be given ownership rights over their homesteads by law with provision for access to the road/village.

(xii) While making land allotments, land acquisition, etc., care should be taken to see that segregation and isolation are avoided and wherever lands are available. Scheduled Castes should be brought into the main village and where no such land is available in the village, land adjacent to the main village of the area should be allotted/acquired.

(xiii) In all the above new housing areas and existing residential areas of Scheduled Castes, all the living and social amenities such as safe drinking water, electricity drainage and convenient access to the main road, to burial/cremation grounds and to educational and medical institutions should be provided.

(xiv) All house site areas allotted for houses to poor persons including Scheduled Castes should be covered with a housing programme in the Sixth Plan period, with suitable annual phasing, so that there is no houseless member of the Scheduled Castes at the end of the Plan Period.

(xv) All works of the above type should be allotted to labour Cooperative Societies of the beneficiaries.

6.14 (i) Identify the link road needed by the Scheduled Caste localities through the following exercise:

(a) Total Number of villages.
(b) Number of villages connected by a feeder road.
(c) Number of such villages in (ii) in which the Scheduled Caste localities are connected to the "main" village or to the feeder road.
(d) List of Scheduled Caste localities in such "connected" villages which have not been linked by a road.

(ii) Take up, on priority the construction of link road to the Harijan localities which have been identified through the above process.

(iii) The construction of these link roads needed by the Scheduled Castes can be taken up also under the N.R.E.P. utilising the Scheduled Caste labour available in the adjoining area.

(iv) Labour Contract societies predominantly with Scheduled Caste member may be encouraged by allotting them the works for the construction of these link roads.

(v) This programme of construction of link roads must be completed within the first two years of the Sixth Plan in respect of all villages where the main village is connected to a road, but the Scheduled Caste locality is not.

(vi) Whenever any future programme of construction of village roads is undertaken it must be specifically ensured that the Scheduled Caste locality is also connected by it.

In a Plan drawn rationally on the basis of relative needs and deprivation a good part of the outlays in the States can and should be in the Special Component Plan.

6.17 (i) Identify the precise magnitude of the problem of electrification through the following exercise:

(a) Listing of villages in the State.
(b) Listing of villages electrified.
(c) Listing of Scheduled Castes localities in those villages which have also been electrified.
(d) Listing of those villages which have been electrified but where electricity has not been extended to the Scheduled Caste locality.

(ii) Take up immediately and with the higher priority the programme for extending street lighting to the Harijan localities identified at (i)(d) above. This programme should be completed as quickly as possible and at any rate within the first three years of the Sixth Plan.

(iii) In all future programmes for the electrification of villages, the Scheduled Castes locality should be the first to get street light.

(iv) In the Scheduled Caste localities which have been identified, provide the internal wiring to all Scheduled Castes houses which are suitable for electrification. This should be done at State cost and provision made in the Budget of the Power Sector, which draws a very large part of the total Plan outlay of each State as part of its duty to the Scheduled Castes.

(v) Simultaneously with the provision of street lighting, in all new villages the extension of house connections to Scheduled Castes must also be provided.

(vi) Arrangements should be made to ensure that the electricity charges are paid and the Scheduled Castes localities actually have street lighting. This will require coordination between Panchayats and local bodies and the Electricity Board. The procedure for Panchayat/Municipal resolutions will also have to be streamlined, so that no time is lost at this stage.

Obviously, in any Plan drawn rationally on the basis of relative needs and deprivation, the bulk of the provision in the rural electrification sector should be brought into the Special Component Plans both for street and domestic light, and for the electrification of existing and new wells for the Scheduled Castes. This will contribute substantially to the solution of drawing up of optimal Special Component Plans, without being baulked by the large size of this so-called 'indivisible' sector of the Power.

6.20 (i) The medical departments should take special measures to acquaint themselves with the health conditions prevalent in the hamlets inhabited by Scheduled Castes.

(ii) The duties of the community health workers should be so organised that visits to Scheduled Caste hamlets are ensured and they get reflected in the reporting system. The extent of assistance given to individuals belonging to Scheduled Castes should also get reflected in their report.

(iii) The doctors at the P.H.C. and district level should specially visit Scheduled Caste hamlets while touring in the rural areas and personally assess the health conditions therein. Special surveys should also be undertaken in the known pockets of high incidence of general or special diseases.

(iv) Health research should be specifically directed to diseases to which each occupational group of Scheduled Castes in characteristically prone, with a view to identifying such diseases, their causes and preventive as well as curative measures.

6.22 (i) Whenever any new health services such as dispensaries, primary health centres, etc., are proposed to be opened in a village, these should be located in the Scheduled Caste locality. Normally there should be no difficulty in locating these facilities in the Scheduled Caste locality.

(ii) If no land or building is available in the Scheduled Caste locality for the dispensary, P.H.C., etc., land should be acquired for the purpose in a site contiguous and adjacent to the Scheduled Caste abadi/residential area.

6.24 There should be specific research on the health problems and hazards of these occupations in which the Scheduled Castes are in large numbers. Specific studies should be undertaken to identify such problems and find and provide preventive and curative remedies.

6.25 (i) A specific effort be made no open shops in the Scheduled Caste localities so that essential goods of every day use can be made available more conveniently.

(ii) These shops which are in the nature of fair price shops should be managed by the Scheduled Caste educated unemployed from the village who should also be given all necessary assistance by way of assistance for mutual investment, working capital loan etc. as part of the self-employment schemes.

(iii) Wherever a single new fair price shop is to be opened in a village, which has a fair population of Scheduled Castes it should be opened in the Scheduled Castes locality, and managed by Scheduled Castes, but open to all communities.

6.30 (i) In slums, which do not have to be relocated the living conditions should be upgraded to acceptable levels by providing municipal and social amenities such as protected drinking water, drainage, electricity, internal roads connected with the main road, fair price shops of essential commodities, educational and medical facilities and community halls with radio, library and recreational arrangements.

(ii) In order to accommodate surplus residents of the above type of slums and residents of slum which are beyond repair and have to be re-located, 50 per cent of surplus land under Urban Ceiling Legislation and Government land not required for any public purpose should be earmarked for Scheduled Castes.

(iii) Social and municipal facilities as prescribed in (i) above may be provided in re-located slums and also in localities other than slums which have a concentration of Scheduled Castes.

(iv) Ownership rights on the sites in slums and other localities with Scheduled Castes concentration should be vested in genuine and deserving residents. Wherever their huts or houses are located on unobjectionable public land and wherever they are located on private land ownership rights should be given to them.

(v) Work relating to slum improvement and slum re-location should be allotted to Labour Contract Societies of beneficiaries.

(vi) The above task should be taken as the priority task of urban local bodies, Central and State level Urban development and housing finance bodies, urban development authorities and State Housing Boards and these should be reflected in the physical programmes, as well as in the allocation of resources.

6.33 (i) A time bound programme should be taken up or the improvement of all slums in which there are large numbers of Scheduled Castes and where they form 51 per cent of more of the population and this should be completed within the Sixth Plan period.

(ii) The responsibility for coordinating and implementing the programme of slum improvement should be given to a specific department/agency (this could be the Municipal Corporations, municipalities, Deptt. of Municipal Administration, Public Health Department, etc.). This programme should be closely monitored and reviewed from time to time.

(iii) Simultaneously with the provisions of services and facilities to slums, arrangements must be made to ensure that there is adequate and efficient maintenance of these services/facilities. Corresponding provisions and outlays should accordingly be made. Here again a clear responsibility must be cast on that Department/Agency which is to be in charge.

7.4 (i) New skill formation is an important input for occupational diversification; every sector of development should locate employment opportunities and identify the skills necessary. Suitable training programmes (both formal and non-formal) for imparting these new skills to potential participant families of the Scheduled Castes must thereafter be devised. While doing so it must be ensured that these are linked up with specific pre-identified employment opportunities so that the Scheduled Castes households can straightway enter a production environment which gives them a regular steam of income.

(ii) After the new skill has been imparted, provision must also be made, as part of a composite programme to provide the Scheduled Caste families with the necessary physical and financial resources to commence the production activity, this could be a loom for carpet weaving; some small machinery for workshops and repair shops, autorickshaws, etc.

Where the newly acquired skill implies paid employment it should be ensured that there is a clear tie-up with the employing agency so that there is no lag between skill acquisition and income generation.

In fact, training for skill formation should logically come as one stage in the process of identification of market opportunities, identification of individuals of the Scheduled Castes to whom those opportunities are suitable and acceptable, identification of gaps in skill and relevant skill formation in order to remove those gaps, while steps for securing subsidies, institutional finance and other facilities are in progress, so that completion of relevant skill formation and commencement of production employment occur at the same point of time.

(iii) A large number of members of the Scheduled Castes are already artisans and craftsman with marketable skills. However, productivity is low and can be substantially enhanced by training them to improve their existing skills. In each such activity the specific training inputs which will improve their skills substantially, should be identified. Suitable programmes for training, again both formal and non-formal must thereafter be drawn up. As with new skills so also with improved skills, suitable linkages with employment opportunities must simultaneously be forged. Further the necessary physical inputs such as machinery, lathes, tool kits, sewing machines, polishing machines for tanned leather, etc. must be simultaneously planned for and made available by the time the training is completed, all as part of a composite programme.

(iv) In each programme of skill improvement, care must be taken to see that infrastructural and institutional arrangements for marketing, raw material supply, credit, etc., are woven into the programme as an integral part. Supporting institutional arrangements must also be made. This is a significant aspect of all human resource development programmes which involve self-employment.

(v) Simultaneously with schemes of training and support outlined above, there should be a clear and specific dovetailing in all programmes for the training of trainers. This is to ensure that a situation is not allowed to arise where we fall short of instructors for any category of programmes relevant to the Scheduled Castes.

(vi) A conscious and systematic manpower planning must be taken up in this area of self-employment-cum-occupational diversification. Such an approach will ensure that we have neither excess nor scarcity in relation to the demand in different fields.

7.7 (i) Each concerned agency must be made responsible to identify the skill development requirements necessary for individuals belonging to the target-groups of Scheduled Castes in order to enable them to taken full advantage of developmental opportunities available in fields with which that agency is concerned. Suitable training courses to meet these needs must be devised by each concerned agency. While doing so, the fullest advantage must be taken of all on-going programmes like TRYSEM, and institutions like ITIs.

(ii) The need for new skills for more efficient production must be recognised, such specific skills identified, and necessary training organised. This along will ensure that the Scheduled Castes are in a position to take advantage of Technological advances in production processes relevant to them.

(iii) Research and production of suitable equipment/machines/ tools which will increase efficiency, reduce laboriousness without displacing labour, or have a favourable impact on the health of those engaged in hazardous or laborious occupations, must be taken up on priority in fields of activities relevant to the Scheduled Castes.

7.9 (i) There should be wide publicity through the mass media of the kinds of opportunities and programmes that are available to the different occupational groups in which there are large numbers of members of the Scheduled Castes. This must be a systematic programme and should be taken up in identified areas with reference to the specific developmental opportunities available. The channels of communication should include the radio, newspapers, television, etc. In addition, all development institutions should also be mobilised to function as important sources and channels of organised mass-communication in the field.

(ii) Visits and tours of potential participants of the Scheduled Castes to areas where similar programmes have been successful in respect of comparable groups, should be arranged. By exposing potential participants from the Scheduled Castes to the experience such successful programmes and ~~projects,~~ a massage similar to that of demonstration effect will be achieved. Such an exposure will make the conscious of the opportunities which are at their door step.

(iii) Since, however, the field situation varies from area to area it is necessary to ensure that the programmes formulated on the basis of identified opportunities take into account the factor of location specificity. Further, there will also be variations in the programme content on account of differences between participant-groups; therefore, programme-formulation must take into account the concept of what may called target-group-specificity or participant-group specificity. It is necessary, consequently, to fully involve participant families in the exercise to programme/scheme formulation. This can only be achieved through close and continuous inter-action between the Governmental-institutional delivery mechanism and the potential participant groups. Such an exercise of interaction must be made an essential pre-requisite before any programme is taken up in any area on a significant scale.

(iv) This process of inter-action must also be used as an opportunity by the delivery system and the developmental field staff to locate individuals from the participant groups who reveal the ability to perceive the interests of their group as a whole, the tendency to speak up for and strive for advancing the interests of their group and the potention to take on the responsibility of organizing the beneficiary-participants as an efficient and effective system which can prevent field-level institutions, agencies and personnel from by passing them. This would apply to each developmental scheme.

When the scheme has a large number of activities of different kinds, such individuals should be located from among participants in each such activity. This should not be done in a manner which will keep the generality of the members of the group un-informed and in the dark, while developing the capabilities of some selected individuals among them. This can result in such individuals getting distorted into a sort of new parasitic middlemen. The alternative model which we recommend requires that (a) such individuals should be thrown up by the group from with in itself and should in fact be its nominees from within itself, (b) the role of public agencies and personnel should essentially be that of recognising such individuals, avoiding any scope for a sort of patronage – factor (c) the human resources of such individuals should be developed, not in isolation, but along with the development of the capabilities of the generality of the members of the group as a whole, so that no dichotomy is allowed to arise between such individuals and the groups to which they belong.

(v) The organisation of the participant groups around activities under composite programmes of development must become a matter of high priority. Such organisation must not be imposed and in fact the participant groups themselves should be enabled to develop this capability. Individuals who are adequately educated, who are held in high esteem by members of the participant-groups and who have been identified for their qualities of representative and organising capacity must necessarily play a pivotal role in this process.

(vi) A cadre of non-formal workers should be built up in the process of enabling the participant groups to organise themselves. In many cases, the individuals found to have representative and organisational qualities, with a minimum level of education (not necessarily of the formal type) and who are held in high esteem in the group will be candidates for this cadre. Suitable arrangements for the payment of honorarium for them with Government support should also be devised.

(vii) The participant groups must be fully aware of the developmental programmes in which they are involved or are likely to be involved and must be given complete information regarding the different alternatives available to them and the role which different agencies are required to play.

(viii) The beneficiary-participants organised as above, must not only be involved in the selection, formulation and implementation of programmes for their own legitimate advancement, but should also act as a healthy and effective pressure group on the different institution/agencies at all levels especially the field level to ensure that they perform well as expected of them. They should also be fully associated with the review, evaluation and monitoring of the programmes.

8.6 (i) Every Central Ministry/Department whose activities have or can have a bearing on the development of the Scheduled Castes, must prepare a Special Component Plan.

(ii) These Special Component Plans should be formulated keeping in mind the needs of the Scheduled Castes and the priority spheres or funds which require attention.

(iii) The Special Component Plans of the Central Ministries must ensure adequate outlays for the different schemes which will ensure:

(a) That 50 per cent of the Scheduled Caste families cross the poverty line in the Sixth Plan, as per the Prime Minister's target.

(b) The provision of Minimum Needs such as Drinking Water, Housing Electricity, Access to education, etc., to the Scheduled Castes.

This would imply the schemes of the Central Ministries must have the capacity to generate an adequate effort from the State Governments and should be able to direct attention at the problems of the Scheduled Castes especially in the priority fields. In particular in view of the facts explained in the foregoing paragraphs, 50 per cent of the benefits of the I.R.D. programme be earmarked and channelised to the Scheduled Castes and similarly a major proportion of the benefits of Operation Flood II be channelised to the Scheduled Castes.

(iv) Every Central Ministry/Department which is particularly relevant to the development of the Scheduled Castes should identify an officer and a unit in the Ministry/Department charged with the specific responsibility of preparing Special Component Plans and Coordinating the work of all the Divisions in the Ministry in this regard.

(v) Arrangements for monitoring and evaluation and for simultaneously assessing the needs for new programmes for the Scheduled Castes in each Central Ministry/Department should be made.

(vi) The Planning Commission in its Annual and Five Year Plan exercise with the Central Ministries must necessarily ensure that adequate and appropriate Special Component Plans for the Scheduled Castes are prepared by each Central Ministry/Department. This emphasis on the Special Component Plans must commence not merely with the plan discussions if the Central Ministry/Departments but also in the preliminary stages of informal and formal interaction between the Planning Commission and the Ministry/Department. It should be useful also to involve the Ministry of Home Affairs, which is the Nodal Ministry for the Scheduled Castes, with such Plan exercises.

8.12 (i) A provision of Rs. 2000 crores of Special Central Assistance for the Sixth Plan period should be made in view of facts outlined in the foregoing paragraphs.

(ii) There should be a clear emphasis on the efforts of the States on the formulation and implementation of their Special Component Plans and the allocation of Special Central Assistance should be related to this effort.

(iii) While in the initial years, stress may be laid on the formulation of Special Component Plans and the relevant effort-based criteria, in subsequent years greater emphasis must be on the performance in the implementation of the Special Component Plans by the States and the criterion pertaining thereto.

(iv) Suitable monitoring and evaluation arrangements for assessing the performance in the implementation of the Special Component Plans should be made in the context of the Special Central Assistance.

(v) Such arrangements must include field visits by multidisciplinary teams from the Government of India including the Planning Commission.

(vi) The Special Central Assistance should be allocated by the States only for programmes of economic development including directly relevant training, directly relevant back-up services and institutional build-up and arrangements for implementation, supervision, monitoring and evaluation and should go to those economic development sectors which do not ordinarily have large Plan outlays.

8.15 (i) Special attention should be paid to mobilising at the State Level, sufficient finance for the Scheduled Castes, this would have to be both from the commercial banking sector and the cooperative sector. While dealing with nationalised banks, arrangements should be made to secure maximum lending at the differential rate of interest.

(ii) It is necessary to formulate suitable and viable family oriented schemes for the Schedule Castes in different areas and occupational groups in the States. The experience gained by the SFDAs/DPAP/IRD, which have also adopted a family oriented target-group approach, should be made use of. The crucial points to be borne in mind are that location specificity and participant group specific are incorporated within the scheme to meet the particular environment of each, and that the parameters of the market and demand are carefully kept in view.

(iii) The Corporations should concentrate on a limited number of selected schemes and ensure that these are taken up in a big way and implemented successfully. For each scheme, the total picture must be kept in view, from raw material supply to the marketing of the products.

(iv) The approach of the Corporations should be to avoid taking up programmes/schemes in a scattered manner merely to increased area coverage. It is necessary to adopt a cluster-cum-saturation approach in which, keeping in view the opportunities available and the potential, the coverage in the group of villages is first completed and the programme is extended to other areas/villages in a phased manner.

Thus for the programme for distributing milch animals, it will not do not assist three or four families in a large number of villages. Instead the approach should be to select clusters of villages along a milk route and Diaries/chilling plants and urban and industrial centres with unsatisfied demand for milk, identify large groups of families in each village who have the capability and the aptitude for dairying, organise the distribution of milch animals with all supporting linkages including fodder, marketing, health care, etc., (with the association of all the relevant Department).

(v) In order to ensure effective coverage, it is extremely important that at the field level suitable and meaningful linkages are established with the existing District and Block level machinery.

(vi) The Corporations, while working out their programmes,

have to fully take into account the on-going programmes both under the State Plan and Central and Centrally sponsored schemes and see than the Scheduled Castes benefit in adequate measure from them. Operation Flood-II is one such important example. The expanded I.R.D. Programme is another.

(vii) The Scheduled Castes Development Corporation should not take up programmes all by itself. The Corporation is envisaged to play a catalytic role providing missing financial and non-financial inputs required to make each programme and schemes viable and successful. It would thus be necessary to establish linkages with various credit and marketing institutions as well as technological departments such as State Leather Development Corporations, Handloom and Handicrafts Boards, K.V.I.C. District Rural Development Societies, etc.

(viii) It is extremely important to ensure that officers with the right attitude and with the requisite level of experience are placed in charge of the Corporations. These officers should also be provided necessary orientation and training. They should have the assured length of tenure and all facilities to deliver the goods.

8.18 (i) A provision of Rs. 100 crores be made in the Centrally Sponsored Scheme of Assistance to States for investment in the share capital to the Scheduled Castes Development Corporations. While this is the minimum requirement for the Sixth Plan period, the scheme should also be treated as an open-ended scheme so that the Government of India are able to fully meet the demands of the States.

(ii) The existing scheme should be modified to include assistance for essential staff expenditure out monitoring and evaluation, recovery, etc., and for taking up promotional activities.

9.5 (i) It should be recognised that the problem of enabling 50 per cent of the Scheduled Castes to cross the poverty line in the Sixth Plan period as a manageable and inescapable task.

(ii) It should be recognised that it is not correct for banks to plead shortage of personnel; it is also not correct for State Governments and State Agencies to talk about the villages beyond the command area of the branches while not taking full advantage of the rich and potential of the existing bank branches.

9.11 (a) Policy level decision for the Banking sector as a whole.

(b) Requirements from the Banking system, whether Cooperative or Commercial Banks.

(c) Requirements from the developmental agencies and the participants families of the Scheduled castes.

(d) Strategy for the field.

9.12 (i) The ensure that there is a definite effort to reach institutional credit to the Scheduled Castes we consider that there should be a specific earmarking of credit, especially long-term and medium-term for the Scheduled Castes. This has been done in respect of Co-operative institutions in certain States. Earmarking is known also to Commercial Bank, for example "40 per cent of the total outstanding is earnested for the priority sector" and a minimum of one per cent for the DRI of which 40 per cent is for the Scheduled Castes and Scheduled Tribes.

(ii) The programmes for reaching the Scheduled Castes families will have meaning only if they are composite and large enough to enable them to cross the poverty line. This requires, as already discussed, the creation of income-generating assets; for this institutional finance essentially in term-lending (long-term and medium-term) is required. In this context composite loans which invariably have a component of term-lending, should be treated as term loans in the implementation, monitoring and evaluation of credit flows, however, no distinction is made between short-term and long-term and medium-term lending. As a result, an impression is often given of larger flows of institutional credit to the Scheduled Castes them justified by the asset creation. We therefore feel that there should be a separate monitoring of term-lending. The Term-lending should be recognised as a major responsibility of the banking sector with regard to the development of the Scheduled Castes.

(iii) The short-term credit to the weaker sections and specially to the Scheduled Castes invariably does not take into account the actual needs of the borrowers in full. This however is not the case with loans to Industries and big entrepreneur; in their case the working capital requirements are specifically taken into account and unit such time as the borrower is able to establish himself, adequate resources are specifically provided for him. In respect of the Scheduled Castes and other weaker sections in the rural areas similar requirements are euphemistically called 'consumption credit' and regarded as extraordinary demands. Thus if milch animals are distributed, the requirements of fodder and even the needs during the period when the milch animal is dry, etc., are looked upon as unusual charges on the banking system. Similarly when a poor family, which is to be provided assistance for development, also needs cash for emergencies and essential social expenditure the banking system does not take these into account; this results in throwing such families back into the grip of the moneylender-cum-land owner. Often it has the consequence of weakening the hold of the poor beneficiary families on the new assets acquired by them with institutional assistance. This is harmful for the institutions themselves. We therefore, consider that a specific policy decision be taken to make available credit for all really inescapable for all such really inescapable requirements along with credit for productive/Self-employment purposes and that appropriate procedures be formulated and suitable systems devised, therefore, in order to avoid room for any misapprehension, it is necessary to clarity that what we are here recommending is not grant of consumption credit in isolation, but alongwith credit for viable productive purposes, where it is really in the nature of "Working Capital".

(iv) A priority sector has already been defined for the banking system. This does not, as it is specifically recognise the area of lending to the Scheduled Castes. We therefore, consider it essential that lending to Scheduled Castes for poverty line crossing – programmes should be specifically monitored and be recognised as the core of priority sector lending. Suitable minimum levels of flows to this core must also be specified, based on the quantum of resource needed for fulfilling the objective of crossing the poverty line in the required magnitude.

(v) The facility of lending at DRI is available to Commercial Banks. No such provision however has been made in respect of loans in the Co-operative Sector. Lending by the Co-operatives, especially in respect of medium and long-term loans, in rural areas, is still considerable and is likely to remain so for some time. We therefore, consider it essential that suitable arrangements be made to provide cheaper credit for the Scheduled Caste from the Cooperative Sector on par with the DRI Scheme now available for Commercial Banks. Necessary refinancing and subsidising arrangements also should be made for the Cooperative institutions. One method of reducing the burden of subsidy on this account can be to have higher rates of lending in the Co-operative Sector in respect of loans to the relatively better-off groups.

(vi) As matter now stand it is extremely difficult to advance loans to non-defaulting members of societies, which as a whole, are in overdues and debarred from refinance facility. The opening of separate credit windows for small farmers, which has been generally approved, is a measure in the right direction. We consider that similar steps and any other steps may be taken to ensure that every Scheduled Caste family which requires loans is made eligible for receiving institutional credit whether from Commercial Bank or from the Cooperative sector. This is particularly necessary since the poor performance of the defaulting society is invariably due to the appropriation of funds by those having relatively large holdings and other grounds similarly placed in a relatively advantageous position in rural society. The sufferers invariably are the small and poor families including and especially the Scheduled Castes.

(vii) There seems to be a general impression in the Banking system at operational levels that usually the poor including the Scheduled Castes do not repay the loans and are therefore bad investment risks. The field experience of the members of this group is quite to the contrary. At the same time we recognise that there is a dearth of reliable and specific material about the repayments by the weaker sections including the Scheduled Castes. We therefore, consider it essential that the correct picture be projected and that suitable studies be undertaken in this context. The blame should not be put on the Scheduled Castes borrowers in cases where only part of the intended loan has gone to the family. Similarly in cases where a non-viable package is given to the poor borrowers, there can be no logic or justification in holding them responsible for the failure of the scheme and consequent failures in lags in repayment. These aspects must be specifically kept in mind while evaluating the flows to the Scheduled Castes.

9.13 (i) Our society at large has an inbuilt and unconscious bias against the Scheduled Castes. This bias also unconsciously afflicts the Banking System, in practice. This bias has to be consciously removed. This Group therefore, recommends that orientation and training programmes be taken up so that the branch officers of Nationalised Banks, the field officers of the Cooperative Financing Institutions and the personnel of development departments and organisations relevant to the Scheduled Castes be given short courses of reorientation and training. Further, in the training programmes of the financing institutions also, a specific element should be introduced to see that a positive approach to the development of the Scheduled Castes is fully adopted in practice at the Branch level.

(ii) Scheduled Castes should be effectively represented on the Board of Directors, Executive Committees, etc., of Banks, Co-operatives and other Financial Institutions.

(iii) In the case of Co-operatives the majority of members of the managing committee should be from landless labourer and traditional artisan groups. A reasonable proportion of this should be reserved for the Scheduled Castes, who are found in these two groups in the largest numbers. A certain proportion of the posts of Presidents should also be reserved for members of the Scheduled Castes by rotation.

(iv) As matters stand, the personnel in the Banks and the Co-operative Financing Institutions are not specifically charged with the responsibility of ensuring adequate and meaningful flow of credit to the Scheduled Castes. This is for a variety of reasons and it is not as if these institutions along are to be blamed for this situation. It is however, necessary to realise this problem and to tackle it. This group feels that among other measures, a charge in personnel policy is required for this purpose.

In respect of the Commercial Banks particularly, who have had their experience initially in the urban areas, some clear directives are essential. In the assessment of the work of a branch officer there should be a clear and adequate weightage given to the officers achievement in the matter of the medium and long-term lending to the Scheduled Castes within the jurisdiction of his branch, in an integrated package large enough to generate adequate incremental incomes to enable poverty line-crossing. The percentage of Scheduled Caste families thus effectively assisted out of the total number on Scheduled Caste families in the command area of the branch could thus be a major criterion for the assessment of the personnel. The present stress on deposit mobilisation and profitability of operations do not adequately serve the purpose. It is imperative, to the Commercial Banks are to play the role envisaged of them, that the significance of this work and of reaching the Scheduled Caste families in a meaningful manner be suitably in built into the personnel polity. Consequent weightage in promotion, attractive postings and the provision of incentives to those who perform well on this scale must be provided for; said similarly, those branch officers who do not fully measure up to the task must be made to realise, through instruments of personnel policy, that their career prospects depend upon the performance in the sector of meaningful lending to the Scheduled Castes, in the desired magnitudes. This Group recognises the importance of recoveries but believe that once a viable and complete package is given in a leakage-proof manner to the Scheduled Castes participants, there is no reason to have any undue apprehensions on this score.

In respect of Co-operative Institutions also a similar personnel policy should be laid down.

(v) An impression has been created that the weaker sections and particularly the Scheduled Castes do not themselves of institutional finance for meaningful programmes. As mentioned earlier, this Group feels that the reasons for this are not fully appreciated and that if institutional finance and composite schemes are properly matched the

Scheduled Castes are more than equal to the challenge of fully taking advantage of the benefits. However there is certainly a lot of work which needs to be done in order to reach the Scheduled Caste families in a meaningful manner. For this however, it will not suffice merely to wait at headquarters for the Scheduled Castes participants to come and press for loans; it is necessary and even essential, that the financing institutions should reach out to the Scheduled Castes and present to them, from their point of view and their perspective the various programmes available to enable them to cross the poverty line.

This Group therefore feels that strenuous efforts should be made by the financing Institutions to identify potential Scheduled Castes participants, assess their situation and see that the difficulties and problems perceived by them are fully dealt with.

(vi) District Credit Plans have been prepared by the lead banks all over the country. The Reserve Bank of India have also issued guidelines to the banks to prepare schemes which will have special relevance for the Scheduled Castes. While this is certainly a welcome step, it is necessary to go much further. In each District, on the basis of the opportunities identified, credit plans must be prepared to cover 50 per cent of the Scheduled Castes families within the sixth Plan period through suitable programmes.

(vii) Overall targets of lending to the priority sector, under the DRI and specifically to the Scheduled Castes and Scheduled Tribes, etc., have been specified. However, at the field level such details are not available. The Branches of the Banks are invariably not in a position to give to members of the Scheduled Castes or to the Development Departments and Corporations a clear idea of the quantum of flows to the Scheduled Castes and other weaker sections under the DRI that has been made available and the quantum still available at any point of time. It is therefore, necessary that at the branch level, at appropriate periodic intervals, there should be a specific publicity of the above information. This will not only help he development agencies in the field but also make the Scheduled Castes and other participants aware of the flows, which has been and which can still be made available to them.

(viii) All Banks, Financial Institutions and Co-operatives must segregate and disclose in their annual reports the quantum of credit that has gone to Scheduled Castes in each category of lending in the year. Certain steps to monitor the flows to Scheduled Castes are already being taken by the Reserve Bank and the Nationalised Banks. This Group however, feels that a much more specific and detailed review is necessary with a view to identifying Branches and Regions where the flow of credit is inadequate and taking timely remedial steps. Further such a review and evaluation must also be done at each branch level of every nationalised bank and disclosed for public information in the area. The Group feels that without such publicity, awareness of the developmental opportunities provided by the Nationalised Banks cannot be created nor can the steps taken by the banks be fully appreciated. Also at the end result the Scheduled Castes cannot avail themselves significantly of the programmes/schemes designed to assist them.

(ix) The problem of lower rates of interest on loans given to the Scheduled Castes and other weaker sections has been a matter of discussion for some time. The Banks have already taken certain steps in this direction and lower rates are in fact now available for certain categories, like for example, the tiny sector. This Group feels however that a much more detailed and closer analysis is necessary to take into account the real and significant differentiation even within the tiny sector. While the DRI Scheme is available to certain categories for schemes within a certain cost ceiling, this does not exhaust the needs and the requirements of the Scheduled Castes. There are many families who may not be eligible for DRI, but who may still be well below the poverty line. There are also purposes which might require a very small level of investment but which may be outside the scope of the DRI scheme. This group is of the view therefore that there should be graded rates of interests ranging from the 4 per cent of the DRI for the Scheduled Castes along following lines:-

S. No.	Quantum of loan	Eligible categories	Recommended rate of interest
1.	Up to Rs. 6500	A per the DRI	4% (existing).
2.	From Rs. 6500 to Rs. 12000	Categories like Agricultural Labourers, Marginal and Small Farmers including share-croppers, leather workers, Weavers and other traditional artisans: Fisherman, Urban unorganised Labour, Educated unemployed, among the Scheduled Castes.	8% (as available for small farmers in certain cases).
3.	From Rs. 12000 to Rs. 15000	-do-	8% plus interest tax.
4.	From Rs. 15000 to Rs. 2000	All Scheduled Castes families	Bank rate plus interest tax.

(x) Under the DRI Scheme credit is now available to families with income of Rs. 2400 in rural areas and Rs. 3000 in urban areas subject to certain other conditions. When the scheme was first envisaged these income limits apparently represented the poverty line. With the passing of years, the poverty line has moved upward. This process of change will naturally continue in future also. This Group feels that in respect of income limit, it would be more appropriate to identify categories of borrowers and to consider them by definition eligible for DRI. As has been done in respect of schemes taken up by the Scheduled Castes Development Corporations, the following categorised of the Scheduled Castes should, automatically be taken to be eligible for the DRI Scheme.

Agricultural Labourers, share-croppers tenants marginal and small farmers, traditional artisans, fishermen, non-agricultural labour, urban non-organised labourers, employed in sectors other than those regularly employed in large and medium scale industries.

(xi) The lending limit of Rs. 6500 may for similar reasons be raised to Rs. 10,000.

(xii) Although there are clear policy decisions that there should be no procedural difficulty in ensuring the flow of and access to institutional finance, in the field there are several problems. They include the following:

(a) Banks ask for guarantees even in respect of loans where the amount is less than Rs. 5000. In fact as per instructions, hypothecation of assets to be created by the loan should suffice. Further in view of the credit guarantee scheme also it is not necessary to seek guarantees for small loans. The very asking for guarantees and sureties and collaterals and securities in such cases, in effect, put off the applicants and throw them back into he exploitative arms of non-institutional money-lenders. It is sometimes argued by bank officers that they are not insisting on guarantees of sureties or securities of collaterals in such cases, but are only asking the applicant to produce them without making it an inescapable condition. Their plea is that in case the applicant comes back expressing his inability to produce such guarantee, etc., they will extend the credit without insisting on such guarantee, etc.

In practice, however, when the applicant is asked to go back to produce such guarantee or the like, the effect of it is that he is put off. Therefore, whatever is not to be insisted upon should not even be asked for. In such cases if some form of guarantee is necessary. Banks can take group guarantees from beneficiaries themselves, which is not a new practice to many banks.

(b) Non-encumbrance certificates are sought even in cases where land is not taken as security. This is also contrary to instructions.

(e) There are enormous delays in the processing of the applications even when these applications have been given to the Banks by agencies like the Scheduled Castes Development Corporations, SFDAS, etc.

(d) In several cases where applications for loans to Scheduled Castes farmers and agricultural labourers have been made in accordance with the District Credit Plan and the Scheme is accepted as bankable, the Branch Officer neither rejects the application nor sanctions it. This leads to increasing frustration among the applicants for the loan and the agencies sponsoring loans and in effect keeps off poor applicants including Scheduled Castes and turns them back into the grip of exploitative non-institutional lending.

(e) The rates of interest charged by the Banks are invariably the normal rates and not the Differential Rate Interest even in cases where this is clearly eligible. In several cases the Branch Managers merely say that the quota under DRI has been already exhausted.

This group feels that clear instructions to the Branches of the Banks should be sent to sort out each of these problems and to ensure that there are no difficulties when applications are actually presented by prospective borrowers to the Banks. Further this Group feels that there must be a periodic and specific review on each of these aspects at different levels including the branch, region and State Level of each nationalised Bank.

9.14 *With regard to the Requirements from Development Agencies we recommend this.* – (i) The Banks are justified in expecting and insisting that schemes sent to them by development agencies should be viable. This group feels that it is necessary for every development agency which sponsors applications and programmes to Commercial Banks and Co-operative Institutions, to adopt the following approach. Programmes and schemes requiring tie-up with institutional finance must be taken up only the basis of clear identified market opportunities. Thus for a dairying programme involving the distribution of milch animals this should be taken up normally in the milk routes of dairies/chilling plants or around urban and industrial centres which have an unsatisfied demand for milk.

Moreover a cluster-cum-saturation approach must be adopted in every such programme. Thus if a group of villages falls within the command area of a dairying programme the development agencies must take up the programme for the distribution of milch animal only in these identified clusters of villages. Further in these villages every scheduled caste family, which can be brought into the programme, must be covered. They should not pick up say 2 or 3 families in a village, but rather these should be in group of say 20 or 30. Such an approach will not only facilities quick scrutiny, sanction and disbursement by banks but also facilitate better management/supervision, local institution building or organisation of the beneficiaries, monitoring and recovery. This will help the beneficiary participants the financial institutions and the development Agencies.

This Group feels that the development agencies responsible for any scheme or programme must invariably send the applications to the Banks in bunches covering entire village which are to be brought under the programme. This will become easy and certainly possible if the cluster-cum-saturation approach and the careful selection of programmes as outlined above is adopted.

(iii) In respect of programmes for the Scheduled Castes there are a large number of agencies operating in the field: Scheduled Castes Development Corporations, the Block Machinery, IRDP, DTCs, etc. There are genuine problems and difficulties for the Financing Institutions if each development organisation approach the Banks separately for similar programmes in the same area as this may lead to overlapping and also problems in implementation. This Group therefore feels that there must be close Co-ordination at the implementation level between different Departments and Corporations and agencies charged with the Development of the Scheduled Castes. This can appropriately be done by a District Committee under the direct responsibility of the Collector/Deputy Commissioner/District Magistrate.

(iv) The constant lament of the Financing Institutions and particularly of the Commercial Banks is that there is insufficient appreciation of the problems of the Banks by the development agencies and that this is specially so when it comes to recoveries from Borrowers sponsored by the Development Agencies. This Group feels that it is important for the development departments and the agencies to demonstrate a visible and continuous support to the financial institutions and especially the Commercial Banks. This involves necessarily assistance in such cases where recovery is difficult. In such cases the development agencies must whole-heartedly assist the Banks.

9.15 (i) This Group is of the firm view that the task of institutional finance to the Scheduled Castes has to be treated as the joint responsibility of the development departments and financing institutions. It will not for the development agencies to regard it as a matter exclusively for the financial institutions nor financial institutions to consider it as the sole responsibility of the Departments charged with the development of the Scheduled Castes.

This Group therefore, consider it essential for the development agencies and the financial institutions to work in close association in this national task of the development of the Scheduled Castes, as a Team. This team approach should precede the sanction and continue through the stages after sanction.

(ii) As part of the Team approach it is necessary for both development agencies and the financing institutions to work together at all stages. The first task is the identification of Scheduled Castes families in the village or groups of villages in question. The Group feels moreover that a specific listing of the Scheduled Castes families (as has been done for small farmers, marginal farmers and agricultural labourers under FDA, MAFALDAs, and IRDs) has to be completed the villages or groups of villages on hand and tie-up made with the programmes of the Bank and Co-operative. For this, close liaison with the development agencies is also necessary. This work of listing and every has already been commenced in several parts the country and it is now only necessary that adequate linkages are forged between development agencies and the financial institutions so that in the old, target-groups of participants are clearly identified.

(iii) When any programme for the Scheduled Castes is taken up on a big scale in any area, development agencies and the financial institutions must meet, discuss and ensure that there are no differences in regard to the package and to the bank ability of the schemes. After this is done this Group feels further, that Banks and the Development agencies must together be involved in the process of identifying the families and obtaining and clearing applications. Day to Day problems must be sorted out in a coordinated fashion and applications should not be tossed back and forth between the development agencies and the financing institutions.

(iv) The District Consultative Committees are an existing instrument available for coordinating and ensuring development programmes which have an element of institutional credit. However, so far they have not been fully utilised, nor have they been made effective. This Group feels that the Distt. Consultative Committees must specifically monitor, review evaluate and apply timely remedies to the programmes for the development of the Scheduled Castes.

This Group further feels that the process of monitoring evaluation and review should not end with discussions in the District Consultative Committee. Linkages between the District Consultative Committees and the Regional and States Officers the Commercial Banks and the development departments must be firmly established. There should also be reporting by the District Consultative Committees to the senior levels of the Commercial Banks on the performance of the Branch Managers with regard to the viable programmes for the Scheduled Castes. The Higher officers of the Bank should promptly act on these reports. This will be in consonance with the emphasis on personnel policy outlined earlier.

(v) In the programme for the development of the Scheduled Castes and in particular for family-oriented schemes of economic development, the Scheduled Castes Development Corporations in the State have an important role to play. By providing margin money loans, these Corporations demonstrate the full association and backing of Government. In the years to come, these Corporations will have an increasingly important role to play. This Group therefore, feels that it is important and necessary for clear procedures and links to be forged between the Scheduled Castes Development Corporations and the Nationalised Banks. This Group recommends for adoption by all Nationalised Banks the arrangements regarding clearance and sanction of schemes and recoveries which have been evolved by the Scheduled Castes Development Corporation of Karnataka and some of the Commercial Banks active in that State. Under this arrangement, recoveries of the Bank loan and the margin money loan of the Corporation are made by the Commercial Banks simultaneously and procedures for adjustments in account have also been laid down. The Karnataka Scheduled Castes Development Corporation shares the cost for any legal proceedings which might arise in these cases and also assists in recovery wherever there are serious problems. Similar arrangements regarding recoveries and regarding Team Approach for clearance and sanction of schemes are necessary and should be established in all States between all Nationalised Banks and the State Scheduled Caste Development Corporations.

(vi) Very often the Banking Institutions take measures to grant special concessions/modify procedures in respect of the Scheduled Castes and other weaker sections. Yet, in several cases this information does not percolate down to the States, leave alone the field offices. Thus for example the IDBI has decided that for Scheduled Castes entrepreneurs the promoters' contribution shall be reduced to just 5 per cent yet in several States this information is not available with the State Finance Corporations, State Scheduled Castes Development Corporations, etc. There is obviously a need to ensure that this communication lag does not occur. Suitable steps require to be taken urgently, by both the financing institutions and the development agencies so that there is continuous contact, communication and interaction.

The State Finance Corporations and Scheduled Caste Development Corporations as well as Banks should make full use of such liberalised terms as are provided for the Scheduled Castes by organisations like the I.D.B.I.

10.9 (i) With the comprehensive strategy recently evolved for the all round socio-economic development of Scheduled Castes, the Scheduled Castes and Scheduled Tribes/Backward Classes Sector can now play the supplementary role originally intended for it. The Schemes under this sector will have to be continued even after substantial flows of funds are available from the Special Component Plans and much larger outlays will be required for such programmes.

(ii) As the Special Component Plans of States as well as Central Ministries develop and thereby any of the development needs of the Scheduled Castes, now catered to from the Scheduled Castes and Scheduled Tribes/Backward Classes Sector, are found clearly to be supported by appropriate general sectors the content of this Sector should be reviewed, with the aim not of reducing or holding down the size of this Sector, but of making its content more meaningful.

(iii) The following outlays should be provided in the Sixth Five Year Plan for each of the continuing Centrally Sponsored Schemes for the Scheduled Castes:

Scheme	(Rs. in crores) outlays
1. Post matric Scholarship for Scheduled Castes and Scheduled Tribes	200.00
2. Pre-matric Scholarships for those engaged in the so-called 'nuclear' Occupations (Classes 1 to 10 only)	4.00
3. Book Banks for Scheduled Castes and Scheduled Tribes	5.00
4. Girl's Hostels for Scheduled Castes	25.00
5. Coaching and Allied Schemes	5.00
6. Aid to 'voluntary organisations' (Scheduled Castes)	10.00
7. Machinery for Implementation of the Protection of Civil Rights Act	15.00
8. Research and Training (Scheduled Castes)	1.00
9. Central Assistance for Scheduled Castes Development Corporations	100.00
	365.00

(iv) The scheme of pre-matric scholarships and girls' hostels should be made open ended schemes like Post-matric scholarship Schemes, so that nobody is denied the benefit of these schemes.

(v) The scheme of Pre-matric Scholarships for those engaged in the so-called 'unclean' occupations should be suitably modified so as to include the children studying in Class 1 to 5 also within the purview of the scheme which is at present covering the children of class 6 to 10 only.

(vi) The following new schemes based on the needs of the Scheduled Castes should be introduced in the Sixth Five Year Plan, with the following provisions:

	(Rs. in crores)
(a) Hostels for Scheduled Castes Boys	50.00
(b) Pre-Matric Scholarships for Scheduled caste children in selected categories such as girls, children of agricultural labourers, leather workers, and other engaged in cottage and village industries, fishermen, other labourers in the un organised sector as compensation for opportunity Cost, and to start with, at the Primary stage (Class 1 to V) — (This scheme will not be necessary in this sector once the	

	Education Ministry provides for this in its Special Component Plan). The outlays for this scheme should be worked out in consultation with the Ministry of Education	700.00
		750.00
(c)	Assistance to Municipalities/Municipal Corporations through States for the conversion of dry latrines into sanitary ones. (This scheme will not be required in this sector. Once the Housing and Urban Development sector provides for it in its Special Component Plan). The outlays required should be worked out in consultation with the Ministry of Works and Housing.	Amount could not be computed at present by us.

11.5 (i) A focus must emerge at the district level for the programmes for the development of the Scheduled Castes families/groups/basties.

(ii) The District Magistrate/Deputy Commissioner Deputy Collector should be assigned a specific responsibility for implementing these programmes.

(iii) The District Magistrate should be assisted by a senior officer of the rank of Additional District Magistrate/Additional Deputy Commissioner/Joint Collector with the sole function of coordination and organisation of the programmes relating to the development of the Scheduled Castes.

(iv) A Committee, whose directions should, by a specific order of the State Government be mandatory and binding on all concerned Departments, should be constituted at the district level with the District Magistrate/Deputy Commissioner/District Collector or Chairman, which should periodically review the implementation of the programmes of the Scheduled Castes by various departments; evaluate the progress and take timely correctional measures.

11.8 (i) Although there will be different programmes for the Scheduled Castes in different areas, the development programmes for the Scheduled Castes can be "projectised" and taken up as distinct, composite and independent units. Thus for example an intensive programme for the distribution of milch animals can be looked upon as a total dairying project for the area; a programme for primary leather workers similarly can be projectised, by bringing in and detailing its several units into a composite whole.

(ii) With the projectisation approach, one special

department/agency must be charged with the overall responsibility for each programme. Thus the Department of Animal Husbandry or of Dairy Development will be expected to look after the Dairying programme and the Department of Agriculture to look after comprehensive land development schemes for the Scheduled Castes.

That Department should integrate other Departments relevant to the project.

(iii) The managerial and staffing requirements for such programmes must be assessed specifically. While doing so the existing implementational and supervisory infrastructure available must be fully taken into account and suitably drawn into the programme. If, after this is done, it is found necessary to have any additional staff inputs, these also must be provided for. But, such additional staff inputs should be directly related to the programme.

(iv) In order to ensure that the programmes are successfully implemented, it essential that the additional staff required for the programmes for the development of the Scheduled Castes must be organised in such a manner as to fit into and become part of the *existing departmental hierarchy* in the field such as for example Additional Deputy Commissioner, Additional B.D.O., Additional E.O., etc. Arrangements for reviews and field visits by the relevant State and District level officers concerned with every programme must also be made.

(v) The special Central Assistance for the Special Component Plans can be utilised to sort out and clear any problems of funding on the staffing side for the successful implementation of the programmes of economic development of the Scheduled Castes, taking care to ensure that there is no overlapping or proliferation.

(vi) An element of answerability for the successful implementation of each programme in the projectised approach must also be clearly built into the programme.

(vii) Simultaneously with the strengthening of the implementation machinery, the machinery for concurrent and continuous monitoring and evaluation, with a view to taking timely remedial measures, wherever necessary, should also be strengthened.

(viii) While the machinery for concurrent and continuous monitoring evaluation will have to be created/strengthened at the district level and below as well as at the State level, the strengthening of the implementation machinery should be essentially at the District level and below. This is not intended as a rigid formulation, but as broad indication, so that there is no proliferation at the wrong levels.

(ix) It is essential for proper implementation that the Planning machinery at all levels should be found. Essential strengthening should, therefore, be undertaken at all required levels, particularly including the district level.

(x) The personnel at all levels – Block, District, State and Central – involved in the formulation of Plans, and programmes/scheme for the development of the Scheduled Castes, their implementation and their monitoring and evaluation, should be given necessary orientation, so that they can be have a perspective of the task of Scheduled Caste development against the background of national development as a whole and the Plan thrust of removal of poverty and inequality. This re-orientation programme should also give them a clear perception of the Scheduled Castes and their problems and needs and the urgency of the task of their development, especially their economic development.

(xi) A new interest of a comprehensive nature has been generated in all the states by the sense of urgency and top priority expressed by the Prime Minister in the development of the Scheduled Castes and matters relating to it such as Special Component Plans, and by the commencement of the Special Central Assistance. The Group feels that implementation at the district level and below will be strengthened by periodical reiteration of this from the highest levels of the Government of India, the Planning Commission and the State Governments.

(xii) Apart from the formal Governmental system, there is also scope for voluntary organisations to participate in the implementation of developmental programmes. Wherever an appropriate, voluntary organisations of proven capability ad competence should be brought into the programme, to the extent of their capability, and given all necessary facilities.

(xiii) The potential of the voluntary organisations is not being fully tapped. There should be a systematic planning by the Central and State Governments, in consultation with the respective voluntary organisations, of the best that they can do and give them necessary facilities to produce their best. In short, the activity of the voluntary organisations should be *planned* with reference to their capability and the priority needs of the Scheduled Castes.

(xiv) There are a number of individual officers who would consider it a privilege to directly work in the field for the development of the Scheduled Castes. They will be an asset for implementation. Such officers should be utilised for gingering up and speeding up the implementation. They should not be made responsible for sanction and routine periodical reporting. Both the Central and State Governments should provide opportunities for such officers to function in the field for Scheduled Castes Development effectively and without being handicapped by routine work. These Governments should create suitable supernumerary posts for them such as Additional Development Commission/Joint Development Commissioner/Deputy Development Commissioner, etc. They should directly deal with the District Magistrate or the State Development Commissioner/Planning Secretary/Secretary in-charge of Scheduled Castes Development, etc.

(xv) Arrangement for this purpose should not be difficult on the analogy of study leave, ensuring their full pay during the period when they do these voluntary services. They should also be allowed to retain the house allotted to them so that their family can stay in the last place or residence of an any suitable place and these officers may be relieved of any worry about their families.

(xvi) There are a number of teachers and hostel inmates of the Scheduled Castes and post-graduate students and other social workers who would also be interested in doing a stint of voluntary service at the field level. They should also be given all facilities and their work should be planned and worked out at the district level in consultation with them by the district authorities, so that their activities meet both their area of interest and capability and also the needs of the Scheduled Castes. They should be suitably monitored. Such voluntary workers may be particularly useful in drawing up the programmes, helping to set up the beneficially-participant system, in helping through with the smooth and effective implementation of special programmes.

(xvii) It must be realised and accepted that, at all levels, the task of preparing the Special Component Plans is essential that of the Planning set-up, like the State Planning Department. No doubt the Planning Department must similarly get the plans prepared by the personnel in each department in respect of their respective sectors. But the task of guiding this exercise and putting the outcome from each Department together into a meaningful Special Component Plans which is capable/sound implementation and monitoring should be undertaken by the Planning Departments. The Planning Department can also fully utilise the capability of the Department Incharge of Scheduled Castes. But to relegate the task itself to the Department in-charge of Scheduled Castes is likely to adversely effect the quality of the plan and will naturally have an adverse bearing on implementation.

(xviii) In view of the importance of the proper implementation of the economic development programmes for Scheduled Castes, it is necessary to have an effective High Level Committee in the Government of India with powers and competence to give mandatory directions in order to ensure that the requisite steps are fully, promptly and competently taken by the various Central Ministries and other Central agencies.

(xix) Each State Governments should set up a similar High level Committee with the Chief Minister as the Chairman.

11.10 (i) It is essential to upgrade the level of Block Development Officer and attract better quality personnel into this important post.

(ii) Every IAS Officer/PCS Officer/direct recruit Gazetted Officer of Development departments such as Agriculture, Animal Husbandry Cooperation, etc., should posted as Block Development Officer for a minimum period before they go on the posts at the district level.

(iii) Subsequently every IAS Officer and PCS Officer before he becomes ripe for District charge and every direct Recruit Gazetted Officer of Departments such as Agriculture, Animal Husbandry, Cooperation, etc., before he becomes ripe for region-level charge should be posted for a minimum tenure as Project Officer in Charge of SFDA/IRDP, etc.

(iv) The total length of service as BDO and Project Officers by personnel in these services should not be less than 3 years and should preferably be 5 years.

(v) Every IAS Officer should also he posted at Additional District Magistrate/Additional Deputy Commissioner/Additional District Collector in-charge of Scheduled Castes Development for at least two years, before he is given District Charge.

(vi) Officers of the IPS must also be appointed to such posts before they are posted as SP. This exposure is essential and useful both from the point of view of orienting the law and order machinery towards the problems of the Scheduled Castes and other weaker sections and also from the point of view of giving a very necessary developmental experience to young IPS officers and tapping their talent in the tasks of development.

(vii) In the training programme of IAS Officers, IPS Officers, PCS Officers and direct recruit Gazetted Officers of Developmental departments such as Agriculture, Animal Husbandry, Cooperation, etc., specific training input regarding the problems and developmental programmes of the Scheduled Castes and other weaker sections must be introduced.

11.12 (i) The beneficiary participants should be educated and trained on the following aspects: –

(a) awareness;
(b) avenues of marketable self-employment the various criteria of their viability and successful working threats to their viability and successful working, preventives and remedies to deal with those threats;
(c) information regarding various departments and agencies concerned with the delivery of programmes of benefit to them, their procedures, the addresses of functionaries at different levels, etc.;
(d) important aspects of implementation of their programmes and the core areas to which their attention should be invited in order that programmes/schemes get successfully implemented;
(e) elements of accounting and management pertaining to their own developmental programmes;
(f) understanding of their rights under various Statutes such as Land Reforms Act, Minimum Wages Act, Protection of Civil Right Act, Bonded Labour Act, etc., and how to secure these rights;
(g) linkage with agencies concerned with at the above;
(h) linkage with law and order agencies for their protection.

(ii) As mentioned in the Chapter on Human Resources Development, they should be assisted and enable to throw up a cadre of non-formal workers/representatives from among themselves. This cadre should be given the benefit of relevant education and training by the appropriate developmental agencies including financial institutions. The payment of essential minimal honorarium to such representatives of the participant groups must figure in each programme. There should be a system of regular meetings of these honorary non-formal workers with the District block authorities, where the details of the progress of implementation should be discussed. They should also be given easy access the District Collector and other officers at the district/block levels and also the concerned State levels officers in respect of the implementation of their schemes and other developmental matters. These representatives should also be invited to the meetings of the district level and block level committees. To these meetings, district level and lower level police officers should also be invited so that the representatives of the Scheduled Castes may be able to bring to their notice any problems of a law and order nature that they may be faced with, for which they may need elective protection of the Police machinery. This is an important aspect of implementation because there are vested interest in society who may try to obstruct and thwart the development of the Scheduled Castes for obvious reasons. It must be perceived by the Scheduled Castes as well as potential obstructions that the law and order machinery is on the side of the Scheduled Castes in their legitimate pursuit of their development.

(iii) In this manner, the participant groups should be fully involved in the programmes of their development right from the formulation stage through implementation and monitoring to post-implementation management.

(iv) They should thus be enabled to fully operate as a genuine pressure group to ginger up implementation.

(v) In this manner, the scope for a parasitic middleman class to emerge between the delivery system of the Govt. and the beneficiary-participants should be totally ruled out.

11.16 (i) Arrangement for concurrent, monitoring and evaluation must be set up covering all levels namely, the Block, District, the State and the Centre.

(ii) Each Department/agency should be responsible for devising suitable reporting, evaluation and timely correctional systems for the development programmes for Scheduled Castes, within its purview.

(iii) In respect of composite schemes the department/agency which has been charged with overall responsibility of each programme for the Scheduled Castes, must be responsible for monitoring and evaluation, etc., as well.

(iv) The Staff and other requirements for enabling effective monitoring and evaluation must be inbuilt in each programme and this should be recognised as an essential input of the composite approach.

(v) Officers at the policy-making and decision-making levels must undertake extensive field visits to assess the implementation of the various programmes for the development of Scheduled Castes.

(vi) Specific evaluation of the various programmes must be regularly and systematically undertaken at all levels.

(vii) Studies on the programmes of the development of the Scheduled Castes must be commissioned by organisations other than Government Departments and independent and expert bodies as well.

(viii) The machinery at the Block District, State and Central levels should be strengthened to meet the demands of the monitoring and evaluation tasks.

12.9 (i) It should be recognised that the Department in charge of the development of the Scheduled Castes has a significant and crucial role to play, that it has so far been regarded as a relatively less important Department and that there is immediate need to improve its status and to make it effective and strong.

(ii) The Department incharge of the development of Scheduled Castes should be adequately strengthened and should also be given sufficient importance so that it is able to attract capable officers.

(iii) It should be made advantageous both economically and career-wise, for personnel in all wings of public services to work for the weaker sections especially the Scheduled Castes. These measures, in the view of what has been explained in the foregoing paragraphs and in the light of what has been stated in the Framework document of the VI Plan, should include the following: –

(a) Compensatory allowances which will not only neutralise the additional cost incurred by those working in this sector, but will also act as an incentive;
(b) Education, medical and other allowances, facilities for housing also in the last place of residence if these are situations like where two establishments have to be maintained;
(c) Foreign deputations, deputation to the United Nations and other International services as also posting in Ministries, which have such attractions, being restricted only to those who have put in substantial period of service in this sector and related fields.

(iv) The personnel policy must stress that work in respect of the development of Scheduled Castes will contribute to the promotion avenues of the officers. In the assessment of the officers also their performance and work in the matter of the development of the Scheduled Castes must be one of the most important criteria.

(v) There should be no shifts and transfers of officers who have been posted to work in post directly relevant to the development of Scheduled Castes, before they put in 3 to 5 years of service in such posts.

(vi) If promotions become due while the officer is working in such posts, these should be given to them in the same post without having to shift them to other departments.

13

WORKING GROUP ON TRIBAL DEVELOPMENT DURING SIXTH PLAN 1980-85, 1980 — REPORT[1]

Chairman Dr. Bhupinder Singh

Members Representative from the Planning Commission; Representative from the Ministry of Finance (Plan Fin.); Representative from the Ministry of Agriculture; Representative from the Ministry of Education and Culture; Representative from the Ministry of Rural Reconstruction; Representative from the Ministry of Health and Family Welfare; Representative from the Ministry of Industry; Representative from the Reserve Bank of India; Representative from the States of Andhra Pradesh, Bihar, Madhya Pradesh, Orissa and Tamil Nadu.

Appointment

The Working Group for the formulation of strategy and plan priorities for the Sixth Plan 1980-85, for the development of Scheduled Tribes, Scheduled Castes and Weaker Sections of the society constituted by the Planning Commission constituted a Group on Development of Scheduled Tribes on July 24, 1980.

Terms of Reference

(a) To review the approach, strategy and priorities in respect of protection and developmental programmes for scheduled tribes/ scheduled castes and weaker sections;

(b) To review the programmes taken up by the States and Central Ministries in respect of these categories;

(c) To formulate concrete proposals for 1980-85 in the context of

1. New Delhi, Ministry of Home Affairs, 1980, 170 p.

a ten year perspective and suggest the phasing of development programmes, indicating financial, physical, legislative and other aspects; and

(d) To review the administrative arrangements for implementation of programmes in States and Centre and suggest measures for improvement.

Contents

Forward; Review of First Tribal Sub-Plan 1974-79; Approach and Strategy; Outlays and Financial Framework; Administration of Tribal Sub-Plan Areas; The Planning Process; Basic Needs of Tribal Communities; Protective Measure; Credit and Marketing; Technology for Tribal Communities; Agriculture and Allied Sectors; Forestry; Shifting Cultivation; Industries; Education; Health; Infrastructural Development; Pockets of Tribal Concentration Dispersed Tribals; Primitive Tribal Groups; Summary of Recommendations; Annexures from I to VIII; Appendices I & II.

Recommendations

CHAPTER 1

Review of First Tribal Sub-Plan 1974-79

(1) Due share should flow from divisible pool of a State Plan to Tribal Sub-Plan. Giving some weightage for backwardness, accrual of due share of benefits to tribal regions from non-divisible component need also to be ensured.

(2) In planning for tribal areas the balance should be redressed in favour of divisible sectors.

(3) Planning process needs to be re-oriented to acquire a bias in favour of beneficiary-oriented schemes, making the scheduled tribe families a target group.

(4) The Centre having a special constitutional responsibility towards the scheduled tribes and Scheduled Areas, the role of Central Ministries is significant and, therefore, quantification of funds by different Ministries/Departments should be made adequately and on a regular basis.

(5) With the emphasis on family approach for development

during the Sixth Plan period, the programmes can take off effectively only with the contribution from the financial institutions. Adequate and timely flow of funds from financial institutions has to be ensured.

(6) Programmes for primitive tribal communities need to be taken up firmly and their problems tackled with vigour and earnestness.

(7) Effective monitoring arrangements in accordance with the recommendations of the Working Group on the subject should be made.

(8) In order to make a fair assessment of the impact of the programmes, independent as well as internal evaluation need to be taken up on a regular basis.

(9) Many factors have been responsible for shortfall in utilisation during 1974-79 of funds of State Plan and Special Central Assistance. Among them are inadequacy of administrative machinery, lack of general preparedness for investments, deficiency in accounting system, procedural delays and delays in issuing sanctions. These inadequacies should be removed expeditiously.

CHAPTER 2

Approach and Strategy

(1) Calculations show that the range of percentage of funds earmarked for beneficiary-oriented programmes is between 0.02 to 15.66 mostly up to 5 per cent. The planning process needs to be reoriented to acquire a bias in favour of beneficiary-oriented schemes.

(2) In the Sixth Plan, the most urgent task would be to create in the economic field, impact of an order which will enable 50 per cent of scheduled tribe families cross the poverty-line, requiring increase in productivity levels in the fields of agriculture, horticulture, animal husbandry, forestry, industry etc.

(3) Education should become the key sector.

(4) The attainment of the two objectives would vitally depend on adequate infrastructure for the creation of which there should be requisite financial and physical effort.

(5) Concomitant with the aforesaid three-fold aims in the Sixth Plan, and the most important, assiduous exertions are necessary to eliminate exploitation of tribals in the fields of land-tenure, money-lending, debt-bondage, trade, excise, forest, labour, etc.

(6) During the Fifth Plan period, tribal sub-Plans covered 65 per

cent of the scheduled tribe population in the country. During the Sixth Plan, 75 per cent of such population should be covered applying the criteria of a minimum of 10,000 total population with 50 per cent or more of scheduled tribe population to identify further pockets of tribal concentration.

(7) In pockets of tribals concentration, the thrust should be towards raising the socio-economic standard of individual tribal family.

(8) The process of planning has to be built up, funnelling upwards from Block through ITDP, district, State to national levels, Inter-weaving of sectoral programmes has to take place at the Block, ITDP as well as State levels. In the formulation exercise, association of tribal representatives would ensure that the plans are reflective of the needs, aspirations and inclinations of the tribal communities.

(9) 'Primitive' tribal groups require sensitive handling an separate project reports for each of the 52 communities should be prepared, in which problems as well as remedial measures therefor should be highlighted. Separate administrative structure for their development should be created.

(10) The delivery system in tribal areas should be overhauled and strengthened. For ending tribal exploitation in credit-cum-marketing. LAMPS should be streamlined and strengthened.

(11) Regulations of anti-exploitative nature should be enforced strictly in the field of land, credit, bondage, labour, etc.

(12) The data base for planning for tribal development should be strong and reliable and steps therefor, are urgently necessary.

CHAPTER 3

Outlays and Financial Framework

(1) Inter-sectoral priority in sub-Plan area should be determined on the basis of specific requirements of the region and relevance of programmes to tribal communities particularly the weakest sections amongst them. Accordingly, the tribal sub-Plan 1980-85 will be a viable area development plan with focus on development of tribal communities.

(2) From the divisible pool of a State Plan, apart from due share, weightage should be given to tribal areas. From the non-divisible portion, accrual of due share should be ensured.

(3) In the States' budget quantified funds are reflected either as sub-head of a minor head in the budget of each sectoral department or as a single demand head whereunder quantified funds of all sectoral departments are reflected. We recommend the second arrangement for better control and easy re-appropriation within tribal sub-Plan sectors.

(4) The Central Ministries should carry out completely the exercise of quantifiable resources for tribal areas, assisting those schemes particularly for which State resources might not be adequate. They may also adopt the budgetary mechanism of reflecting the share of tribal areas separately.

(5) The Central Ministries may determine the possible supplementation which they expect to make to the States from their plans for key programmes.

(6) The basic investments in tribal areas are to be made from the State Plans and funds of the Centrally-sponsored and Central schemes. The role of Special Central Assistance of the Home Ministry is that of a gap-filler, i.e., to make available resources for specially relevant schemes for which funds are otherwise not in sight.

(7) The formula for distribution of special Central assistance among States should also contain a factor relating to performance.

(8) Institutional finance should augment State funds more for schemes of individual benefits, than has been the case so far.

(9) Full modalities should be worked out to operationalise availability of differential rate of interest finance in tribal areas.

(10) To bridge the gap in performance, there should be constant dialogue and concerted effort between the development agencies and financial institutions, particularly in the field.

(11) The effort of financial institutions should be quantified separately in respect of each of the three sections, i.e., scheduled tribes, scheduled castes and other weaker sections.

(12) For the Sixth Plan period, the national projection of the tribal sub-Plan may be Rs. 2700 crores from State Plan, Rs. 750 crores from Central Ministries, Rs. 1000 crores of Special Central Assistance and Rs. 550 crores of institutional finance, making in all an estimated total of Rs. 5000 crores.

(13) As in the case of State Plan outlays, earmarking of funds from the non-Plan side also for tribal areas should be undertaken by the State Government.

(14) Review should be undertaken by each State Government of the State of administration in the Scheduled Areas and proposals made

to the Government of India for upgrading it to a satisfactory level, so that the question of securing funds under the First Proviso of Article 275(1) could be initiated.

(15) The grants made by the Seventh Finance Commission for payment of compensatory allowance to State employees working in tribal areas and for construction of residential accommodation for State employees posted in these areas should be utilised expeditiously and their impact assessed.

(16) The example of Gujarat Government of issue of financial sanctions for a five-year period indicating annual phasing and assuring field agencies availability of funds every year without having to wait for the annual formal sanctions, might be followed with advantage by other State Governments.

(17) A supplement of State budget for the tribal sub-plan area giving a clear picture of project-wise financial position would be helpful.

(18) Financial discipline should be followed rigorously. Departmental as well audited statements of accounts should be prepared regularly and punctually. If necessary, specific staff should be appointed for the purpose.

CHAPTER 4

Administration of Tribal Sub-Plan Areas

The Fifth Schedule

(1) The delivery system for tribal areas should be made effective.

(2) Multipurpose village level workers have been found more useful for tribal areas than the specialist village agricultural workers, as the tribal economy is, by and large, undifferentiated. The coverage should be intensive at the gross-root level.

(3) Integration should be ensured of technical and administrative cadres at Block and Project levels.

(4) The Block should be an integral part of the command-chain-Village-Panchayat-Block-ITDP-district-Division-State.

(5) Development Blocks may be rationalised by reorganising them into smaller Blocks (adopting norms similar to those for TD Blocks) with reference to tribal demographic situation. They may be strengthened to underpin ITDPs.

(6) The Project Administrator (Class I Officer) in-charge of ITDP should have full control over Blocks or Talukas and the BDOs or Taluka Development Officers. He should have a definite standing in the district administrative hierarchy.

(7) In States having large tribal areas, semi-autonomous regional bodies might be created, comprised of both official and non-official elements. In Bihar, the *status quo* anto may be restored by unifying the three regional Authorities into a single Authority for Chota Nagpur and Santhal Parganas.

(8) The Tribal Development Department in a State should be made the nodal department for tribal development programmes. It should be consulted by the Administrative Departments and Planning Department at the stage of formulation of such programmes for five-year and annual plans.

(9) Administration for tribal areas should be comprehensive and unified, combining development, regulatory and public distribution systems. Such combination should be effected in the Project Administrators at the ITDP-level definitely and at Block level if feasible.

(10) State-level Committees should be activated.

(11) Tribes Advisory Councils and Tribes Advisory Boards should be made active.

(12) The quality of personnel is crucial to implementation of development programmes. Only suitable officers, i.e., those having the requisite aptitude, empathy and dedication should be posted in tribal areas. The State Governments may adopt the recommendations of the Maheshwar Prasad Committee for attachment of incentives to posts in tribal areas and selection of suitable personnel. The award of the Seventh Finance Commission for construction of residential accommodation for and payment of compensatory allowance to State employees posted in tribal areas should be utilised expeditiously and the results assessed.

(13) Personnel in tribal areas have to be built up by continuous exposure to work situations in those areas. In States having sizable tribal areas, sub-cadres within the selected State cadres, whose members should have an obligation to serve tribal areas for a period of 5-15 years, should be constituted. In the recruitment of field-level functionaries, whose cadres are generally regional or district-based, preference should be given to tribal and local persons, particularly in departments like Police, Revenue, Forest and Education.

(14) Development of backward classes, including tribal develop-

ment, should be a full subject to all entry-training programmes of State, Central and all India Services.

(15) Not only the statutory Panchayats, but also traditional tribal institutions should be revived and reinforced and made vehicles of tribal participation in development works.

(16) Tribal participation will become a reality if their involvement is effected in both planning and implementation stages. At the Panchayat level, a committee should be constituted of the Sarpanch, a ward member and the Panchayat Secretary to execute simple programmes of development such as excavation of drinking-water wells, laying of roads, construction of buildings for educational and health institutions, etc. Panchayat should also form an audit committee to comment on the work done and report to the Panchayat. Similar implementational committees should be formed at the Panchayati Samiti (Block) level.

(17) Reservation in Panchayat bodies proportional to population of scheduled tribes should be made to make them representative and reflect the demographic reality.

(18) Participation of youthful elements among scheduled tribes and youthful dormitories for development purposes should be enlisted. Camps for the young and the old should be held.

(19) Voluntary organisations should be enabled to play an adequate role for stimulating tribal leadership and training tribals. Non-formal workers capable of performing grass-root extension and cooperative functions should be picked up from among the tribal communities. The potential of tribal youth institutions should be exploited fully.

(20) State Regulations dealing with alienation of tribal land, undesirable activities of money-lenders, debt bondage, and the Act of Labour Ministry dealing with inter-State migration should be enforced strictly. States may also consider adoption of a Regulation for regulating the activities of unscrupulous contractors and intermediaries in industrial zones located in Scheduled Areas.

(21) To counter exploitation of tribals in the fields of trade, commerce and credit, LAMPS should be streamlined and made purposeful.

(22) A sound monitoring system should be established and the monitoring channels should flow through State, divisional, district, ITDP, Block down to the grass-root levels.

(23) At the Centre, the Central Ministries, the Planning Commission and the Ministry of Home Affairs each should have in-built

monitoring assemblages.

(24) Periodic evaluation should be undertaken through independent bodies, utilising feed-back for policy formulation. General all-round evaluation should be carried out periodically through concurrent and post-facto performance audit.

(25) The role of the State Governor should be readdressed by the concerned States to enable him to play a positive role in tribal development.

CHAPTER 5

The Planning Process

(1) The process of planning has to be built up from below funnelling upwards, implying realistic integrated effort.

(2) It has to be initiated simultaneously at three levels; the Development Block, the ITDP and the State. At each level, balanced inter-sectoral programmes relative to the natural resource endowment, the needs, aspirations, skills, and aptitude of the people and resource availability should emerge.

(3) Block planning should particularly relate to sectors having a bearing on family-oriented schemes such as agriculture, horticulture, animal husbandry, forestry, minor irrigation, tiny cottage, village and small industries.

(4) The projects for the Sixth Plan period of ITDPs in a State should determine the size and character of the State Tribal sub-Plan.

(5) The five-year Block plan should be ready at least six months before submission of the State Tribal sub-Plan to the Planning Commission. The ITDP should take not more than three months to complete the project report. The State Tribal Development Department should not take more than three months to draft the tribal sub-Plan. At each level, the Plan should be a product of intense study and consultation.

(6) A 20-year perspective plan will help the planning process greatly.

(7) The exercise of Annual Plan for the following year of a Block should be completed within June of the financial year and the ITDP should complete its formulations by the end of August. The State's tribal sub-plan should emerge by October to enable its discussion in the Planning Commission in November leading to its finalisation. The

process should culminate in incorporation of the financial provisions in the State budget for the succeeding year.

(8) If the share of each ITDP could be reflected under the single demand head of the State budget relating to tribal development, it would mean knowledge of financial resources for the ITDPs in advance.

(9) Greater attention should be paid to the divisible sectors in a State Plan budget, as benefits from such sectors can make a direct impact on the socio-economic development of a tribal family.

(10) An ITDP should be given planning staff support to enable it to carry out the various tasks.

CHAPTER 6

Basic Needs of Tribal Communities

(1) The concept of minimum needs in the case of tribal communities would need close scrutiny, particularly in regard to the primitive groups. The general concept may not apply *in toto*.

(2) To ward off starvation for a few weeks in a year, which is a normal feature in some tribal areas, creation of employment potential off-season should be regarded as one of the basic needs.

(3) On account of the prevalent low level of nourishment in tribal areas, nutrition programmes should have universal coverage therein.

(4) At least one safe drinking-water source should be available within one kilometre of a village or a hamlet in tribal areas within the Plan period.

(5) The norms for establishment of health institutions in tribal areas should be lowered.

(6) Concomitant with the attempt to improve their nutritional levels, the 'primitive' tribal groups should be brought within the fold of genetic, preventive and curative medical sciences.

(7) The norm for establishment of a school should be examined by each State Government in the light of the scattered population in tribal areas and the low rate of literacy among the tribal communities. Elementary and middle education should be made more functional and relevant for tribals.

(8) Local material for a reasonable house for every tribal should be accepted as a priority charge in forest produce.

(9) For countering exploitation, stationary and mobile multi-

purpose cooperative societies should be set up in the remote interior tribal areas.

CHAPTER 7

Protective Measures

Land Alienation

(1) The existing laws relating to transfer of land belonging to scheduled tribes should be continuously reviewed to plug loopholes.

(2) Areas of high incidence of land alienation in each State should be identified and suitable remedial measures taken on a time-bound basis.

(3) In areas where land restoration work is sizable, adequate machinery should be created to settle the issues expeditiously.

(4) Necessary inputs to develop the restored land should form a part of the developmental programmes.

(5) Formal records of rights of tribals over land must be prepared within a time-frame.

(6) Progress of restoration of land should be reviewed regularly at the State and national levels.

Excise Policy

(7) The excise policy for tribal areas, as evolved by the Government of India, should be implemented within a specified period.

(8) Tribals should be allowed to brew liquor for personal consumption and social purposes. A strict watch should be kept to ensure that the concession to brew liquor is not misused.

(9) Sustained social work enlisting the assistance of voluntary organisations should be undertaken to wean the tribals away from the habit of drinking.

(10) Regulations for money-lending and debt bondage should be enforced strictly. Schemes of rehabilitation of freed bonded labour should be effective.

CHAPTER 8

Credit and Marketing

(1) LAMPS may be static or mobile. Weekly Hats might be the most suitable sites for establishment of LAMPS. "Integrated co-operative development centre" or a 'growth centre' comprised of a

LAMPS, a godown, a branch of cooperative or commercial bank, a post office, a market yard and such other ancillary services should be encouraged.

(2) The States should examine whether the constitution of LAMPS and withdrawal or disappearance of older societies have not resulted in depletion of facilities. The effort should result in further provision of facilities.

(3) LAMPS should adopt model by-laws so that they acquire tribal orientation. Barter system should be allowed. Public distribution should be in-built in LAMPS.

(4) For credit purposes, LAMPS may be liked to district-cooperative banks supplemented with lines of credit with other financial institutions like commercial banks for free flow of credit.

(5) For marketing purposes, to the extent possible, LAMPS should be affiliated to a single apex level marketing body like the Tribal Development Corporation. In certain circumstances, however, multiple-affiliation may be necessary.

(6) The Reserve Bank of India may refinance consumption credit advances to tribals made by central financing agencies.

(7) The differential rate of interest finance should be operationalised. For the purpose, if necessary, the State Governments should bear the difference between actual administrative costs and 4 per cent through subsidy financed from the State Plan resources or Special Central Assistance. Secondly, coordination should be ensured at different hierarchical levels between the corresponding developmental and financing agencies. District credit plans should be prepared by district credit councils and the requirement to be distributed over various banks.

(8) DRI finance should flow through commercial banks and where branches of such banks are not available through LAMPS as per the decision of the Government of India. For the purpose, commercial banks may supply adequate DRI finance to LAMPS.

(9) State Governments should review their programmes with a view to full availment of the assistance of the National Cooperative Development Corporation (NCDC) for strengthening share capital base of LAMPS, establishment of small and medium sized units for processing of agricultural, horticultural and minor forest produce, construction of godowns, purchase of transport vehicles, rehabilitation, expansion and modernisation of existing processing units and establishment of bakery units, cold storages, etc.

(10) Vehicles provided under NCDC's Rural Consumer Scheme could be used for mobile LAMPS.

(11) At the national level, a Federation of Tribal Development Corporation called TRIFED might be set up to handle problems of State Tribal Development Corporations, Forest Development Corporations and other such State bodies.

(12) At present, there is no satisfactory arrangement for providing seasonal working capital to marketing bodies like LAMPS, TDCs, etc., for farm and forest produce. Since marketing is crucial for providing effective protection to tribals, the need should be met on an assured and priority basis by the Central Cooperative banks and the Reserve Bank on a concessional rate of interest.

(13) The guiding principle in pricing should be a fair return to the tribal, obtained in market place deducting therefrom cost elements. Where labour only is involved, the statutory minimum wage should be taken into account.

(14) A suitable regulation placing curbs on undesirable activities should be promulgated for marketing centres, permitting an effective say of the local community in the management of the market. The practice of auctioning weekly markets should be discontinued, as the potential for harassment of tribals by outside elements is great.

(15) Each State should examine the position of personnel manning LAMPS and devise procedures for the selection of persons having the requisite competence, sympathy, knowledge and experience for being posted to LAMPS. They must not only have proper orientation but also familiarity with cooperative laws, minor forest and farm produce, etc. Cooperative training institutes should produce specific course contents for officials to be posted to tribal areas.

(16) In the State Directorates of Cooperation, there should be a separate wing to handle LAMPS and connected bodies, under a Joint/Deputy Registrar of Cooperative Societies. The Managing Director, Tribal Development Corporation may be conferred ex-officio status of the Additional/Joint/Deputy Registrar.

(17) The position of overdues in tribal areas may be reviewed and genuine cases shifted from the spurious ones. In case of genuine overdues, effort should be made for recovery. The work of recovery should be completed within a year under the overall guidance of a Project committee.

(18) Simple procedures should be devised for landing and recovering advances.

(19) At the State-level, a Review and Implementation Committee comprised of the Tribal Commissioner, Registrar-Cooperative Societies, Managing Director-Tribal Development Corporations, the Join/Deputy Registrars heading the wing in the Directorate, Managing Director Forest Development Corporation, a representative of NCDC, may be set up to take stock of progress made in implementation of various schemes and providing directions. It should meet quarterly and report to the State and Central Government.

CHAPTER 9

Technology for Tribal Communities

(1) The pace of technology transfer to scheduled tribe communities has to be tempered with constraints of long isolation, slow cross-fertilisation of ideas, constricted educational and informative systems and technology-ritual conflict.

(2) Prototype technology transfer models should have relevance to the existing economic-socio-cultural milieu and its absorption capacity. In theory, in consonance with the wide range of variation among the various tribal communities, it might be desirable to evolve a number of such models equalling the number of scheduled tribe communities, but practical considerations would limit the number in a given situation.

(3) Each prototype model should be cast in a project approach and not be of piecemeal character.

(4) Consideration of the agricultural sector has to be on national, regional and micro levels. From the national point of view, dry-farming techniques have to be evolved, integration in the field of agriculture, horticulture, animal husbandry and forestry effected and the policy of establishment in tribal areas of experimental and seed multiplication farms followed. At the regional level, the policy has to be given a concrete shape by both national and State agencies for promotion of dry-farming. At the local level, the ethos of each tribal community should govern the plan for technology transfer and the schemes have to be specific and relevant.

(5) In the ayacut of irrigation, projects, command area concept should be applied.

(6) The horticultural potential of tribal areas should be fully exploited through upgraded technology, marketing and processing ar-

rangements.

(7) The traditional expertise of tribals in animal husbandry should be relied upon for development plans, particularly in respect of the small animal.

(8) In the field of industries, upgradation of intermediate technology might be apt, examples being tassar, oil-seed extraction, sabai grass treatment.

(9) Bullock-cart should be introduced in those tribal areas where it has not reached. The cart should supplant as much as possible the high-cost petrol or diesel automobile.

(10) Advance planning and action for imparting education in skills to tribals has to be undertaken in areas where industrial and mining complexes are being inducted or are proposed to be inducted.

(11) Special training should be imparted for unstructured, non-formal employment without insistence on essential qualifications.

(12) In forestry, sector, training in lodging, carpentry, wood-working should be organised and the tribal involved in advanced methods of working of forest.

(13) Training of tribal women, as in mixed farming, would yield rich dividends.

(14) In the field of health, in view of the endemic communicable diseases, sickle-cell, anaemia and other genetic abnormalities, through careful mapping of tribal communities, genetic counselling methods would have to be adopted.

(15) In the plan for tribal technology, holding of training courses in the relevant field should be an integral part.

(16) Like the Design Institute at Ahmedabad, regional institutes may be located in tribal areas for evolving relevant technological modules for the synergy, individual techniques and equipment in the tribal context.

(17) Technology transfer of the right grade will require personnel of sensitivity, competence and perspective for which pursuit of the right type of personnel policies is indispensable.

CHAPTER 10

Agriculture and Allied Subjects

Agriculture

(1) For meaningful agricultural development plans of tribal areas, the agro-climatic conditions, the traditional agronomic practices and

cultural constraints of the tribal areas have to be kept in view. The proved technology and practices of tribal areas should be subjected to adaptive research and scrutinised with reference to acceptability and assimilation among tribals.

(2) From the national standpoint, dry-farming techniques need to be evolved for tribal areas. The existing low-grade economy with little surplusage, barred access to high-cost inputs such as fertilisers, pesticides, etc., and the local manurial resources in the form of forest little and dung-waste should be fully reckoned with. However, adoption of modern technology should be considered as linked to not merely its availability but more to the existing technological practices conjoined with religious, ritualistic and cultural mores. The policy, in effect, should have multiple perception resting on agronomical, economic sociological, cultural and other dimensions.

(3) At the regional or State level, the national policy has to be concretised by the State farms by undertaking multiplication of seed varieties as a part of adaptive research and experimentation. Local energy and manurial sources should be brought into the fold of drive and extension to reduce cost. Different practices and techniques should be subjected to field trials.

(4) At the local or micro level, the ethos of each tribal community should govern plans of technology transfer.

(5) The Ministry of Agriculture might assign the tasks to specific organisations at the national, State and local levels. The concerned institutions at the three levels should form a national grid for development of tribal agriculture. The three tiers should have constant and meaningful interaction among them.

Irrigation

(1) The potential of irrigation in tribal areas being reportedly high, clear perspective in each State for its development should be framed.

(2) Master plans for irrigation development should be prepared which should include flow irrigation major, medium and minor, lift irrigation and ground water development.

(3) Areas of growing pressure of population, with limited agricultural land, should be identified and given priority in the irrigation plans.

(4) There should no financial constraint for excavation of small

irrigation dug wells each at a moderate cost. The risk of infructuous expenditure on digging of well, e.g., on encountering rock strata, should be borne by the State.

(5) Development of land, construction of channels should be part of irrigation projects, in so far as tribals are concerned.

(6) Irrigation project reports should provide for scheme for rehabilitation of displaced tribals along with the requisite finance.

(7) Intensive extension support should be provided in the irrigated areas so that the cultivator gets full benefit of new investment. Full water-rates should be realisable only after, say, a period of six years or so. The first three-year period may be treated as free demonstration.

(8) On account of multi-agency operation, the tribal carries substantial risk in obtaining irrigation due to default on the part of any one of the agencies. Tribals should be usually protected from this risk and made liable for payment of water-rate only when irrigation is actually provided.

Horticulture

(1) Tribal areas are generally favourable for horticulture. Hence extensive programme of horticultural development should be taken up.

(2) *In situ* horticultural plantations have been found to be one of the answers to the problem of shifting cultivation. The methodology allows, low administrative cost and greater involvement of tribals.

(3) The problem of marketing in horticulture is crucial and advance action is called for. Small processing plants run by tribals in fruit growing areas should be set up.

Animal Husbandry

(1) Traditionally tribals have been keepers of animals, particularly small animals. Hence, there is potential for cattle-breeding, poultry, piggery, sheep-rearing, goat-keeping, pisciculture and dairying.

(2) Overall perspective for development for each of the fields including effort to be made therein should be drawn up.

(3) Reliance should be more on improvement of local breeds rather than exotic breeds.

(4) Areas like hinterlands of industrial complexes, mining complexes, urban peripheries, etc., should be specially selected for

priorities in animal husbandry programmes.

(5) Adequate marketing arrangements, where possible through cooperative structure, are essential.

(6) For the weaker sections of the community and shifting cultivators, plantation of fodder trees and upgradation of local stock through artificial insemination would be helpful.

(7) The size of the units in each scheme should be small enough as to be manageable by an average tribal.

Fisheries

(1) For tribals fishing provides a supplemental avocation and nutrition.

(2) Scientific management of the existing reservoirs particularly tanks, is needed.

(3) Change in management of tanks or reservoirs from the control of the community to a statutory panchayat or a cooperative should be brought about only where it is anticipated to bring some tangible benefit to the members of the local community.

(4) Number of fish farmers development agencies in tribal areas should be increased.

Consolidation of Institutions

(1) In tribal areas a high degree of specialisation on the part of institutions is wasteful, particularly in terms of technical manpower. The institutional support, therefore, should be multi-disciplinary, the same centre catering to more than one requirement.

(2) Existing level of utilisation of the institutions in tribal areas already establishment should be reviewed at the local level by the project committees and institutions made multi-purpose. They should also be assigned the responsibility of extension in the surrounding villages.

Orientation and Adaptation

(1) Orientation of technical personnel should be taken up on a priority basis for not only understanding the physical parameters but also the sociological factors of tribal situation.

(2) The technical skills of the tribal people have to be taken as a

key condition for introduction of new practices.

(3) Women play an important role in tribal areas. Hence, they have to be trained in a big way under the training programmes.

Integration of Programmes at ITDP Level

(1) Since the ITDPs have a wide range covering total investment from all the schemes in State Plans as well as Central Ministries' plans, all programmes meant for specific target groups or aimed at solving specific problems should be built into the ITDPs, defining clearly the basic purpose of each of the programmes within the overall frame of the ITDP.

(2) All financial flows may emerge at the ITDP level below which they should emerge as balanced set of programmes. A suitable accounting system at the ITDP level would be necessary. But full integration of all programmes should be aimed at.

CHAPTER 11

Forestry

(1) The significant role that forests play in tribal economy has to be clearly recognised and the forest policy under formulation should have appropriate orientation.

(2) While the management of forests and vegetal resources should be such as will provide for maximum goods and services for the well-being of all sections of the country's population, there has to be a judicious balance between the national and the local particularly the tribal needs.

(3) The national goal of covering one-third of the area under forests necessitates a land-use pattern, calling for identification of areas fit for agriculture and silviculture.

(4) Reserve forests should be demarcated for production forestry to meet the national demands of industries, communications, defence, etc. Secondly, the growing needs of the community in the way of fuel, fodder, agricultural implements, house construction, domestic furniture, fruit, flower, herbs and medicines have to be satisfied through social forestry in village forests, protected forests and other waste-land around villages. Thirdly, the needs of environment and conservation can be met through tree-cover planted on land falling outside the

aforesaid two categories.

(5) In forest-rich regions, forestry oriented tribal development programmes should be framed in which agriculture may occupy secondary position. For such ITDPs separate working (management) plans would be necessary for linking the forestry programmes with economic development of tribals.

(6) For the achievement of the area under forests to the optimal one-third level, the pace of reforestation of 13 per cent existing degraded forests will have to be quickened and afforestation of 10 per cent of the country's total area scattered as waste-land and strips of land alongside of roads, railway lines, canals, river banks, etc., will have to be effected. The tree-cover programme being colossal, the State Forest Departments by themselves may not be in a position to mount it, let alone achieve it. Besides governmental efforts it would therefore, be necessary (a) to actively invest panchayats, corporate bodies voluntary organisations and individuals with the responsibility of forestry in and around villages, (b) raise a "tree army" for undertaking silvicultural operations in the more distant degrated, marginal and sub-marginal lands outside the forest areas.

(7) As a matter of broad perspective, the relative areas required for production forestry, social forestry and conservation forestry should be indicated clearly in each State.

(8) The State Forest Department should consider themselves responsible for development of tribals as well as forests. The tribals also should recognise the need to preserve forests. The partnership should inform the new policy.

(9) Forestry operations should be executed through cooperatives of forest labourers which should be encouraged by the forest department as a protective device for the existing forests. The Cooperatives should be given a share in the profits from those operations. Cooperatives should substitute contractors.

(10) Association of the tribals should be ensured in large scale plantation programmes giving them right to the usufruct.

(11) Minor Forest Produce (MFP) plays an important role in tribal economy. The right of tribals to collection of MFP should be conferred by all States.

(12) To ensure remunerative price to tribal marketing of MFP should be organised through cooperatives such as LAMPS. The price should be based on market value. In rich-forested States, MFP Corporations may be created for tackling different matters connected with

MFP collection, grading, collection of marketing intelligence, export and improving the resource base. At national level there should be TRIFED.

(13) In all plantation programmes there should be a mix of species which yield fuelwood, minor forest produce items, fruit, fodder and small timber useful to the local community.

(14) Item-wise survey of MFP, higher exploitation of the potential better methods of collection and grading, improving resource base, developing a system of marketing and distribution, ensuring proper processing and utilisation are necessary.

(15) First processing of MFP through cooperatives of primary collectors should be ensured or value-addition.

(16) Some of the cottage, small and medium forest-based industries, e.g., paper and pulp plants should be located in the tribal area to take advantage of raw material like bamboo and infrastructure that exists in the area.

(17) Research and development of the various items of MFP should be undertaken by the various centres of ICSIR, FRIs and SFRIs, etc., particularly relative to their discovery and multiplication.

(18) Tribals living in forest villages should be given heritable and inalienable rights over the land which they cultivate in the forest villages. All social and economic development programmes should be extended to these villages on the same lines as for residents of tribal villages.

(19) On the pattern of Gujarat schemes, Tribal families should be involved for undertaking silvicultural work as per forest department plans. Tribal families involved in this work should be paid fair wages during gestation period and the profits from the usufruct may be shared on 50 : 50 basis. "Kumra" cultivation as per Andhra Pattern also is commended.

(20) Human resource development through training and extension is essential for conversion of the natural resource endowment into a ready economic asset.

(21) Training and orientation of foresters have to be paid special attention.

(22) Institutional finance may be attracted for forestry schemes, as done by the Gujarat Forest Development Corporation.

CHAPTER 12

Shifting Cultivation

(1) A perspective may be prepared for resettlement of shifting cultivators in 233 blocks spreading over 62 districts of 16 States.

(2) The tribal has evolved harmony between technology and ritual in shifting cultivation. The problem is how to usher in technological advancement in such circumstances without alienating the tribals. The solution may not lie in legal ban on shifting cultivation.

(3) An integrated approach incorporating forestry development on hill tops, horticulture plantations in the intermediate slopes and terrace cultivation in the foot-hills may be a broad strategy. But each contextual micro-situation should be studied to formulate comprehensive programme of resettlement of shifting cultivator.

(4) Pilot rehabilitation schemes may be instituted including rubber, coffee, tea, cashew and horticulture (in situ or otherwise) plantations. Such schemes should be prepared on small regional area basis keeping a mini-catchment or water-shed as the area of operation.

(5) A definite proportion of the total outlay on agriculture and allied sectors in the States having sizable shifting cultivation should be allocated with an additional nucleus funds, in favour of the concerned Project Administrators.

(6) Each project should be executed by multi-disciplinary team working under the guidance of a project officer whose job should be to co-ordinate.

(7) At district level there should be a Supervisory Committee consisting of Collector, Divisional Forest Officer, District Agriculture Officer, District Education Officer, District Medical Officer, etc., as well as tribal M.P. and M.L.As and other non-officials.

(8) Since settlement of shifting cultivator is a sensitive problem, it is advisable to have Watchdog Committee at the State level and nation-levels. These Committees should provide technical support and constantly review programmes of action.

(9) Measures for regulating shifting cultivation should be carried out within the existing social framework in the best interest of the individual family, the community and the ecology.

CHAPTER 13

Industries

(1) In Central India, the tribal belt straddling across the States of West Bengal, Bihar, Orissa, Madhya Pradesh, Andhra Pradesh has become, since a few decades, a zone of intense industrial and mining activity. In this area, the tribals have lost land which is their basic resource and have not, by and large, been able to secure alternative source of livelihood.

(2) The tribals may be prepared before hand to participate in industrialisation or, in the alternative, to make gainful living notwithstanding the establishment of a new modern industry.

(3) Project reports, feasibility studies, etc., preceding establishment of major and medium industries should contain consideration of future of the local communities based on study of all related aspects like the present socio-economic status, the cultural profile and the anthropology of prospective development. Interdisciplinary teams composed of plant technologists, administrators, economists, sociologists, anthropologists and others concerned should go into the matter.

(4) Those members of the tribal communities who can absorb education and skills speedily should be employed in the industrial projects, while others should be got engaged in production sectors in the hinterland of industrial and mining projects.

(5) In order to have clear perception, the Bureau of Public Enterprises should take up leadership role at the national level for location of industries in tribal areas in public sector.

(6) Licensing committees of Ministries should have a member from the Home Ministry and in the State representatives of Tribal Development Departments may be associated with similar committees or bodies.

(7) Traditional tribal handicrafts and products of arts and crafts should be encouraged and markets found therefor. A Committee should be set up to locate vanishing tribal arts and crafts for revival, promotion and development.

(8) To the extent possible, the technology of the tribal artisan may be upgraded.

(9) Forest-based cottage, village and small industries have good scope, e.g., honey-extraction, lac culture, *beedi* leaves processing, on

extraction, tassar culture, tamarind-conversion, wood-based industries, gums and resins, broomsticks manufacture, carpet-making, etc. Some like tassar, oilseeds and *beedi* leaves have major scope. A long-term perspective for the development and marketing of all items with clear targets for the Sixth Plan period should be spelt out. A federated cooperative structure can play a substantial role in boosting economy, while the KVI Commission should become responsible for certain specific items.

(10) The entire Scheduled Area, except the industrially advanced pockets, should be treated as industrially backward.

(11) The anomaly of co-existence of unemployed trained technicians and unfilled skilled jobs should be removed through appropriate measures.

(12) A substantial programme of training in entrepreneurial skills, with follow-up in helping and getting financial support, marketing outlets, supply of raw materials, etc., should be built up.

(13) For tribal migrants, a small advance in the beginning will come in handy and guidance should be provided during migration period, so that they do not fall into the clutches of unscrupulous labour contractors. The provisions of the Inter-State Migrant Workmen (Regulation of Employment and Conditions of Service) Act, 1979 should be enforced strictly.

(14) To safeguard the interests of tribal labour and save them from malpractices employed by contractors in Scheduled Areas, the Regulation suggested by Ministry of Home Affairs may be promulgated by States.

CHAPTER 14

Education

(1) While core economic sectors might hold primacy in planning, education is the key to tribal development. It is an input not only for economic development, but also for inner strength of the tribal communities so that they can meet the new challenge on terms of some degree of equality.

(2) Education has to be tackled on both the non-formal and formal levels.

(3) In the non-formal education programmes in tribal areas, coverage and enrolment of members of scheduled tribes should be

given high priority and quantified. Further, the preparation of curricula and reading material need perceptive and sensitive handling by both the Central and State agencies. The course content should include instruction as to how a tribal should deal with problems connected with land, credit, currency, weights and measures, hygiene, local geography, local administration lower government functionaries, liquor-vendors, etc.

(4) On the formal educational side also, both the qualitative and quantitative aspects should engage serious attention. Steps should be taken to work out syllabi for education, taking into account the culture, technology, ethos and assimilative power of tribal communities. Care should, however, be taken to see that the new syllabi do not place the tribal students in any position of disadvantage with reference to entry into higher educational institutions or employment.

(5) At the national level, the Ministry of Education might set up a body to evolve broad guidelines for imparting the requisite orientation to the conventional educational system. The content and bias may, however, have to differ from one tribe to another, in view of variation in the socio-cultural backgrounds among the various scheduled tribe communities in a State and, as such, in each State expert committees may be have to be constituted to prepare syllabi and courses in accordance with guidelines to be issued by the national body.

(6) The States should be asked to consider and take action for instruction at the primary stage in mother tongue of tribal children.

(7) By the end of Sixth Plan period, at least 5 per cent of schools in tribal areas in a State should run primary classes as per the revised syllabi.

(8) Vocational facilities in such field as agriculture, industry, sports, etc., should be provided in adequate number of educational institutions.

(9) Low literacy pockets, backward communities and areas where intensive economic programmes have been or are being taken up, should be identified and special educational effort mounted.

(10) Weaknesses of the educational system to equip tribal students for job opportunities should be located and steps taken to overcome them.

(11) Vocational guidance centres should be set up in tribal areas so that tribal boys and girls get sound advice regarding their competence and qualifications *vis-a-vis* job opportunities.

(12) Attention needs to be paid to low enrolment ratio, sparseness

of educational institutions serving tribal areas, high wastage rate, absentee teachers. Inducements might be in the form of a more comprehensible educational system, scholarship assistance, attendance incentive, uniform, mid-day meals and compensation for opportunity costs.

(13) Pre-matric and post-matric scholarships should be disbursed in advance in order to meet the contingencies of advance payment of initial fees, caution money, hostel dues, etc. Arrangements for disbursement of scholarships should be reviewed and strengthened.

(14) Incentive should be given to teachers serving in tribal areas.

(15) Teacher should become the fulcrum of development activities in the village.

(16) Norms for establishment of educational institutions at the primary, middle and secondary level should be scrutinised once again with a view to ensure their relevance for tribal areas in the context of the low density of population and scattered habitations. The structural balance among the primary, middle and secondary institutions should be properly struck and maintained.

(17) Multiplicity of government organisations running educational institutions should be rationalised. Co-ordination in the Education Department should be ensured by the concerned organisations.

(18) Particularly with a view to boost education among tribal girls, recruitment of women teachers should be paid special attention.

(19) There should be a special drive to locate and appoint tribal men and women as teachers.

(20) In order to reduce costs and delays in availability of construction materials, indigenous material and specifications, with such refinements as may be necessary, may be adopted for school buildings, teachers residential accommodations, etc.

(21) A sound monitoring system should be set up in a State from grass-root level through State to national level. In the State Directorates of Education, officers in the rank of a Joint Director or Deputy Director may be appointed to specifically attend to the problems of education among scheduled tribes.

CHAPTER 15

Health

(1) In the field of health, attention has to be directed more

towards preventive side, sanitation and hygiene. However, the curative aspect should not be neglected.

(2) Under certain conditions, allopathic treatment may be necessary but, it might be advantageous to enable the tribal to also avail of the homeopathic, ayurvedic and his own system of medicine.

(3) State Governments might take financial and physical steps to have adequate research conducted into the tribal system of medicine.

(4) Surveys should be conducted to ascertain the extent of prevalence of incidence of diseases to which some tribal communities are particularly prone like tuberculosis, malaria, yaws, veneral diseases, leprosy, etc., Where diagnosed, vigorous remedial measures should be commenced straightway.

(5) Genetic mapping and counselling are urgently necessary for the survival and health of some small primitive tribal groups. This matter should receive the attention of the Ministry of Health, the All India Institute of Medical Sciences, the Indian Council of Medical Research, etc.

(6) Tribal areas being deficient in health institutions, the relative norms for PHCs and sub-centres should be relaxed. For the former, population norms of 20,000 and for the latter norm of 3,000 may be adopted. Deficiencies with reference to these norms should be made up.

(7) Mobile units, whether motorised or non-motorised, should be used for tribal areas.

(8) All vacancies in the tribal areas should be filled up.

(9) If more than one doctor are posted in a PHC, one may be posted at the headquarters and the others at suitable places in the interior. Shortage of medicines should not be allowed to occur, since the requirement of tribal area is small.

(10) The community health volunteers scheme may be continued in tribal areas drawing the volunteers from the local tribal village community. It might be preferable to utilise the services of tribal medicine-men for the purpose, training them in the modern system of medicine.

CHAPTER 16

Infrastructure Development

(1) The special conditions and requirements of the tribal areas

were not broadly taken into account while preparing the 20-year plan of road development (1961-81). Road development in tribal areas should support economic activity and tribal development. However, in certain tribal areas if road development is unaccompanied by effective protective measures, it is likely to help exploitative forces to the detriment of tribal interests.

(2) Important administration centres such as Tehsils and Blocks should be made accessible as early as possible. Further, weekly market centres should be connected on priority, say within a period of one or two years. Health sub-centres should be the next priority.

(3) The problem of tribal areas has been separately reviewed by the P&T Board and a special programme of communications development in these areas has been agreed to. This network plan should follow the needs of economy and should provide support for effective implementation of programmes. Tehsil and Block headquarters should come in the first priority, the headquarters of LAMPS, weekly market centres and headquarters of village clusters following.

(4) It is necessary to review the entire situation in the large tribal tracts which are without any railway facilities and prepare for them a phased programme of development of railways for which different financial norms may be adopted.

(5) A great interface between the rural electrification programme and economic programmes in tribal areas is necessary to make heavy investments economically productive. The scheme of rural electrification involving subsidy on behalf of the Central Government should be cleared on project-by-project basis ensuring appropriate linkage between rural electrification and economic activity.

(6) All tribal areas in the country which have not reached the minimum level of rural electrification should qualify for special attention under the scheme.

CHAPTER 17

Pockets of Tribal Concentration and Dispersed Tribals

(1) Of the estimated 4.10 crores scheduled tribe population in the country, 2.30 crores constituting about 65 per cent are covered by the tribal sub-Plan. Outside the tribal sub-Plan area, about 26 lakhs population has been iden fied in pockets of tribal concentrations. Thus, about 73 per cent of the total scheduled tribe population is covered.

(2) Since the tribal concentration pockets are part of administrative unit like a Development Block or a Taluka, area development approach generally adopted for the tribal sub-Plan areas may not be feasible for them. The benefits of the infrastructural and family-wise schemes of the Block or Taluka plan should normally accrue to the pocket area and population and alongside, special target-group plans should be fitted therewith. The target-groups plans should be prepared accordingly.

(3) Notwithstanding such guidelines, the State Governments have not prepared pockets development plans. This may be done expeditiously.

(4) Development programmes for the dispersed tribals (living outside the tribal sub-Plan area and pockets of tribal concentration) should be adequately built into the general rural development programmes. The flows of the general development sectors may be supplemented by funds of the backward classes welfare sector for these programmes.

(5) Separate administrative arrangements within the general sectors may be made to implement and monitor programmes.

CHAPTER 18

Primitive Tribal Groups

(1) The guidelines of the Planning Commission indicate that special attention and high priority should be given to areas and groups facing special problems including primitive tribal groups in backward pockets, shifting cultivators and tribals affected by the major projects.

(2) The tribal sub-Plan must attempt in broad terms answers to the main issues facing these tribal communities.

(3) The basic policy frame for these backward communities could vary from the general approach and be unfettered by the existing formal, procedural or legal frame.

(4) The starting point would be identification of the primitive tribal groups in accordance with the guidelines.

(5) A project report should be prepared for each tribal group separately. The project report should contain a unique programme for each group taking into consideration its eco-system. The first phase of development proposed should aim at conservation and re-organisation of the traditional skills of the group and the second phase should spell

out the development programmes as such.

(6) The problem of these groups may not be mainly economic, genetic and patho-genetic mapping among them is called for. The All India Institute of Medical Sciences, the Indian Council of Medical Research and other such bodies should take the lead for establishment of a national centre for such studies. Regional centres in Madhya Pradesh, Orissa, Bihar and Andaman and Nicobar Islands may support the national centre.

(7) No single task relating to primitive tribal groups can be complete without appropriate administrative structure and sensitive personnel manning it. Separate organisational structure may be created, if necessary. A special officer may be appointed each in the States of Madhya Pradesh, Orissa and Bihar to look after these groups.

(8) The help of voluntary organisations should be enlisted.

(9) Special Regulations might be promulgated to protect the command over resources of the groups.

14

ALL INDIA COMMITTEE ON JAIL REFORMS, 1980-83—REPORT[1]

Chairman	Justice Anand Narain Mulla
Members	Shri Yogendra Sharma; Miss Saroj Khaparde; Dr. (Mrs.) M. Sarad Menon; Shri C.S. Mallaiah
Co-opted Members	Shri Prakash Mehrotra; Prof. Rasheeduddin Khan; Shri D.J. Jadhav; Shri H.C. Saksena; Dr. Hira Singh; Shri K.L.N. Reddy; Dr. (Mrs.) Jyotsana H. Shah
Permanent Invitee	Bibi Amtus Salam
M. Secy.	Shri K.S. Rastogi

Appointment

Prison administration in India has been, off and on, a subject of criticism in the press, the Parliament and the Judiciary, overcrowding in prisons, prolonged detention of undertrial prisoners unsatisfactory living conditions, lack of treatment programmes and allegations of indifferent and even in human approach of person staff have repeated by attracted the attention of the critics over the years.

The judiciary, as the agency responsible for the lawful deprivation of an offender's liberty, has occasionally denounced the degeneration of a term of sentence into servitude. Through some of its recent judgements, it has extended its jurisdiction over the execution of the terms of sentence to ensure that a prisoner is neither subjected to dehumanized treatment in jail, nor is he incapaciated for future social reintegration. It has observed that a sentenced offender cannot be treated as a person denuded of all his fundamental human rights and that his restoration to the law-abiding community is, and ought to be, the ultimate policy behind judicial sentencing.

Prisons are expected to re-educate one who has been declared a

---

1. New Delhi; Ministry of Home Affairs; 1983; 2 Vols.

criminal in order to help him eventually to be rehabilitated in an atmosphere of healthy social interactions and to promote the prospects of his reclamation in the social milieu. The existing prison conditions in general are however, not conducive to the fulfilment of the desired objective. The unsatisfactory situation existing in jails had attracted the attention of the Government of India and the State Governments from time to time. Valuable recommendations were made by various bodies at the national and state levels for effecting improvement in prison administration but progress in the follow-up-action and implementation of the recommendations has been slow in most of the States and Union Territories. In the recent past there were widespread agitations both by prison staff and the prison inmates demanding improved service conditions and better living conditions in prisons. There were even reports of occasional violence from some of the States and Union Territories. The States and Union Territories which witnessed large-scale and protected incidents of prison violence and indiscipline include Bihar, Madhya Pradesh, Manipur, Orissa, Rajasthan, Tamil Nadu, Chandigarh and Delhi.

The Government of India, taking stock of the situation and motivated by the desire for improvement in the prison administration decided to set up a committee to study all aspects of prison administration in the country and to devise measures for its effective improvement, with particular emphasis on the area of women, adolescents, children and mentally sick persons in jails. The Ministry of Home Affairs accordingly set up the All India Committee on Jail Reforms under its Resolution No. VI. 14016/3/80-GPA. IV of July 25, 1980.

Terms of Reference

(i) To review the laws, rules and regulations governing the management of prisons and the treatment of prisoners and to make recommendations keeping in view the overall objective of protecting the society and rehabilitating the offenders;

(ii) To examine the living conditions of prisoners with specific reference to their basic needs and provision of facilities compatible with the dignity of human life and to suggest improvements as considered necessary;

(iii) To reappraise the policies governing the recruitment, training and development of prison personnel in relation to the objective of custody and correction and to find ways of ensuring that persons with requisite talent, aptitude and ability man the prison service;

(iv) To look into the procedure regarding the internal management of prisons with a view to raising the present level of prison security and institutional discipline and to suggest appropriate change;

(v) To review the programmes of institutional treatment, education, vocational training, industry, agriculture and such other occupational activities and to suggest measures with a view to develop prisons as correctional centres;

(vi) To suggest measures for the specialised treatment of women, adolescents, children and mentally sick persons;

(vii) To review the working of open air prisons and to suggest measures for improvement;

(viii) To scrutinise the system of remission of prison sentence, parole and probation and to lay down guidelines for bringing about uniformity and standardisation in approach; and

(ix) Any other matter relating to prison administration that the Committee may like to consider.

The Committee was specifically asked to look into the affairs of Tihar Jail, and to make recommendations with regard to improvement in its administration within one month.

Contents

Recommendations

CHAPTER III

REALITIES IN INDIAN PRISONS

1. For making the present prison system conducive to the achievement of desired objectives, certain basic pre-requisites should be ensured which would constitute the foundations on which the Indian prison system can be restructured. (Paras 3.45.1 to 3.45.15)

CHAPTER IV

LEGISLATION

2. Directive Principle on National Policy on Prisons should be formulated and embodied in Part IV of the Constitution. (Para 4.34.1)

3. The subject of prisons and allied institutions should be included in the Concurrent List of the Seventh Schedule of the Constitution of India. (Para 4.34.2)

4. All the Acts pertaining to prison administration should be consolidated and a new uniform and comprehensive legislation enacted by the Parliament for the entire country. (Para 4.34.3)

5. In case the subject of prisons and allied institutions is not brought under the Concurrent List, the Government of India should prepare a model Bill for being adopted by all the States and Union Territories. (Para 4.34.4)

6. Immediate steps should taken by the State Governments/ Union Territory Administrations to frame rules under the prison statute. (Para 4.34.5)

7. Revision of jail manuals of the States and Union Territories should be given top priority. (Paras 4.34.6, 4.34.7)

8. Standing executive instructions issued for meeting certain situations or for efficient running of prison administration should be separately bound as reference material for the prison personnel. (Para 4.34.8)

9. Operation manuals on various subjects of prison management should be prepared and made available to the staff for guidance. (Para 4.34.9)

10. A separate legislation for young offenders should be passed to

replace the present Borstal School Acts. (Para 4.34.10)

11. Civil prisoners should not be detained in jails meant for convicted and criminal prisoners. (Para 4.34.11)

12. The Union and State Governments should conduct a qualitative and quantitative analysis of legislation, etc., to examine possibilities of delegalising certain areas of human and social behaviour and take necessary action in this regard. (Para 4.34.12)

13. Serious thought should be given to policies of discriminalisation, depenalisation and deinstitutionalisation at the legislative level. (Para 4.34.13)

14. In the preamble of the Indian Penal Code specific mention should be made about protection of society through the reformation and rehabilitation of offenders as objective of punishment. (Para 4.34.14)

15. The Indian Penal Code should be suitably amended in the light of the contemporary ideology of reformation and rehabilitation of offenders, e.g., it may provide alternatives to prison sentences and eliminate distinction between simple and rigorous imprisonment. (Para 4.34.15)

16.(a) Section 302 of the Indian Penal Code should be suitably amended so that (i) it is only in cases of murder with aggravating circumstances that death is prescribed as one of the punishments; and (ii) in other cases of murder, courts are given discretion to impose imprisonment for life or imprisonment for a lesser term. (Para 4.34.16)

16.(b) Imprisonment for life should be imprisonment for a fixed term extending over a reasonable period of time which may be determined by the legislature and incorporated in the Indian Penal Code.

17. Section 303 of the Indian Penal Code should be deleted and its provision brought suitably under the proposed section 302 of the Indian Penal Code. (Para 4.34.17)

18. Undertrial prisoners continue to be detained in prisons for long periods. A review on an all India basis should be undertaken to find out whether the provisions of the Code of Criminal Procedure in this regard have been fully implemented. (Para 4.34.18)

19. The Code of Criminal Procedure should be so amended as to provide that as soon as an undertrial prisoner completes period of detention equal to half of the maximum sentence award able to him on conviction, he is released immediately and unconditionally. (Para 4.34.19)

20. Section 433A of the Code of Criminal Procedure should be

suitably amended so that such lifers as offer good prognosis for reformation and rehabilitation can generally be released after 8 to 10 years of actual imprisonment. (Para 4.34.20)

21. Preventive sections of the Code of Criminal Procedure, specially Section 109, should be reviewed and amended suitably to restrict their use only in very genuine cases. (Para 4.34.21)

22. Section 428 of the Code of Criminal Procedure should be suitably amended so that the period spent by an undertrial in detention during investigation, inquiry or trial could be computed as sentence served in case he is sentenced to life imprisonment. (Para 4.34.22)

23. The Code of Criminal Procedure should be amended so as to provide for presentence investigation in case of all offenders liable to be sentenced to life imprisonment. (Para 4.34.23)

24. The Probation of Offenders Act, 1958 should be fully impleMented in every district of each State and Union Territory. (Para 4.34.24)

25. Non-criminal lunatics should not be detained in prisons. The Mental Health Bill should be passed expeditiously. (Para 4.34.25)

26. Children Act should be enacted and implemented in every district of each State/Union Territory. (Para 4.34.26)

27. Disposal of mercy petitions should be expeditiously done and in no case should it take more than six months. (Para 4.34.27)

28. Habitual Offenders Acts should be amended in the light of the provision of Chapter XLIII of the Model Prison Manual. (Para 3.34.28)

CHAPTER V

PRISON BUILDINGS

29. The State Governments and Union Territory Administrations should undertake an immediate survey, to be completed within a year, of prison buildings with regard to minimum needs essential to maintain standards of comfort and cleanliness in consonance with human dignity. (Para 5.8.1)

30. The work plan which may be prepared as a result of the survey should be executed within 2 years. (Para 5.8.2)

31. Old prison buildings which have outlived their utility should be demolished. Each State/Union Territory should prepare a comprehensive plan for re-modelling and renovation of other existing prison buildings so as to make them functional. Funds for the purpose

should be made available by the Central Government. (Para 5.8.3)

32. The State Governments and Union Territory Administrations should draw within one year a Master Plan for the constructions of prison buildings on the principles laid down. (Para 5.8.4)

33. The estimated financial outlay on new buildings would be about Rs. 376 crores. This amount should be made available by the Central Government. (Para 5.8.5)

34. The National Commission on Prisons, the National Buildings Organisation and the National Institute of Social Defence should coordinate to evolve standards and norms for buildings of different categories of prisons. The National Commission on Prisons should monitor the observance of these standards and norms. (Paras 5.8.6, 26.13.5)

35. A special cell with necessary staff and expertise from Prison Department should be established at the National Buildings Organisation to design model plans of buildings for different categories of prisons. (Paras 5.8.7 to 5.8.12, 5.8.24 and 5.8.26)

36. There should be four types of living accommodations.

(a) Barracks with accommodation for twenty inmates;
(b) Dormitory accommodation, each dormitory providing accommodation for four to six prisoners;
(c) Single seated room accommodation for prisoners needing privacy for pursuing studies, etc.; and
(d) Cells for segregation of inmates for purposes of security and punishment. (Para 5.8.10)

37. Cells should be fitted with flush type latrines, and existing cells should not be used till this facility is provided in them. (Para 5.8.13)

38. There should be a separate kitchen for every 200 inmates. (Paras 5.8.14, 6.8.9)

39. Each prison should have an independent stand-by arrangement for water supply in the form of tube-wells or hand-pumps. (Para 5.8.15)

40. Annual repairs/renovation of prison buildings should be done by the prison department for which adequate funds should be placed at its disposal. (Para 5.8.16)

41. New works costing up to Rs. 2 lakhs should be executed by

the prison department. (Para 5.8.17)

42. A special cell under a Superintending Engineer should be set up at the prison headquarters of each state. (Para 5.8.18)

43. All constructions in prison department should adhere to ISI standards. (Para 5.8.19)

44. New prison building should be constructed close to cities but away from crowded areas. (Para 5.8.20)

45. No building other than prison building should be constructed within 100 metres of the prison campus. (Para 5.8.21)

46. Old prison buildings surrounded by crowded localities should be remodelled to house undertrial prisoners. (Para 5.8.22)

47. All additional institutions to accommodate any future increase in convict population should be of open or semi-open type. (Para 5.8.23)

48. Housing for prison staff should be developed on modern lines with adequate community facilities. (Para 5.8.25)

CHAPTER VI

LIVING CONDITIONS IN PRISONS

Diet

49. The system of purchasing food articles through contract system should be discontinued. Food articles should be purchased from Government distribution agencies or cooperative societies. Fuel should be purchased from the forest department. (Para 6.8.1)

50. Food articles should be of good medium quality. The system of purchasing cereals/pulses of the cheapest rate wherever in vogue should be discontinued. (Para 6.8.2)

51. There should be two types of diet, one for the labouring and the other for non-labouring prisoners.

52. Adequate and nutritious diet should be given to nursing women and to children accompanying women prisoners. (Para 6.8.4)

53. Norms of prison diet should be laid down in terms of calorific and nutritional value, quality and quantity. Adequate checks should be provided to ensure prisoners get diet as per rules.

54. Cooking and serving utensils should be made of appropriate metals. (Para 6.8.6)

55. Management of kitchens or cooking or food on caste or

religious basis should be totally banned in prisons. (Para 6.8.7)

56. Prisoners should get special diet on religious festivals and national days as may be specified in rules. (Para 6.8.8.)

57. Each kitchen should cater for not more than 200 prisoners. (Paras 6.8.9, 5.8.14)

58. There should be two shifts of workers in the kitchen. Paid cooks should be employed wherever necessary. (Para 6.8.10)

59. Prison kitchen should be modernised in terms of substitutes of fuel. (Para 6.8.11)

60. To break the monotony of prison menus should be prepared in advance, under the the guidance of nutrition experts. (Para 6.8.12)

61. Prisoners' Panchayats, under proper supervision of prison staff, should be associated with preparation and distribution of food, etc. (Para 6.8.13)

62. Some prison officials should be given special training in dietary and management of kitchens and such of officials should be put incharge of supervising kitchens. (Para 6.8.14)

63. Prison officers should supervise every aspect of the prison diet system. (Para 6.8.15)

64. Medical officer should ensure that food in cooked under hygienic conditions and is nutritious. (Para 6.8.16)

65. Prisoners should be given such food as is normally eaten by people in the region. (Para 6.8.17)

66. Clean drinking water should be supplied to prisoners and it should be tested periodically. (Para 6.8.18)

67. Prisoners should be served food in clean, hygienic and covered places. (6.8.19)

68. Normally the time for serving evening meals should be 7.30 p.m. For this purpose the time of lock-up should be shifted further by 2 to 3 hours.

69. Bartering of food articles should be totally banned. (Para 6.8.21)

70. Prisoners should not be allowed to have their own mini kitchens inside the prison/barrack. (Para 6.8.22)

Sanitation and Hygiene

71. Open spaces and roads inside the main wall of the prison should be asphalted leaving enough space for flower beds. (Para 6.12.1)

72. Open gutters and sewers should be covered. Wherever possible prisons should be connected to the public drainage and sewer systems. (Para 6.12.2)

73. The ratio of latrines to prisoners should be 1 : 6. (Para 6.12.3)

74. The system of open basket-type latrines should be discontinued. The system of carrying night soil as headloads should be stopped forthwith. (Para 6.12.4)

75. Flush/septic latrines should be provided in every barrack and cell. (Para 6.12.5)

76. Adequate number of separate urinals should be provided. (Para 6.12.6)

77. Every prison should have arrangements for storing enough water for at least a week. (Para 6.12.7)

78. Every prison should provide cubicles for bathing at the rate of 1 for 10 prisoners, with proper arrangements to ensure privacy. (Para 6.12.8)

79. Separate platforms for washing clothes should be constructed. (Para 6.12.9)

80. Properly equipped laundries for periodic washing, disinfection and fumigation of clothing and bedding should be set up at each central and district prison. (Para 6.12.10)

81. Medical officers of the prison must look after all aspects of prison sanitation and hygiene. (Para 6.12.11)

82. Every prison should be got thoroughly inspected by the local public health officer periodically. (Para 6.12.12)

Clothing, bedding and equipment

83. Clothing supplied to prisoners should be proper and adequate. (Paras 6.17.1 to 6.17.9, 6.17.11, 6.17.13)

84. Children allowed to stay with women prisoners should be given suitable clothing similar to that normally used by children in the free community. (Para 6.17.7)

85. The period of life of each article of clothing should be fixed in accordance with the type of cloth used and the wear and tear involved. (Para 6.17.10)

86. Every prison should maintain a repair unit where prisoners' clothing can be repaired. (Para 6.17.12)

87. Prisoners' clothing, bedding and other equipment should be washed, sterilized disinfected or fumigated regularly. (Paras 6.17.14

and 6.17.17)

88. Bedding and other articles issued to prisoners should be adequate. (Para 6.17.15)

89. Prisoners should be allowed to purchase footwear at their own cost from prison canteens. (Para 6.17.16)

90. Each housing unit should have certain minimum facilities. (Para 6.17.18)

91. All articles of prisoners' bedding, clothing and other equipment should be inspected by the superintendent at least once a week to ensure that proper standards are maintained. (Para 6.17.19)

Letters

92. Each prison should have a section under the control and supervision of an experienced assistant superintendent to deal with all matters pertaining to the mail of inmates. (Para 6.18.1)

93. On initial admission or on admission on transfer from another prison, a printed card should be sent to the family of the prisoners containing detailed information about him. (Para 6.18.2)

94. Whenever a prisoner is transferred from a prison, intimation of such transfer should be sent to the family of the prisoner. (Para 6.18.3)

95. Spouse/family members/close relative of a prisoner should be telegraphically informed about prisoner's serious illness, serious injury, and removal to a hospital for medical treatment or for treatment of mental illness. (Para 6.18.4)

96. On admission each prisoner should be asked to given a list of persons with whom he wants to correspond. (Para 6.18.5)

97. There should be no limit on incoming letters for prisoners. (Para 6.18.6)

98. There should be no restriction on the number of letters prisoners may send at their own cost. However, at government cost an undertrial should be allowed to writer two letters per week whereas a convict should be allowed to write one letter per week. (Para 6.18.8)

99. Illiterate or semi-iiterate prisoners should be provided help in writing letters. (Para 6.18.8)

100. Guidelines for censorship of letters should be formulated so that censorship of letters is done on the basis of human considerations. (Para 6.18.9)

Interviews

101. The scale of interviews for convicted and undertrial prisoners should be liberalized. (Paras 6.10.1, 12.17.16)

102. Facilities for interviews of prisoners should be humanized and conditions/procedure governing grant of interviews rationalized. (Paras 6.19.2 to 6.19.8)

103. A senior officer in charge of interviews should be responsible for grant of interviews as per rules. (Para 6.19.9)

Canteens

104. Canteens should be organized in all the central and district prisons. (Paras 6.20.1 to 6.20.3)

105. Canteen facilities should extended to all prisoners. (Para 6.20.2)

106. Çanteens should be run on the basis of marginal profit. (Para 6.20.4)

107. Each prisoner should have a canteen card in which the canteen credits and debits should recorded. (Para 6.20.5)

108. Prisoners should be allowed to spend not more than half of the wages earned in prisons on purchases from canteens. In addition, prisoners should be allowed to spend up to Rs. 30 per month from their private cash for purchasing articles from the canteen. (Para 6.20.6)

109. Canteen accounts should be got audited every month. (Para 6.20.7)

110. Prisoners panchayats should be associated with the management of canteens. (Para 6.20.8)

Other facilities

111. Certain other basic facilities should be provided to prisoners. (Para 6.21)

Prison visitors

112. There should be a Board of Visitors in each State/Union Territory. (Para 6.22.1)

113. Correspondents of prisons should be appointed in each State/Union Territory. (Para 6.22.2)

114. A Board of Visitors should be constituted for each central prison, district prison and sub-jail. (Paras 6.22, 6.22.4)

115. The functions of the Board of Visitors should be clearly laid down. (Para 6.22.5)

116. The Board of Visitors for an institution should visit such institution at least once in a month. (Para 6.22.6)

117. A copy of remarks entered in the Visitors Book by the Chairman or by any member of the Board should be forwarded by the Superintendent to the Inspector General of Prisons along with his comments for necessary action. (Para 6.22.7)

118. It should be the duty of the Deputy Inspector General of Prisons and the Inspector General of Prisons to meet the Board of Visitors whenever they visit the prison. (Para 6.22.8)

119. It should be obligatory on the part of both official and non-official visitors to pay visits to prison as per the schedule fixed by the Chairman of the Board. (Para 6.22.9)

120. Classification of prisoners into A, B, C, or I, II, III classes on the basis of their social, economic and educational backgrounds should be abolished. (Para 6.23)

CHAPTER VII

MEDICAL AND PSYCHIATRIC SERVICES

121. (a) Medical officers should be deputed from the State Medical Service to prisons. (Para 7.13.1)

121. (b) The term of deputation of medical officers to prisons should be 3 to 5 years. (Para 7.13.2)

122. Immediately before or soon after joining at the prison, the medical officer should be required to undergo a short-term orientation course. (Para 7.13.3)

123. Every central and district prison should have two or more medical officers. A central prison with an inmate population of more than one thousand prisoners should have three medical officers. (Para 7.13.4)

124. At every prison where there is a sufficiently large number of woman prisoners (say, 25 or above), a whole-time lady medical officer should be appointed. At other prisons arrangement should be made for part time lady medical officers. (Para 7.13.5)

125. Every central and district prison should have the services of a

qualified psychiatrist who should be assisted by a psychologist and a psychiatrist social worker. (Para 7.13.6)

126. The prison hospitals should have full contingent of staff according to their requirements. (Para 7.13.7)

127. A senior officer of the rank of Joint/Deputy Director in the Medical Department should be deputed at the headquarters of the Department of Prisons and Correctional Services. (Para 7.13.8)

128. Medical officers posted at a prison will function under the control of the Inspector General of Prisons and immediately under the superintendent of the prison. For professional work they will consult senior medical officers. (Para 7.13.9)

129. The Inspector General of Prisons and superintendent of prisons should make the work of medical officers stimulating by encouraging and involving them in research in collaboration with the Medical and Public health departments. (Para 7.13.10)

130. Adequate incentives should be provided to medical officers, psychiatrists and para-medical personnel deputed to prisons. (Paras 7.13.11, 7.13.12)

131. Medical officers associated with prisons on part-time basis should be paid proper honorarium or fee. (Paras 7.13.13, 7.13.14)

132. Duties of medical officers, Psychiatrists and psychiatric social workers connected with prisons should be clearly defined. (Para 17.13.15)

133. All central and district prisons should provide hospital accommodation for 5% of the daily average inmate population. (Para 7.13.16)

134. Buildings, equipment and other facilities for prison hospitals should to certain norms. (Paras 7.13.17 to 7.13.23)

135. Visiting specialists from local hospitals should be arranged for treatment of ailments requiring specialised services. (Para 7.13.24)

136. Each State should have a fully equipped prison hospital manned by specialists for the treatment of prisoners requiring specialised treatment from all over the State. (Para 7.13.25)

137. Non-criminal lunatics should not be kept in or sent to prisons. (Para 7.13.26)

138. Criminal lunatics should be sent to the nearest prison having the services of a psychiatrist. (Para 7.13.27)

139. All criminal lunatics under observation of a psychiatrist should be kept in one barrack. (Para 7.13.28)

140. If a criminal lunatic undergoes trial and is declared "guilty but insane" be should be sent to the nearest mental hospital for further

management. (Para 7.13.29)

141. If a criminal lunatic, after standing trial following recovery from his mental illness, is declared guilty of the crime he should undergo his term in the prison but should be under the care and treatment of the psychiatrist. (Para 7.13.30)

142. If an undertrial criminal lunatic fails to recover from his mental illness even after he has completed half or the maximum term awardable on conviction, his case should be submitted to the State Government for considering the withdrawal of the criminal case against him. (Para 7.13.31)

143. If a convict while undergoing his imprisonment becomes mentally ill, he should be shifted to the psychiatric wing of the prison hospital and placed under the observation of the prison psychiatrist. (Para 7.13.32)

144. There should be at least one separate prison hospital with a capacity for too inmates fully equipped for the care and confinement of criminal lunatics in each big State. (Para 7.13.33)

145. Sick women prisoners should be treated in a separate enclosure attached either to the hospital section or to women section of the prison. (Para 7.13.34)

146. Proper medical facilities should be provided in sub-jails. (Para 7.13.35)

147. Proper arrangements should be made for the care and treatment of old, infirm and debilitated prisoners in a separate ward. (Para 7.13.36)

148. Requirement of drugs for three months should be stocked in the prison hospital. (Para 7.17.37)

149. The medical officer incharge of prison hospital should, in accordance with prison rules and in consultation with the superintendent, work out criteria for the prescription of special medical diet to prisoners and these criteria and the special medical diets prescribed under them should be reviewed from time to time. (Para 7.13.38)

150. The medical officer will assist the superintendent in an emergent situation. (Para 7.13.39)

CHAPTER VIII

SECURITY AND DISCIPLINE

151. From the point of view of security and discipline, prisons

should be classified into special security prisons, maximum security prisons, medium security prisons and minimum security prison – (semi-open prisons, open prisons and Sanganer type open camps). (Para 8.34.1)

152. Every prison should be provided with adequate custodial staff to ensure that no one is required to work for more than 8 hours a day, besides a day's rest every week. (Para 8.34.2)

153. A time-bound plan for the improvement of old prison buildings with a view to ensuring proper security should be drawn and implemented. (Paras 8.34.3, 5.8.3)

154. Each jail should be provided with basic requirements of security. (Para 8.34.4)

155. An officer of the rank of deputy superintendent should be appointed at each special security and maximum security prison for discharging the duties of a whole time security officer. (Para 8.34.5)

156. Adequate staff should posted at jail gates for conducting searches. (Para 8.34.6)

157. A statutory provision should be made to make it obligatory on the part of police to inform the superintendent of the prison about the antecedents of every dangerous convict of undertrial admitted to the prison. (Para 8.34.7)

158. Prison staff should be trained in the use of devices for dispersing mobs in order to minimise use of force. (Para 8.34.8)

159. Jails should be inspected at odd hours by range Deputy Inspectors General of Prisons to ensure proper observance of security measures. (Para 8.34.9)

160. The institution of convict officers discharging supervisory and disciplinary duties at present should be abolished in a phased manner. (Para 8.34.10)

161. All well-behaved convicted prisoners in good health who have completed one month's confinement and who know counting should by rotation, be employed in two-hour shifts for counting of prisoners inside barracks at night. (Para 8.34.11)

162. Preventive measures for ensuring security through segregation and imposition of fetters should be very discreetly used. Prisoners should have the right to appeal to the Inspector General of Prisons against the restrictions imposed on them. (Para 8.34.12)

163. The superintendent should have the power to use preventive measures to the extent prescribed for ensuring security and control. (Para 8.34.13)

164. Any use of preventive measures beyond the prescribed limits should be subject to approval of the District Judge or the Chief Judicial Magistrate having visitorial powers over the prison. (Para 8.34.14)

165. Fetters and handcuffs should not be imposed undertrial prisoners except when they have a credible tendency to violence or escape. (Para 8.34.15)

166. Provisions regarding segregation and imposition of fetters as measures for ensuring security contained in the Prisons Act, 1894 should be suitably revised. (Para 8.34.16)

167. Contingent of special security guards should be posted at each jail for escorting prisoners to and from hospitals for specialized treatment. (Para 8.34.17)

168. Each district hospital should have a separate prisoners' ward with a room for the guards so that sick prisoners are not made to stay with other patients in the general ward. (Para 8.34.18)

169. Provisions with regard to security and custody of prisoners contained in Chapter XVI of the Model Prison Manual and those for meeting emergent situations in prisons contained in Chapter LIII of that Manual should be implemented. (Para 8.34.19)

170. Disciplinary problems in prisons should be tackled with fairness, politeness and firmness. (Para 8.34.20)

171. Progressive stage system should be introduced in the Jails. (Para 8.34.21)

172. Acts and omissions identified in Chapter XXXI on 'Discipline' of the Model Prison Manual should constitute prison offences. (Para 8.34.22)

173. Some of the existing prison punishments should be abolished and some new ones introduced. (Para 8.34.23)

174. The procedure for dealing with complaints against prisoners should be rationalised. (Para 8.34.24)

175. Newly admitted prisoners should be given a booklet printed in local language containing information regarding regulations governing various aspects of prison life. (Para 8.34.25)

176. Facilities available to prisoners to life appeal/ revision/review or to make other applications in regard their criminal cases should be improved. Prisoners may also be provided free legal aid in such matters. (Para 8.34.26)

177. The procedure for dealing with genuine complaints and grievances of inmates should be rationalised. (Para 8.34.27)

178. Prison administration should exercise constant vigilance and

alertness to locate areas of discontent among prisoners which may lead to mass indiscipline and take quick remedial measures. (Para 8.34.28)

179. Prisoners panchyats should be involved in matters pertaining to inmates/self-management and self-improvement in day to day life. (Para 8.34.29)

180. The intelligence branch of the local police should be actively involved in the detection and prevention of smuggling of contraband articles in the prisons. The vigilance cell in the headquarters organisation of the Department of Prisons should also pay proper attention to this aspect of prison security and discipline. (Para 8.34.30)

CHAPTER IX

SYSTEM OF CLASSIFICATION

Diversification of institutions

181. Diversification of institutions should be evolved for basic segregation and treatment of homogeneous groups of prisoners. (Para 9.7.1)

182. Each State/Union Territory should evolve a system of classification of prisons according to its requirements. (Para 9.7.2)

183. Homogeneous groups of inmates should be kept in appropriate classified institutions. (Para 9.7.3)

184. In large States classification of prisons be done on a regional basis. (Para 9.7.4)

185. Small States and Union Territories where diversification of institutions in not feasible because of a very small number of prisoners and institutions should utilise this facility in neighbouring State or apply principles of diversification in separate yards/enclosures/wings of each institution. (Para 9.7.5)

186. Diversified institutions should be set up by each State/Union Territory according to its requirements. (Para 9.7.6)

187. With the construction of new prison buildings and establishment of semi-open and open prisons the pressure on existing prisons will be reduced to a great extent. These institutions can be converted into medium, maximum and special security institutions for adult offenders and into Reception Centres and Kishore/Yuva Sadans for Young offenders. (Para 9.7.7)

188. In every central and district prison a reception centre should

be established for initial classification of convicted prisoners. (Para 9.7.8)

189. Panels of experts should be appointed by Government of India on a regional basis to assist the States and Union Territories in the region to prepares a basic plan for setting up a system of classified institutions. (Para 9.7.9)

Classification of Prisoners

190. The principles of classification included in the report of the All India Jail Manual Committee 1957-59 should be adopted on an all India basis. (Para 9.12.1)

191. The aims and objectives of classification as laid down in Chapter XIX of the Model Prison Manual should be kept in view while undertaking classification of prisoners. (Para 9.12.2)

192. A reception centre should be set up in every central and district prison where prisoners sentenced to more than one year should be initially classified by a classification committee consisting of professional staff. (Para 9.12.3)

193. The principles of keeping a prisoners as near his home town as possible should be broadly kept in view at the time of classification of inmates. (Para 9.12.4)

194. Provisions of the Model Prison Manual regarding procedure for initial classification, stage of classification and reclassification procedures decisions of the classification committee, progress reports review of progress re-classification contents of the inmates case file should be adopted by each State and Union Territory. (Para 9.12)

195. Proper forms of history sheet, initial classification sheet and progress report should be adopted. (Para 9.12.6)

Typology of crime

196. Research should be undertaken to develop a typology of crime in the context of the current patterns of crime in India. (Para 9.19.1)

197. Newly admitted prisoners should be broadly categorised into socially conditioned criminals and individualised criminals. (Para 9.19.2)

198. In each State and Union Territory study groups should be set up for the purpose of undertaking studies of various patterns of crime. The reports of these study groups should be utilised for evolving clas-

sification of prisoners on scientific basis. (Para 9.19.3)

199. The existing legal provisions in regard to the classification of habitual offenders should be suitably amended. (Para 9.19.4)

200. Every prison officer should be given thorough training in behavioural sciences and techniques of social work. (Para 9.19.5)

CHAPTER X

TREATMENT PROGRAMMES

201. Treatment programmes should be properly planned and developed. They should be regarded as an integral part of prison programmes. (Para 10.28.1)

202. The atmosphere of prisons should be surcharged with positive values and the inmates should be exposed to wholesome environment with opportunities to reform themselves. (Para 10.28.2)

203. Inmate-personnel relationship in prisons should be based on mutual trust and confidence. (Para 10.28.3)

204. Discipline in prisons should be firm and positive so that treatment programmes may be carried out uninterruptedly and effectively. (Para 10.28.4)

205. Treatment programmes should be individualised. (Para 10.28.5)

206. Prison staff should promptly attend to the immediate need of newly admitted inmates. (Para 10.28.6)

207. Treatment of offenders through diversified work programmes and vocational training should be the focal point of prison activities. (Para 10.28.7)

208. Each State/Union Territory should reformulate its prison educational policy and programmes. (Paras 10.28.8 to 10.28.17 and 10.28.26 to 10.28.28)

209. Educational programmes in prisons and in Kishore/Yuva Sadans should be integrated with the educational system in the States/Union Territories. (Para 10.28.18)

210. Diversified educational programmes should be organised for different groups of inmates. (Para 10.28.19)

211. Inmates who have reached a certain stage of education should be allowed to continue their education either as regular students of schools/colleges or through correspondence courses. (Para 10.28.20)

212. Special attention should be paid to the development of

suitable educational programmes for women prisoners. (Para 10.28.21)

213. The Inspector General of Prisons and Director of Correctional Services should formulate a detailed educational programme for each institution in consultation with the State education department. (Para 10.28.22)

214. It should be one of the primary responsibilities of the prison superintendent and other prison personnel that programme of education is implemented in its proper spirit. (Para 10.28.23)

215. Programmes of adult education, social education and moral education should also be organised in sub-jails. (Para 20.28.24)

216. Literate inmates whose conduct is good should given training in imparting education to other inmates and they should assist the educational personnel of the institution. (Para 10.28.25)

217. The strength of educational personnel at each institution should be fixed in accordance with its requirements. (Para 10.28.29)

218. Social, moral and health education lectures should be organised. (Para 10.28.30)

219. Each State and Union Territory should accept and adopt the basic essential elements of recreational and cultural activities. (Para 10.28.31)

220. The Inspector General of Prisons of each State/Union Territory should formulate a plan for recreational and cultural activities for each institution. (Para 10.28.32)

221. Recreation should be properly designed and planned. It should also be adequately guided and supervised. (Para 10.28.33)

222. Recreation should be treated as incentive for good behaviour and self-discipline. (Para 10.28.34)

223. Appropriate recreational and cultural activities should be provided in prisons. (Para 10.28.35)

224. Each central and district prison and Kishore/Yuva Sadan should have a 16 mm film projector. (Para 10.28.36)

225. Library of good films should be developed at the headquarters organisation. (Para 10.28.37)

226. Every prison and allied institution should have a proper library with sufficient number of newspapers, periodicals and books. (Para 10.28.38)

227. Every prison and allied institution should have annual sports meet. Inter-institution and inter-state sports meets of inmates should also be organised. (Para 10.28.39)

228. Every prison and allied institution should have a committee

for recreational and cultural activities comprising carefully selected inmates. (Para 10.28.40)

229. The Department of Prisons and Correctional Services should maintain close liaison with the Department of Sports and committees for recreational and cultural activities at the district and state level. (Para 10.28.41)

230. Continuity of contacts of prisoners with their family members and the community should be maintained.(Para 10.28.42)

231. Various incentives of the prison system should be judiciously used to promote self-discipline and modification of behaviour of inmates. (Para 10.28.43)

232. Techniques of case work, group work, individual and group guidance, and counselling should be applied in prisons as measures of treatment of offenders. (Para 10.28.44)

233. Anti-social value schemes of offenders should be replaced by proper habits and attitudes through individual guidance. (Para 10.28.45)

234. Psychotherapy which has been recognised as an effective measure for treatment of prisoners suffering from mental disorders should be used in prisons. (Para 10.28.46)

235. Supportive therapy should be used as technique of treatment of inmates. (Para 10.28.47)

236. Prison personnel should present such models of behaviour in their conduct before the inmates as would be useful for the offenders to imitate. (Para 10.28.48)

237. The impact of treatment programmes should be regularly reviewed through independent agencies. It should also be reviewed through in-built mechanisms in the prison system (such as periodical review of progress of inmates, re-classification of inmates, review of sentences, after-care, follow-up, etc.) (Para 10.28.49)

238. Community participation in treatment programmes should be encouraged. (Para 10.28.50)

239. A prisoners' Welfare Fund should be set up in each State/Union Territory. (Para 10.28.51)

240. Daily routine in prisons and allied institutions should be regulated to provide for diversified treatment programmes. The locking-up time may be shifted by two to three hours after sunset. (Para 10.28.52)

CHAPTER XI

WORK PROGRAMMES AND VOCATIONAL TRAINING

241. Prison work programmes and vocational training should be integrated with national economic policies and development plans. (Para 11.33.1)

242. Certain specified objectives should form basic foundation for the development of work programmes and vocational training in correctional institutions. (Para 11.33.2)

243. Undertrial prisoners who volunteer to work should be encouraged to take up work programmes and receive vocational training. (Para 11.33.3)

244. Vocational training programmes in self-employing trades and occupations should be organised in every central and district prison. (Para 11.33.4)

245. Prison industries should be organised on business-cum-commercial basis. (Para 11.33.5)

246. While designing employment and production policies in prisons the composition of inmates coming from rural and urban areas should be taken into consideration and a variety of opportunities of work and vocational training should be created to cater for the heterogeneous inmate population. (Para 11.33.6)

247. Production units should be semi-mechanised and, where possible, fully mechanised. (Para 11.33.7)

248. Inmates should be given work experience in every section of a trade/industry. (Para 11.33.8)

249. In the plan of re-organisation of work programmes modernisation and diversification of existing prison industries should receive due priority (Para 11.3.9)

250. The possibility of introducing products according to market trends should be explored so that prison products may be able to reasonably satisfy customers' expectations. (Para 11.33.10)

251. Various products of prison industries should be standardised in terms of specifications, patterns, designs, etc, (Paras 11.33.11, 11.33.13 and 11.33.14)

252. Tools and equipment should be such as would facilitate production of articles of good quality and should be standardized. (Paras 11.33.12, 11.33.15 and 11.33.16)

253. In every institution there should be a separate and properly

organised maintenance workshop. (Para 11.33.17)

254. Adequate funds should be provided for annual replacement of equipment, accessories, spare parts, etc. (Para 11.33.18)

255. Technical supervision should be improved and a system of quality control should be introduced at every stage of production. (Para 11.33.19)

256. A policy for purchase of raw material, consumable articles, stores, tools and equipment, etc., should be laid down. (Para 11.33.20)

257. The accounts and stores organisation should be modernised on business-cum-commercial principles. (Para 11.33.21)

258. Costing of prison products should be done on a rational basis taking into account the various limitations and handicaps of prison management. (Para 11.33.22)

259. Comprehensive and detailed statistics for each service unit and production unit should be maintained on systematic basis. (Para 11.33.23)

260. An autonomous board for work programmes and vocational training vested with full fiscal and administrative powers, should be set up at the headquarters organisation of the Department of Prisons and Correctional Services. (Para 11.33.24)

261. At the prison level there should be a committee to implement the policies and programmes as chalked out by the board. (Para 11.33.25)

262. Qualified technical personnel should be appointed in adequate numbers in every production unit and for every programme of vocational training. (Para 11.33.26)

263. The executive and supervisory personnel should be given training in modern methods of management. (Para 11.33.27)

264. Account branches should be constituted at the institutional, regional and headquarters level. (Para 11.33.28)

265. Accounts of production units should be properly audited. (Para 11.33.29)

266. Work programmes in an institution should be planned taking into consideration various relevant factors. (Para 11.33.30)

267. Based on plans of each institution a master plan should be prepared for the whole department. (Para 11.33.31)

268. The requirements of government departments, semi-government agencies, etc., in respect of prison products should be consolidated in the office if the board. (Para 11.33.32)

269. The targets of production for each unit for the ensuing year

should be fixed in advance. (Para 11.33.33)

270. Plans for employment and production in each institution should be prepared for each quarter on the basis of relevant factors. (Para 11.3.34)

271. The chain of command, lines of authority and spans of staff control should be clearly defined at the institutional, regional and board level. (Para 11.33.35)

272. Staff meetings and joint staff consultations for evaluating manufacturing processes, personnel effectiveness, production targets, time schedule, etc., should be held regularly. (Para 1.33.36)

273. The performance of technical, executive and supervisory personnel functioning in the field of work programmes and vocational training at every level should be evaluated on the basis of the performance of individual staff member. (Para 11.33.37)

274. Every State and Union Territory should have a clear policy for the employment of inmates and for production programmes. (Paras 11.33.38, 11.33.39)

275. Tasks for each operation and sub-operation should be standardised and specified with reference to time schedule and the requirements of manpower. (Paras 11.33.40 and 11.33.44)

276. Correct work-sheet for each prisoner should be maintained by the technical personnel. (Para 11.33.41)

277. (a) There should be a complete ban on the use of inmate labour in the offices or at the residential quarters of prison personnel. (Para 11.33.42)

(b) The system of half task and two-thirds task should be discontinued except in specified cases.

278. Every prisoner who starts giving prescribed task should be brought on the wage system. Newly admitted prisoners should be given some token remuneration till they start performing the prescribed task. (Para 11.33.43)

279. Rationalised wage system should be introduced in prisons and allied institutions of every State/Union Territory. (Paras 11.33.45 to 11.33.51)

280. Hours of work for each group of prisoners should be prescribed in accordance with the programme content of each institution. (Para 11.33.52)

281. The daily routine, time schedule, etc., should be worked out for each institution on the basis of the principles laid down in Chapter XXI of the Model Prison Manual. (Para 11.33.53)

282. Prisoners should not be made to work in the production units after lock-up of the prisons. (Para 11.33.54)

283. Certain basic minimum facilities should be provided in work-sheds and other places where prisoners work. (Para 11.33.55)

284. Conditions of work in every factory, work-shed, etc., in every institution should be regularly inspected. (Paras 11.33.56, 11.33.57)

285. The traditional conservative policy of minimum investment in prison work programmes should be discarded and new realistic financial policy in all these matters should be adopted by each State/Union Territory. (Para 11.35.58)

286. The performance and economic aspects of each unit of work programmes should be got evaluated periodically by a committee consisting of experts. (Para 11.33.59)

287. Flow process charts should be introduced in every prison industry. (Para 11.33.60)

288. Department of Prisons and Correctional Services should concentrate on the production of articles and supply of services which are readily marketable. (Para 11.33.61)

289. Sales should be promoted through establishment of show-rooms and participation in exhibitions. (Para 11.33.62)

290. Training programmes should be designed and planned to suit the needs of prisoners sentenced to short, medium and long-term of imprisonment. They may consist of apprenticeship training, on-the-job training and vocational training (Paras 11.33.63, 11.33.64)

291. Details of the duration of each training course, syllabus and time-schedule should be worked out by the board. (Para 11.33.65)

292. Adequate number of instructors should be appointed for organising vocational training programmes. (Para 11.33.66)

293. Vocational training programmes should be developed in liaison with the Department of Technical Education, etc., and the inmates successfully undergoing training programmes should awarded regular certificates by that Department. (Para 11.33.67)

294. Adequate provision of finances should be made in the annual budget for vocational training projects. (Para 11.33.68)

295. The perspective master plan for the development of work programmes and vocational training should be prepared by each State/Union Territory. (Para 11.33.69)

296. Diversification of programmes of work and vocational training should be done in such a way that opportunities of work and training are available to different groups of inmates at the institutional,

regional or State/Union Territory level. (Paras 11.33.70 to 11.33.73)

297. Production units should be classified into (i) principal and (ii) ancillary and cottage industries. Agricultural farms should be classified as large, medium and small size farms. (Para 11.33.71)

298. Agricultural work programmes on agricultural farms should be diversified. (Para 11.33.72)

299. Diversification of prisons and classification of prisoners should be planned and executed simultaneously with diversification of programmes of work and vocational training. (Para 11.33.74).

300. Prisoners sentenced to medium and long-terms of imprisonment should be given training in multiple skills. (Para 11.33.75)

301. Background of inmates should be taken into consideration while planning their employment on work programmes. (Paras 11.33.76, 11.33.78)

302. Work camps and work centres should be developed in areas of community services. (Para 11.33.77)

303. Each State/Union Territory should appoint a committee of experts for the re-organisation and development of programmes of work and vocational training. (Para 11.33.79)

Agriculture

304. Agriculture, other allied activities and agro-based industries should be given high priority in the planned development of work programmes and vocational training in correctional institutions. (Para 11.39.1)

305. A systematic survey of the agricultural land available with various prison institutions should be undertaken to plan for its maximum utilization. (Para 11.39.2)

306. All farm lands should be examined in terms of soil analysis, irrigability, fertility, requirements of drainage, etc. (Para 11.39.3)

307. Each new prison building should have farm land. (Para 11.39.4)

308. Farms should be divided into suitable plots according to the cropping schemes to be prepared well in advance. (Paras 11.39.5, 11.39.6)

309. Project of land development should be undertaken on priority basis. (Para 11.39.7)

310. All uncultivated government land in the vicinity of a prison institution should be attached to the institution for agricultural pur-

poses. (Para 11.39.8)

311. Land belonging to the prison development should not be surrendered for the use either of other government departments or of private agencies. (Para 11.39.9)

312. Institutional land should be properly fenced. (Para 11.39.10)

313. A regular plan for maximum utilization of the existing irrigation facilities for providing additional facilities should be prepared and implemented for each firm. (Paras 11.39.11 to 11.39.15)

314. Necessary buildings should be constructed on each farm. (Para 11.39.16)

315. All necessary equipment and spare parts should be made available at each firm. (Para 11.39.17)

316. Pucca approach roads and pucca internal roads should be provided for all farms. (Para 11.39.18)

317. A maintenance shop should be set up at each large farm. (Para 11.39.19)

318. Transport facilities should be provided according to the actual requirements of each farm. (Para 11.39.20)

319. Petrol/diesel depots should be provided at large farms. (Para 11.39.21)

320. Requirements of labour at each farm should be met. (Para 11.39.22)

321. The practice of putting prisoners working on farms in ankle ring and fetters should be discontinued forthwith. (Para 11.39.23)

322. Inmates for open agricultural farms should be properly selected. (Paras 11.39.24, 11.39.35)

323. Before the prisoners are transferred to open institutions, they should be allowed to work for some time in semi-open institutions. (Para 11.39.25)

324. Prisoners working on farms should be given adequate and proper wages. (Para 11.39.26)

325. Adequate funds should be provided for the development of agriculture and allied activities. (Para 11.39.27)

326. Accounts of agriculture and allied activities should be separately maintained. (Para 11.39.28)

327. Requisite personnel should be provided at each agricultural unit and their duties and responsibilities should be clearly laid down. (Paras 11.39.29 and 1.39.30)

328. Costing of agricultural and other produce should be done on business-cum-commercial lines. (Para 11.39.31)

329. The efficiency of each unit should be evaluated in terms of targets fixed. (Para 11.39.32)

330. The inmate population of an agricultural farm should not exceed 200. (Para 11.39.33)

331. Sites for open agricultural prisons should have all infrastructural facilities. (Para 11.39.34)

332. Dairies should be developed on open prison farms on commercial lines under proper technical guidance. (Paras 11.39.36 to 11.39.41)

333. Dairies in closed prisons should be discontinued. (Para 11.39.42)

334. Wherever possible poultries should be organised on open farms. They should be run on commercial lines under proper technical supervision. (Paras 11.39.43 to 11.39.46)

335. In Jail Training Schools and Regional Training Institutes, prison personnel should imparted training in various aspects of agriculture and other allied activities. (Para 11.39.47)

336. Bio-gas plants, windmills, solar-cooking ranges etc., should be introduced in open institutions. (Para 11.39.48)

337. Vocational training in agriculture and other allied activities should be organised on agricultural farms. (Para 11.39.49)

338. The benefit of extension services for agriculture and allied activities should be availed of by the Department of Prisons and Correctional Services. (Para 11.39.50)

CHAPTER XII

UNDERTRIAL AND OTHER UNCONVICTED PRISONERS

339. A review of all the police lock-ups should be taken up in each State/Union Territory and the living conditions in them should improved. (Para 12.17.1)

340. A Board of Visitors should be appointed in each district to visit regularly all police lock-ups. (Para 12.17.2)

341. Undertrial prisoners should be lodged in separate institutions away from the convicted prisoners. (Para 12.17.3)

342. Institutions meant for lodging undertrial prisoners should be as close to the courts as possible and there should be proper arrangement for the transportation of undertrial prisoners. (Para 12.7.4)

343. The recommendation of the Law Commission with regard to

speedy trials and simplification of bail procedures made in its 77th and 78th Reports`should be accepted and implemented. In addition, bail should be granted to the accused as a matter of right unless proved by the prosecution that his being at large might endanger the security of the society. (Para 12.17.5)

344. The feasibility of launching bail hostels on the lines of those sponsored and financed by Xenia Field Foundation (U.K.) should be examined under Indian conditions. (Para 12.17.6)

345. Release of accused persons on personal recognizance should be encouraged. (Para 12.17.7)

346. The provisions of Section 167 of the Code of Criminal Procedure with regard to the time limit for the police investigation in case of accused undertrial prisoners should be strictly followed both by the police and the courts. (Para 12.17.8)

347. The classification of undertrial prisoners into class I, II and III or A, B, and C on the basis of their socio-economic status should be abolished. (Para 12.17.9)

348. The time spent by inmates in Jails, awaiting investigation and trial, should be put to use for the benefit of both the prisoners and the community. (Para 12.17.10)

349. Rights of undertrial prisoners including facilities of access to legal material, legal counsel and legal aid should be protected. (Para 12.17.11)

350. All undertrial prisoners should be effectively produced before the presiding magistrates on the dates of hearing. (Para 12.17.12)

351. Undertrial prisoners should be allowed to obtain cooked food from their families. (Para 12.17.13)

352. Those undertrial prisoners who do not have sufficient clothes should be supplied clothes at government cost. (Para 12.17.14)

353. There should be no restriction on the number of letters undertrial prisoners may send at their own cost. However, at government cost they should be allowed to write two letters per week. (Para 12.17.15)

354. There should be no restriction on the number of interviews sought by undertrial prisoners for the sake of legal assistance. Interview with family members and friends should, however, be restricted to two per week. (Para 12.17.16)

355. Undertrial prisoners should be allowed the facility of canteen available to other prisoners in the prison. (Para 12.17.17)

356. The daily routine of undertrial prisoners should include

programmes of diversified education and recreational activities. (Para 12.17.18)

357. Habitual undertrial prisoners should be segregated from other undertrial prisoners. (Para 12.17.19)

358. The management and discipline of undertrial prisoners should be the responsibility of only the paid staff. (Para 12.17.20)

359. (a) An effective mechanism of review of the cases of undertrial prisoners regularly both at the district level and the State level should be evolved.

(b) The Code of Criminal Procedure should be suitably amended to provide that as soon as an undertrial prisoners completes the period of detention equal to half of the maximum sentence awardable to him on conviction, he should be released immediately and unconditionally. (Para 12.17.21)

360. Broad guidelines about the arrest of persons, specially those involved in minor violations of law, should be laid down. (Para 12.17.22)

361. Non-criminal lunatics, persons needing protective custody and children should not be sent to prisons at all. (Para 12.17.23)

362. Preventive sections of the Code of Criminal Procedure, specially Section 109, should be reviewed and amended suitably to restrict their use only in very genuine cases. (Para 12.17.24)

363. Persons detained under executive orders made under provisions of special legislations should be kept away from convicted and undertrial prisoners. (Para 12.17.25)

CHAPTER XIII

WOMEN PRISONERS

364. All police investigations involving women must, as far as possible be carried out in the presence of a relative of the accused or her lawyer and of a lady staff member. Women should not be called to the police station for investigation. (Para 13.11.1)

365. Police personnel should treat women with due courtesy and dignity during investigation and while they are in police custody. (Para 13.11.2)

366. Women in police custody should invariably be under the charge of women police officials. (Para 13.11.3)

367. Instructions of the Ministry of Home Affairs for the guidance

of the police on the subject of handling women offenders should be followed. (Para 13.11.4)

368. A separate place with proper toilet facilities should be provided on court premises for women prisoners a waiting production before presiding magistrates. (Para 13.11.5)

369. Bail should be liberally granted to women undertrial prisoners, and those not able to furnish surety may be released on personal recognizance. (Para 13.11.6)

370. The Probation of Offenders Act should be extensively used for the benefit of women offenders. (Para 13.11.7)

371. Women prisoners should be lodged in separate institutions/annexes meant exclusively for them. (Para 13.11.8)

272. Enclosures for women in common prisons should be so renovated as to ensure that women prisoners do not come in view of male prisoners. Their enclosures should have a proper 'double lock system'. (Para 13.11.9)

373. All prisons/annexes for women must be staffed by women personnel only. (Para 13.11.10)

374. All general duties with regard to women offenders should be performed by women staff only. (Para 13.11.11)

375. Women guards should be arranged to look after women prisoners in sub-jails. (Para 13.11.12)

376. The staff posted at institutions for women should be properly trained and their service conditions should be on par with those of the male staff. (Para 13.11.13)

377. A senior lady officer, if available at the headquarters or organisation, should be entrusted with the job of looking after the problems of women prisoners. (Para 13.11.14)

378. Newly admitted women prisoners should be medically examined for pregnancy. Pregnant women prisoners should be transferred to local maternity hospital for purposes of delivery. (Para 13.11.15)

379. While registering the birth of a child to a women prisoner, the place of birth should not be mentioned as 'prison', if such a birth takes place there; instead the name of locality should be mentioned. (Para 13.11.16)

380. Pregnant and nursing women prisoners should be prescribed special diet and exempted from unsuitable types of work. (Para 13.11.17)

381. There should be proper arrangement for the segregation of

various categories of women prisoners. (Para 13.11.18)

382. Women needing protective custody should not be confined prisons. (Para 13.11.19)

383. There should be a separate ward for women in prison hospitals. (Para 13.11.20)

384. Women prisoners should be permitted to retain their *mangal sutra*, glass or plastic bangles, etc. (Para 13.11.22)

385. Women prisoners should be given adequate and proper clothing and facilities for personal hygiene and personal maintenance according to their custom. (Para 13.11.23)

386. Adequate and proper work and treatment programmes should be organized for women in prisons. (Paras 13.11.24 to 13.11.26 and 13.11.28)

387. Some self-contained units for groups of 8 to 10 women prisoners should be constructed to provide them a kind of family/group living. (Para 13.11.29)

388. Women prisoners should be given the facility of maintaining contacts with their families through letters, visits from relatives and leave. (Para 13.11.29)

389. Children (up to the age of 5 years) accompanying women prisoners may be allowed to be kept with them in specially organized creches outside the main prison building. (Para 13.11.30)

390. Prisons and annexes for women offenders in common prisons should be open for frequent visits by lady visitors. (Para 13.11.31)

391. Special consideration should be given to women prisoners in the matter of premature release. (Para 13.11.32)

392. Proper pre-release preparations in respect of women convicts should be made. Avenues for the settlement of marriage after their release may be explored. On release, women prisoners should, as far as possible, be escorted by women guards in plain clothes. (Para 13.11.33)

393. State Governments should encourage and support voluntary women organizations is looking after women offenders. (Para 13.11.34)

394. There should be a women's non-official organisation at the national level to look after the interests of women prisoners. Such an organisation should be given financial assistance by the Central Government. (Para 13.11.35)

CHAPTER XIV

CHILDREN IN PRISONS

395. Children Act should be expeditiously enacted/enforced in every district of each State/Union Territory. (Para 14.11.1)

396. Necessary infrastructure required under the Children Act should be immediately set up in every district. (Para 14.11.2)

397. Cases of children kept in prisons should be brought before the Children's Courts. Children not involved in delinquent acts or those who have committed delinquent acts of a minor nature should be placed under the care of voluntary probation officers, etc. (Para 14.11.3)

398. Persons actually working in the field of social work or who voluntarily offer to work in the field should be recognised as voluntary probation officers, fit persons and approved persons for the purposes of Children Acts. Good educational institutions having hostel facilities should be recognised as approved institutions. (Para 14.11.4)

399. Voluntary probation officers and voluntary organisations should be paid honorarium/maintenance allowance for taking care of children. (Paras 14.11.5, 14.11.8)

400. Government should exercise effective supervision on voluntary organisations and individuals. (Para 14.11.6)

401. Voluntary organisations should be encouraged and given financial aid to set up children institutions for such children as cannot be released on probation or on licence. (Para 14.11.7)

402. The head of the department of child welfare should be the Chief Authority under the Children Act. (Para 14.11.8)

403. Prison superintendent should take a monthly review of children confirmed in prison and send a report to the appropriate authorities for necessary action. (Para 14.11.9)

404. Ministry of Home Affairs and the Ministry of Social Welfare should take necessary action for ensuring removal of children from prisons in various State and Union Territories. (Paras 14.11.10, 14.11.11 and 14.11.12)

405. Juvenile probation and non-institutional services for children should be effectively organised. (Para 14.11.13)

406. A child should be sent to children's institution only as a last resort. As far as possible, he should be allowed to stay with the family. (Para 14.11.14)

407. There should be a statutory ban on keeping boys below the age of 16 years and girls below the age of 18 years in police custody on in a police lock-up. (Para 14.11.15)

408. In every district there should be a separate wing in the police organisation to be named as Juvenile Aid Bureau. (Para 14.11.16)

409. There should be a statutory ban on committing children below the age of 16/18 years to prisons either as undertrials or as convicted persons. (Para 14.11.17)

410. The high courts should issue standing orders to all subordinate courts that under no circumstances a child below 16/18 years should be committed to police custody or to judicial custody in prisons. (Para 14.11.18)

411. If any court commits a child to the prison, the prison superintendent should be authorised to refuse his admission to the prison. (Para 14.11.19)

412. If any court insists on committing a child to a prison, the prison superintendent should immediately take all necessary steps for the removal of the child from the prison. (Para 14.11.20)

413. Each State and Union Territory should prepare a master plan for setting up a network of non-institutional and institutional services for children. (Para 14.11.21)

414. Each State/Union Territory should be formulate a policy containing guidelines regarding handling of various problems relating to children in need or children in conflict with law. (Para 14.11.22)

415. It should be made a statutory responsibility of local bodies to set up child welfare services in their areas. (Para 14.11.23)

416. Government of India should prepare a comprehensive Model Bill for children embodying various aspects of child welfare services. (Para 14.11.24)

417. The extent and quality of services in children's institutions should be improved. (Para 14.11.25)

418. Necessary financial provision should be made for developing child welfare services. (Para 14.11.26, 14.11.27)

419. The National Children Fund should utilised on a high priority basis for developing services for the socially and economically handicapped children, specially in such parts of the country where these services have not yet been developed. (Para 14.11.28)

420. A separate department of child welfare should be established in every State/Union Territory. (Para 14.11.29)

421. Children who have difficult behaviour pattern and who attain

the age of 16/18 years, while in children institutions should, if necessary, be sent to a Kishore/Yuva Sadan. Under no circumstances should they be sent to a prison. (Para 14.11.30)

422. Children, dependent on prisoners, should preferably be kept with the relatives or friends of such prisoners. (Paras 14.11.31)

423. A common platform of all organisations involved in the work of child welfare could be set up so that child welfare services could be co-ordinated and developed in all parts of India. (Para 14.11.33)

424. A committee should be set up at each district headquarters to oversee all matters relating to child welfare. (Para 14.11.34)

425. A State level committee should be constituted to advise the Government on all matters pertaining to child welfare. (Para 14.11.35)

CHAPTER XV

YOUNG OFFENDERS

426. The subject of treatment of young offenders should be included in the Concurrent List of the Seventh Schedule of the Constitution. (Para 15.8.1)

427. A new uniform legislation for young offenders should be enacted on the lines of the Chapter Scheme given in Annexure IV-C attached to Chapter IV on 'Legislation'. (Para 15.8.2)

428. In case the subject of treatment of young offenders is not brought under the Concurrent List, the Government of India should prepare a Model Bill on the lines recommended in Chapter IV on 'Legislation' for being adopted by all the State and Union Territories. (Para 15.8.3)

429. A wing at the headquarters of the Department of Prisons and Correctional Services under a senior officer of the rank of Additional/ Joint Director of Correctional Services should be created for dealing with the problems of young offenders. (Para 15.8.4)

430. Separate courts for young offenders should be established. Pre-sentence investigation reports of the probation officers should be a statutory requirement for deciding the cases of young offenders. (Para 15.8.5)

431. Pre-sentence investigation report should include all relevant antecedents of the young offender and should also attempt a prognosis for his resettlement in a socially useful way of life. (Para 15.8.6)

432. Young offenders involved in minor violations should, instead

of being kept in police custody, be kept with their families/guardians/ approved voluntary agencies on the undertaking that they will be produced before the police as and when required for investigation. (Para 15.8.7)

433. Young offenders, involved in serious offences, while in police custody should be kept separate from adult criminals and the police custody should be only for a minimum period required for investigation. (Para 15.8.8)

434. The investigation of cases of young offenders must be expeditiously done. (Para 15.8.9)

435. Bail should be liberally granted in case of young offenders. (Para 15.8.10)

436. When it is not possible to release a young offender on bail, he should be kept in a Reception Centre/Kishore/Yuva Sadan during the pendency of his trial. (Para 15.8.11)

437. In case it becomes necessary to keep young offenders in a sub-jail during investigation and trial, it should be ensured that they do not come in contact with adult criminals there. (Para 15.8.12)

438. Young offenders should be sent to institutions only as a last resort. When a young offender is found guilty and is likely to be punished with imprisonment not exceeding one year, the court should take recourse to non-institutional measures. Suitable cases of young offenders likely to be sentenced to periods above one year should also, as far as possible, be processed through the non-institutional approach. (Para 15.8.13)

439. The existing Borstal schools and juvenile jails should be converted into a system of diversified Kishore/Yuva Sadans and Reception Centres. Besides this, additional institutions (Kishore/Yuva Sadans) as worked out in Chapter V on 'Prison Buildings' may be set up. These Kishore/Yuva Sadans should be developed as centres of scientific study and correctional treatment for young offenders. (Paras 15.8.14)

440. There should be separate institutions for young offenders to be called Reception Centres and Kishore/Yuva Sadans. (Para 15.8.15)

441. There should be separate institutions for girl young offenders. (Para 15.8.16)

442. Reception Centres should be organised at district or regional level as per the requirements of each State/Union Territory. The period of detention in a Reception Centre should not normally exceed eight weeks. (Para 15.8.17)

443. Kishore/Yuva Sadans should be properly diversified. (Para

15.8.18)

444. In Kishore/Yuva Sadans all basic operations for treatment and rehabilitation of young offenders should be adopted. (Para 15.8.19)

445. Initially all hopeful cases of young offenders offering good prognosis may be kept in institutions recognised as approved Kishore/Yuva Sadans or in semi-open Kishore/Yuva Sadans. Later on, on the basis of their response to training and treatment, suitable young offenders should be transferred to open Kishore/Yuva Sadans. Difficult, discipline and problem cases and escape risks should be sent to special Kishore/Yuva Sadans. In due course after observing their response to institutional programmes, these young offenders may be transferred to semi-open Kishore/Yuva Sadans and later to open Kishore/Yuva Sadans. (Para 15.8.20)

446. Decisions about placement of young offenders in the diversified Kishore/Yuva Sadans should be taken by the classification committee. (Para 15.8.21, 9.12.3)

447. Gradation in custody and contents of correctional programmes should be the criteria for diversification of institutions into open, semi-open and special Kishore/Yuva Sadans. (Para 15.8.22)

448. Placement of young offenders under non-institutional treatment will result in considerable economy. The savings so effected should be fruitfully diverted for the development of non-institutional programmes and other services for young offenders. (Para 15.8.23)

449. Scientific classification should be adopted for young offenders. This will help in their individualised treatment and training. (Para 15.8.24)

450. At each institution there should be a Review Board. (Para 15.8.25)

451. At the end of every six months the Review Board should examine the case of every young offender and determine his suitability for release on licence. (Para 15.8.26)

452. Young offenders offering good prognosis may be kept in Kishore/Yuva Sadan till they attain the age of 25 years. (Para 15.8.27)

453. Young offenders requiring institutionalisation for more than 5 years should be continued in a Kishore/Yuva Sadan through the review procedure. Of these, deserving young offenders should be released on licence on certain conditions. Only such young offenders as are intractable, violent, criminal psychopaths, hardened or dangerous, should be transferred to prisons. (Para 15.8.28)

454. Specially selected and adequately trained personnel should be

made available for implementing various programmes for young offenders. (Para 15.8.29)

455. Suitable and adequate staff should be provided at institution for young offenders. In this connection reference to Chapter XXIV on 'Development of Prison Personnel' may be made. (Para 15.8.30)

456. Adequate funds for all programmes connected with young offenders should be provided. (Para 15.8.31)

CHAPTER XVI

PRISONERS SENTENCED TO LIFE IMPRISONMENT

457. Section 443A of the Code of Criminal Procedure should be amended. (Para 16.11.1)

458. The Code of Criminal Procedure should be amended to provide for a pre-sentence study of offenders liable to be sentenced to imprisonment for life. The judge concerned should make use of this material while passing the sentence. (Para 16.11.2)

459. On admission of a life convict in a prison a comprehensive, social and psychological study should be made for the purpose of designing a suitable diversified programme of training and treatment for him. (Para 16.11.3)

460. A life convict should be allotted work taking into account his aptitude and potentialities and should be imparted multiple skills. (Para 16.11.4)

461. Life convicts coming from rural areas should be given training in trades suited to their needs. (Para 16.11.5)

464. Special attention should be paid to diversified educational programmes for life convicts (Para 16.11.6)

463. A classification committee of the prison should review the case of every life convict every three months. (Para 16.11.7)

464. The planning and research unit at the headquarters of the Department of Prisons and Correctional Services should be under take studies of the pattern of murders committed by individual offenders and by a socially conditioned criminals. (Para 16.11.8)

465. Broad guidelines for the Review Board/Advisory Board/Review Committee should be laid down. (Para 16.11.9, 16.11.10)

466. The facilities of interviews, letters, and release on leave and special leave should be liberalised in case of life convicts to enable

them to maintain contacts their families and the community. (Para 16.11.11)

467. Life convicts who offer good prognosis should be transferred to semi-open and open prisons. (Para 16.11.12)

468. The scale of remission for life convicts in semi-open prisons should be liberalised and they should be given the facility of staying with their family members in to be constructed on the premises of such institutions. (Paras 16.11.12, 16.11.14, 19.33.18 and 19.33.22)

469. Provisions of Chapter XLII of the Model Prison Manual regarding life convicts should be adopted by all the States/Union Territories. (Para 16.11.15)

470. Techniques of supportive therapy should be used to maintain interest in life of a life convict who has to spend a long period in the prison. (Para 16.11.16)

471. Pre-release preparation, and planning for after-care and follow-up should be paid special attention in case of life convicts. (Para 16.11.17)

472. The Advisory Committee should hold a separate meeting for reviewing the cases of life convicts only and the final orders in such cases should be passed expeditiously. (Para 16.11.18)

CHAPTER XVII

PRISONERS SENTENCED TO DEATH

473. Section 30 of the Prisons Act, 1984 should be replaced by a fresh legislation providing for a more human and dignified treatment to prisoners under sentence of death. (Para 17.7.1)

474. Immediately after admission, or soon after conviction of an undertrial as the case may be, the superintendent should explain to the prisoner sentenced to death the rules regarding appeal and mercy petitions. Those who require legal assistance should be extended facilities available for free legal aid. (Para 17.7.2)

475. Every State should have one or more specified jails where prisoners under sentence of death should be confined. These jails should have proper arrangements for the confinement of such prisoners and for their execution. (Para 17.7.3)

476. Security arrangements in the enclosure where prisoners under sentence of death are kept should be on twenty four hour basis. (Para 17.7.4)

477. Prisoners under sentence of death should be provided with the same diet, clothing and beddings, feeding utensils, etc., as are given to other prisoners. (Para 17.7.5)

478. Prisoners under sentence of death should be encouraged to employ themselves on some useful work, and should be provided with suitable work, if they so desire, in their own enclosures. (Para 17.7.6)

479. Those who have some healthy hobby should be given facilities to pursue it subject to rules. (Para 17.7.7)

480. They should be allowed to avail of recreational facilities available in the jail. (Para 17.7.8)

481. Those who are interested in education may be extended necessary facilities. Books, newspapers and magazines should also be provided to them. (Para 17.7.9)

482. They should be allowed to follow their own religion and belief subject to rules and requirements of discipline, and to retain religious and other books. (Para 17.7.10)

483. They should be given liberal facilities for interviews with and letters to and from relatives and legal counsels. (Para 17.7.11)

484. Canteen facilities, as available to other prisoners, should also be provided to prisoners under sentence of death. (Para 17.7.12)

485. Special attention should be paid to their personal and domestic problems. (Para 17.7.13)

486. When the death sentence becomes finally executable the prisoner should immediately be transferred to a separate enclosure where arrangements should be made to keep him in a cell under constant watch. During the day he may be allowed to associate with other such prisoners. (Para 17.7.14)

487. Before execution arrangements should be made for the prisoner to meet his near and dear ones even at State cost, if necessary. (Para 17.7.15)

488. Provisions of paragraphs 10 to 20 of Chapter XLVI of the Model Prison Manual should be incorporated in the State Jail Manuals. (Para 17.7.16)

CHAPTER XVIII

SUB-JAILS

489. A sub-jail should be located at each place where a criminal court functions. (Para 18.9.1)

490. A daily average number of 10 inmates/undertrial prisoners detained during the past one year should justify the construction of a new sub-jail at an administrative unit where a criminal court functions. (Para 18.9.2)

491. The necessity of construction of new sub-jails should not be brushed aside only for financial consideration. (Para 18.9.3)

492. Sub-jails should not be linked up with police or excise lock-ups. (Para 18.9.4)

493. Persons in police custody should not be kept in sub-jails. (Para 18.9.5)

494. Sub-jails housed in improvised insecure buildings should be abolished. (Para 18.9.6)

495. All new-sub-jail buildings should have living barracks and dormitories at a reasonable distance from the main wall. (Para 18.9.7)

496. Each sub-jail building should have a separate annexe for women prisoners. (Para 18.9.8)

497. There should be two types of sub-jails: (i) Class-II sub-jails for an average daily population up to 50 inmates and (ii) Class-I sub-jails for an average daily, population exceeding 50 but up to 100 inmates. (Para 18.9.9)

498. A time-bound programme for the construction of new sub-jail buildings should be drawn up and implemented by each State Government/Union Territory Administration. (Para 18.9.10)

499. All sub-jails should immediately be brought under the administrative control of the respective Inspector General of Prisons and only an officer of the Prison Department should be appointed as officer-in-charge of the sub-jail. (Para 18.9.11)

500. Sub-jails should be adequately and property staffed. (Paras 18.9.11, 18.9.13)

50.1 Guarding of sub-jails should be done exclusively by prison staff. (Para 18.9.14)

502. Whenever women prisoners are admitted in a sub-jail, arrangements for appointing women guards on purely temporary basis should be made. (Para 18.9.15)

503. Sub-jails should have suitable residential accommodation for all the staff members posted there with an independent guard room attached to the sub-jail building. (Para 18.9.16)

504. Living conditions in sub-jails should be compatible with human dignity and should be in accordance with the recommendations made in Chapter VI on 'Living Conditions in Prisons'. (Para 18.9.17)

505. Stand-by reserve stock of beddings and serving utensils should be kept in sub-jails. (Para 18.9.18)

506. An effective system of regular/periodic disposal of unserviceable articles should be evolved and strictly followed. (Para 18.9.19)

507. A regular stock of clothings should be kept both for men and women for issuing them to needy inmates. (Para 18.9.20)

508. Vehicles should be provided/arranged for transportation of prisoners confined in sub-jails. (Para 18.9.21)

509. The system of supplying cooked food to prisoners in sub-jails on contract basis should be discontinued and proper cooking facilities should be provided to the prisoners as per scales prescribed in the jail manuals. (Para 18.9.22)

510. The scale of diet for inmates of sub-jails should be the same as that for inmates of district or central prisons. (Para 18.9.23)

511. Proper medical facilities should be provided at each sub-jail. (Para 18.9.24)

512. Proper employment on work programmes and recreational facilities should be provided to prisoners at sub-jails. (Para 18.9.25)

513. Arrangements should be made for imparting adult education/non-formal education on a regular basis to inmates of sub-jails. (Para 18.9.26)

514. A Visiting Committee should be constituted by the District Magistrate for each sub-jail under his jurisdiction. (Para 18.9.27)

515. The District Magistrate should constitute a committee to review the position of undertrial prisoners in each sub-jail under his jurisdiction. The Inspector General of Prisons should review the situation of undertrials in sub-jails with State Home Secretary once in every three months. (Para 18.9.28)

516. State prison rules should be made applicable to sub-jails in all respects. (Para 18.9.29)

517. Habitual offenders should not be lodged in sub-jails. (Para 18.9.30)

518. Provisions in State jail manuals permitting handcuffing or fettering of inmates lodged in sub-jails should be re-examined. (Para 18.9.31)

519. Sub-Jails should be regularly inspected by the Inspector General of Prisons and the Deputy Inspectors General of Prisons. (Para 18.9.32)

520. Accounts and the record of release of inmates should be annually audited. (Para 18.9.33)

CHAPTER XIX

OPEN INSTITUTIONS

521. Open camp movement should be developed as a positive measure of correctional treatment. (Para 19.33.1)

522. The scope and purpose of open institutions should be clearly defined in the statute. (Para 19.33.2)

523. There should be 3 types of open institutions namely, semi-open, open and Sanganer type open institutions. (Para 19.33.3)

524. Conditions of eligibility of prisoners for admission to open institutions should be liberalised. (Para 19.33.4)

525. The inmate capacity of existing open institutions should be fully utilized. (Para 19.33.5)

526. Open institutions in any State should be able to accommodate at least 20 per cent of prisoners sentenced to one year and above. (Para 19.33.6)

527. All additional institutions for accommodating any future increase in convict population should be open type. (Para 19.33.7)

528. Open camps (Sanganer type) should be developed in each State/Union Territory as the final stage in open camp movement. (Para 19.33.8)

529. Land attached to closed prisons should be converted into semi-open or open institutions. (Para 19.33.9)

530. Open camps, mobile and permanent, should be set up at public projects to provide employment to prisoners sentenced to less than one year. Ticketless traveller should be employed on railway projects in camps to be financed by the Railways. (Para 19.33.10)

531. Diversified work programmes including those relating to agriculture and industry should be provided at open institutions. (Para 19.33.11)

532. 'Day release system' should be introduced as a measure of semi-open facility for suitable in mates confined in prisons. (Para 19.33.12)

533. The system of wages in open institutions should be rationalised. (Para 19.33.13)

534. All work programmes including agriculture in open institutions should be carried out by prisoners themselves under the supervision and management of the prison department. (Para 19.33.14)

535. The inmates in open institutions should be granted liberal

facilities for functional literacy, recreation, cultural activities, community participation, visit to neighbouring towns for marketing and recreational purpose, continued contacts with family, remission of sentences, leave and premature release. (Paras 19.33.15 to 19.33.21)

536. Family reunion of short durations should be allowed to inmates of open institutions by allowing them to stay with their families in huts to be constructed on the premises of such institutions. (Para 19.33.22)

537. Before being transferred to an open institution prisoners should be oriented about the requirements and responsibilities of living in such an institution. (Para 19.33.23)

538. Prison offences and punishments for inmates in open institutions should be separately defined. Inmates not abiding by the rules of the open institution should be sent back to closed prisons. (Para 19.33.24)

539. The maximum inmate capacity of an open institution should be 200. (Para 19.33.25)

540. The staff posted at open institutions should be carefully selected, trained and oriented to correctional philosophy. (Para 19.33.26)

541. The working conditions of the staff at open institutions should be improved. (Para 19.33.27)

542. Model rules laying down minimum standards for open institutions should be framed. (Para 19.33.28)

CHAPTER XX

SYSTEM OF REMISSION, LEAVE AND PREMATURE RELEASE

Remission system

543. The rules of eligibility in respect of various categories of convicted prisoners for earning ordinary and special remission should be reviewed and rationalised. (Paras 20.7.1 to 20.7.7)

544. The Government of India should lay down uniform guidelines to be followed by State Government/Union Territory Administrations for grant of State remission. (Para 20.7.8)

545. The practice of granting remission on occasions or for reasons not justifiable should be immediately stopped. (Para 20.7.9)

546. At the institutional level, a committee should be formed to

consider grant of remission. It should also recommend grant of special remission by the Inspector General of Prisons. (Para 20.7.10)

547. Grant of remission should be properly recorded and authenticated. (Para 20.7.11)

548. Prisoners with substantive sentences of 2 months and above but up to 5 years should be sanctioned remission each month while those sentenced to over 5 years (including life convicts) should be granted remission once in a quarter. (Para 20.7.12)

549. Ordinary remission should be calculated for full calendar months. It should not be granted for fraction of a calendar month. (Para 20.7.13)

550. For purposes of special remission any fraction of a year should be counted as one complete year. (Para 20.7.14)

551. Maximum limit of remission which a prisoner can earn should be half of the substancive sentence awarded to him. (Para 20.7.15)

552. Grant of remission to prisoners sentenced by Court Martial should be on the same principles as those applicable to other prisoners. (Para 20.7.16)

Leave

553. To bring about uniformity in terminology for prisoners' temporary release from prisons, there should be two types of leave: (i) Leave and (ii) special leave. (Para 20.12.1)

554. Rules for eligibility of convicted prisoners for being released on leave and special leave should be reviewed, rationalised and liberalised. (Para 20.12.5)

555. Inspector General of Prisons should be the authority competent for grant of release on leave or special leave. However, special leave may be granted by the superintendent of the prison concerned in the event of an emergent situation. (Paras 20.12.2 to 20.12.6)

556. The period spent on leave should count as sentence served while that spent on special leave should be treated as sentence suspended. (Para 20.12.7)

557. Rules regarding surety for release on leave or special leave should be liberalised. (Para 20.12.8)

558. The procedure for grant of leave and special leave should be reviewed and liberalised. (Para 20.12.9)

559. Record of release of prisoners on leave and special leave should be properly kept. (Para 20.12.10)

Premature release

560. Rules for eligibility of convicted prisoners for consideration of premature release should be reviewed and rationalised. (Paras 20.17.1, 20.1.2)

561. The case of each prisoner eligible for review and premature release should initially be examined by the institutional classification committee before being forwarded to the Review Board. (Para 20.17.3)

562. Review Boards should be constituted in each State/Union Territory for consideration of premature release. (Para 20.17.4)

563. The case of every prisoner which is ripe for review should be decided within a maximum period of six months from the date of eligibility. (Para 20.17.5)

564. Each State/Union Territory should formulate a set of guidelines to be uniformly applied to govern the working of Review Boards. (Para 20.17.6)

565. Section 433 A of the Code of Criminal Procedure should be suitably amended. (Paras 20.17.7, 4.34.20, 16.9.1)

566. The management of record relating to review of sentences and premature release should be streamlined. (Para 20.17.8)

CHAPTER XXI

COMMUNITY INVOLVEMENT IN CORRECTIONS

567. Public participation in prevention of crime and treatment of offenders must be made a part of our National Policy on Prisons. (Para 21.17.1)

568. An intensive public education drive should be taken up to make the society aware of the role it can play in the prevention of crime and treatment of offenders. (Para 21.17.2)

569. At the national level, the National Commission on Prisons should locate and enrol individuals and community groups volunteering to serve in the correctional field. (Para 21.17.3)

570. A committee should be constituted in each State/Union Territory to identify and enrol voluntary workers and agencies at the state, district and sub-divisional levels. (Para 21.17.4)

571. Selection of volunteers should be done very carefully and cautiously. (Para 21.17.5)

572. The government should give due patronage, financial assis-

tance and recognition to voluntary agencies and individuals working in correctional field. (Para 21.17.6)

573. Voluntary workers should be properly trained and given statutory authorisation for working in the correctional field. They should be given all possible help and advice at all levels. (Paras 21.17.7, 21.7.8)

574. Special voluntary social service institutions should be helped to come up for the protection and welfare of children and youth. (Para 21.17.9)

575. Voluntary services in the treatment, after care and rehabilitation of offenders should be organised on a systematic basis. Modalities for the utilisation of voluntary services should be specified; they should be further developed through interaction of voluntary workers with the Department of Prisons and Correctional Services. (Paras 21.17.10, 21.17.11 and 21.18)

576. The Inspector General of Prisons and Director of Correctional Services should be empowered to derecognise and delist voluntary organisations or individuals and discontinue their involvement in correctional programmes, wherever grounds for such action exist. (Para 21.19)

CHAPTER XXII

AFTER-CARE, REHABILITATION AND FOLLOW-UP

577. After-care of prisoners discharged from prisons and allied institutions should be the statutory function of the Department of Prisons and Correctional Services. (Para 22.13.1)

578. (a) There should be a properly staffed After-care and Follow-up Unit in the headquarters organisation of the Department of Prisons and Correctional Services in each State/Union Territory.

578. (b) In the districts, probation officers should be incharge of after-care and follow-up work. In large States, Regional Probation Officers should be appointed to supervise and coordinate the work of probation officers in the districts.

(c) At the institutional level this work should be done by officers incharge of prisoners' welfare in close liaison with the classification committee. (Para 22.13.2)

579. The After-care and Follow-up Unit should evolve an objective method of assessing Post-release needs of inmates. (Para 22.13.3)

580. There should be at least one voluntary organization in each district to which the work of extending help to released prisoners could be entrusted. (Para 22.13.4)

581. At the institutional level the classification committee should formulate pre-release plans and should provide the After-care and Follow-up Unit at the headquarters with all necessary data projecting the post-release needs of inmates. (Para 22.13.5)

582. Close liaison with prospective employers should be established for the employment of released prisoners. (Para 22.13.6)

583. Self-employment work programmes should be devised for prisoners which they can independently pursue after release. Necessary arrangements for adequate Finances from various sources should be made before the prisoner is actually released. (Para 22.13.7)

584. Officer incharge of welfare of prisoners should, as a pre-release preparation, chalk out, in definite terms, the rehabilitative programme that the inmate has to follow on release. (Para 22.13.8)

585. After-care services should include all kinds of help which could result in proper readjustment of the released prisoners in the society. (Para 22.13.9)

586. After-care homes should be established to meet the immediate needs of released prisoners. (Para 22.13.10)

587. Restriction on employment of ex-prisoners in government service or public sector undertakings should be removed by suitable amendment of the rules. (Para 22.13.11)

588. Small Scale Industries Departments of State Governments/ Union Territory Administrations should formulate schemes of small production units which could be run by ex-prisoners on cooperative basis. There units could be financed by State Finance Corporation, Cooperative and other Banks under their innovative banking schemes. (Para 22.13.12)

589. State Tenancy Acts should be suitably amended to protect the rights of prisoners in agricultural land. (Para 22.13.13)

590. Women prisoners willing to get married after their release should be rendered all necessary help in settling them in matrimony. (Paras 22.13.14, 13.11.33)

591. The Department of Prisons and Correctional Services in collaboration with the State Department of Information and Publicity should make proper use of mass media to educate public about the need for rehabilitation of ex-prisoners in society. (Para 22.13.15)

592. Government should encourage formation of voluntary or-

ganizations for taking up programmes for the help of released prisoners and should give them necessary financial and other help. Services of voluntary workers in the field should be appropriately recognised. (Para 22.13.16)

CHAPTER XXIII

ORGANIZATIONAL STRUCTURE

593. There should be a separate Department of Prisons and Correctional Administration in the secretariats of the States. At the Centre, the set-up dealing with prisons in the Ministry of Home Affairs should also be upgraded to the status of a Department. Senior officers having experience of correctional administration should be posted in the secretariats. (Para 23.15.1)

594. The prison department in each State/Union Territory should be responsible for institutional training and treatment, probation and after-care of both the adult and the young offenders. This integrated department should be called the Department of Prisons and Correctional Services, and the head of this department should be designated as the Inspector General of Prisons and Director of Correctional Services. (Para 23.15.2)

595. The Department of Prisons and Correctional Services in all States/Union Territories should invariably be headed by an officer from this department. (Para 23.15.3)

596. The Inspector General of Prisons and Director of Correctional Services should, at his headquarters, be assisted by senior officers in various aspects of prison administration. (Para 23.15.4)

597. A regional set-up should be established in each large State. (Para 23.15.5)

598. Each prison and allied institution should have adequate personnel in accordance with its requirements and the specified norms. (Paras 23.15.6, 23.15.7, 23.15.9, 23.15.10 and 23.15.11)

599. Each district should have a district prison with a whole-time superintendent. (Para 23.15.8)

600. Adequate number of probation officers of various categories should be appointed to look after probation and after-care work in the field. (Para 23.15.12)

601. All posts in the Department of Prisons and Correctional Services except where specialised services are required should be manned

by persons belonging to the department. (Para 23.15.13)

CHAPTER XXIV

DEVELOPMENT OF PRISON PERSONNEL

602. (a) There should be an in-built mechanism in the prison department for continuous and systematic study of the man-power needs.

602. (b) Direct entry into various wings of the prison service should be at appropriate levels. (Para 24.44.1)

603. Conditions of recruitment and promotion should be so fixed as to ensure that persons with requisite qualifications, experience and professional competence are available in the prison service at all levels. (Para 24.44.2)

604. Every direct recruit in the service should have opportunities of at least three promotions during the span of his career. (Para 24.44.3)

605. Physical fitness and psychological tests should be essential prerequisites for direct recruitment. (Para 24.44.4)

606. Officers and staff for specialised services in the prison department should be taken on deputation from respective departments of the State Governments. They should be given proper incentives. (Paras 24.44.5, 24.44.6 and 24.44.7)

607. Ministerial staff should be borne on the strength of the prison department. The executive staff should in no case be put on ministerial work. (Para 24.44.8)

608. An all India service to be called the Indian Prisons and Correctional Service should be constituted. (Para 24.44.9)

609. Prison personnel should be paid salaries and allowances at par with those of equivalent ranks in the police department. (Para 24.44.10)

610. Uniform including badges should be prescribed for all security and executive staff in the prison department. (Para 24.44.11)

611. Three-shift system of duties should be introduced in prisons. (Para 24.44.12)

612. Every member of the staff should be allowed a day off once a week (Para 24.44.13)

613. Adequate leave reserve staff should be provided. (Para 24.44.14)

614. The systems of convict officers discharging supervisory and

disciplinary duties should be abolished in a phased manner. (Para 24.44.15)

615. Residential quarters should be provided to all members of the staff. (Para 24.44.16)

616. Prison staff which is entitled to rent-free accommodation but is not provided with such accommodation should be paid 10 per cent extra house-rent allowance in addition to the house rent allowance allowed to Government employees in general. (Para 24.44.17)

617. Certain facilities as provided in Chapter XI of the Model Prison Manual should be extended to prison personnel. (Para 24.44.18)

618. The Government of India should institute medals for rewarding prison personnel. State Governments/Union Territory Administrations should suitably recognise special services rendered by prison personnel. (Para 24.44.19)

619. All good work done by prison personnel should be given proper publicity. (Para 24.44.20)

620. Prison personnel meeting with serious injuries, accidents, etc., while on duty, should given financial assistance. (Para 24.44.21)

621. In case of death of a prison personnel in lawful discharge of his duties, a lump sum of Rs. 20,000 should be paid to the survivors in his family. (Para 24.44.22)

622. A welfare fund for prison and correctional personnel should be established in each State/Union Territory. (Para 24.44.23)

623. Proper forum should be provided at the institutional and State levels for prison personnel to ventilate grievances. (Para 24.44.24)

624. Staff meetings and conferences should be regularly held. (Para 24.44.25)

625. All new recruits should be given basic initial in-service training. Officers and staff on deputation should be given a short orientation course. (Para 24.44.26)

626. Adequate training reserve should be provided in each cadre of the service. (Para 24.44.27)

627. Training of staff should be taken at three different levels: state level, regional level and national level. (Para 24.44.28)

628. Qualified persons with aptitude for training and teaching should be posted at these institutions. (Para 24.44.29)

629. Directors of Regional Training Institutions should be from the Prisons and Correctional Service and should be of the rank of Inspector General of Prisons. Principals of State level training schools should of the rank of superintendents of Central prisons. (Para 24.44.30)

630. Permanent academic staff of the training institutions and experts invited to them should be properly informed of the training requirements. (Para 24.44.31)

631. Details of syllabi, etc. should be properly evolved and reviewed once every three years. (Para 24.44.32)

632. Proper literature should be prepared for meeting the training needs of various categories of prison personnel. (Para 24.44.33)

633. Basic initial training, in-service training, refresher courses and special training courses should be organised by the training institutions for various categories of personnel. (Para 24.44.34)

634. The Inspector General of Prisons and Director of Correctional Services should prepare a panel of officers for attending conferences and special training courses in the country and abroad. (Para 24.44.35)

635. Study teams of senior officers should be deputed to visit prison institutions in various States in the country as also those in other countries. (Para 24.44.37)

636. The Central Government, the State Governments and the Union Territory Administrations should encourage setting up of a professional non-official registered body at the national level with its branches in all the State and Union Territories and should provide necessary financial and other assistance to them for their proper functioning (Para 24.44.38)

CHAPTER XXV

PLANNING, RESEARCH AND DEVELOPMENT

637. The new legislations should clearly define the general objectives of correctional system in the country. (Para 25.8.1)

638. Each State Government/Union Territory Administration should lay down specific objectives and goals not only for the department but also for individual institutions. (Para 25.8.2)

639. Organisational and institutional goals should be reviewed at least once a year. (Para 25.8.3)

640. The National Commission on Prisons should be functionally linked with State correctional organisations to review the achievement of goals and objectives, etc., and to plan their future organisational, personnel and functional structure in consultation with them. (Para 25.8.4)

641. There should be an appropriately manned unit for planning

and research at the headquarters of the Department of Prisons and Correctional Services of each State and Union Territory. (Para 25.8.5)

642. Each State/Union Territory should develop an integrated process of long-term and short-term planning and prepare plans for administrative and operational functioning. The National Commission on Prisons should coordinate these plans and monitor their progress so as to have an all India perspective of the development of prisons. (Paras 25.8.6, 25.8.7)

643. The National Commission on Prisons should work out and finance some pilot projects to serve as demonstration projects for the development of prison administration. (Paras 25.8.8, 25.12.6)

644. Research in the correctional field should be problem oriented and practical. Cooperation of outside agencies should be sought in this work. (Para 25.8.9)

645. There should be a systematic collection of statistical data on uniform pattern throughout the country. The National Commission on Prisons should publish an annual statistical report on corrections. (Paras 25.8.10, 25.8.11)

646. A scientific method of keeping and weeding of record in prison department should be evolved. (Para 25.8.12)

Prisons and national plans

647. Programmes for reformation and rehabilitation of offenders should find a place in our national plans. (Para 25.12.1)

648. Funds for renovation of old buildings and construction of new buildings should be made available to the State Governments by the Central Government under plan. (Para 25.12.2)

649. Sufficient outlays should be earmarked under plan by the Central Government for initiating certain centrally sponsored schemes for the welfare of prisoners. (Para 25.12.3)

650. Training of personnel should find place under the plan sector. (Para 25.12.4)

651. Central financial assistance in the form of matching grants or long-term loans should be extended to the State Governments for modernization or the mechanization of prison industry and agriculture. (Para 25.12.5)

652. Other programmes for the development of prisons and reformation of prisoners should be included in the State Plan. (Para 25.12.7)

653. Under the pretext of economy, cuts should not be effected in

the non-plan budget of the prison departments.

CHAPTER XXVI

NATIONAL COMMISSION ON PRISONS

654. Government of India should immediately set up a National Commission on Prisons. (Paras 26.13.1, 26.13.2 and 26.13.3)

655. The Objectives and functions of the National Commission on Prisons should be clearly laid down. (Para 26.13.4)

CHAPTER XXVII

NATIONAL POLICY ON PRISONS

656. Government of India should finalize the National Policy on Prisons on the lines suggested, and notify it. (Paras 27.1, 27.2, 27.2.1, to 27.2.31)

CHAPTER XXVIII

ACTION PLAN

657. Implementation of important recommendations should be phased into immediate, short term and long term action plan. (Paras 28.2, 28.3)

658. Estimated financial outlays for improvement in certain important areas of prison management have been worked out taking into account board principles and need for achieving basic minimum standards. (Paras 28.5 to 28.16)

15

RAILWAY ACCIDENT INVESTIGATION REPORT ON THE OUTBREAK OF FIRE IN FIRST CLASS COACH NO. CR-2934 OF NO. 149 UP QUTAB EXPRESS BETWEEN TEHARKA AND NIWARI STATIONS ON THE JHANSI-MANIKPUR BROAD GAUGE SINGLE LINE SECTION OF CENTRAL RAILWAY'S JHANSI DIVISION AT ABOUT 03.45 HOURS ON SEPTEMBER 9, 1980 — REPORT[1]

One Man Commission Shri N.P. Vithal.

Appointment

The Commission was appointed under Ministry of Tourism and Civil Aviation (Commission of Railway Safety) in accordance with Rule 4 of the Statutory Investigation into Railway Accidents Rules 1973 Vide Notification No. RS.13-T(8)/71 dated April 19, 1973 on September 9, 1980.

Terms of Reference

To enquire into the Outbreak of Fire in First Class Coach No. CR-2934 on the Qutab Express between Teharka and Niwari Stations on the Jhansi-Manikpur Broad Gauge Single Line section of Central Railway's Jhansi Division at about 03.45 hours on September 9, 1980.

Contents

Summary; Inspection and Inquiry; Composition of Train and Damage, Summary of Evidence, Tests and Observations; Discussion; Conclu-

1. Delhi, Controller of Publications, 1983, 21 p., 1 Chart.

sions; Remarks and Recommendations; Railway Board's comments on various paras of the Report.

Conclusions

Cause of the Accident

(a) Upon full consideration of the factual, material and circumstantial evidence at my disposal I have come to the conclusion that the outbreak of Fire in FC Coach No. CR-2934 at about 03.45 hours on 9-9-1980 was in all probability due to the ignition of some inflammable material in its 'E'. Compartment which came into contact with some naked fire-inducing material such as a burning cigarette-end or burning math-stick which was inadvertently left behind by an unalert passenger as he vacated this compartment to detrain at Mauranipur Station.

(b) This Accident is accordingly to be classified under the category of "Failure of persons other than Railway Staff".

Responsibility

(a) The responsibility for this accident lies with an unknown outsider, who in all probability was the passenger who was travelling in the 'E' Compartment of FC Coach No. CR 2934 up to Mauranipur Station.

(b) Minor infractions, such as those referred to in para 38 and 39 of the report, which came to light during my Inquiry, have been separately referred to the Railway for action.

Recommendations

Improvement in the Fire-resisting Capability of Coaches

42. (a) As brought out earlier [para 37(c)], any fire-retardent or fire-resistant measures so far taken have actually proved to be of little avail, once a fire gets going. Also, the description of the gutted Coach [para 25] is proof enough to the presence of substantial quantities of fire-excitable, fire-supporting and fire-propagating substances that variously go into a Coach by way of furnishings/fittings. It is, of course, economically meaningless to think in terms of fire-proofing a

Coach. Indeed, even protection against fire, once it has, gone beyond a certain point, cannot be regarded as an economically practicable proposition, however desirable and laudable the idea may be. Hence, the only pragmatic solution would lie in the improvement and upgradation of the inherent or intrinsic resistivity of the various inputs into coach-building to withstand a limited fire-attack, which might be expected to occur within the first few minutes of its outbreak. It is accordingly recommended that the Railway Board should take a long term perspective of this vexing problem and accord high priority to the development, through the expertise available in the RDSO, of appropriate surface-treatment techniques and of fire-resistant products, not only for the purposes of manufacturing new Coaches at the ICF, Perambur, but also for their progressive incorporation into the existing Coaches on a programmed basis, giving preference initially to the more expensive FC and AC Coaches.

(b) In this context, reference is also invited to Railway Board's Case No. 76/Safety (A&R)/1/6/ on the Inquiry into the Fire in Coach No. 746 A on 433 Down Local at Western Railway's Jogeshwari Station on 7-3-1976, and the correspondence resting with letter No. RX. 23-T (3)/76 dated 28th August 1980 from the Chief Commissioner of Railway Safety, wherein attention was drawn to certain products recently developed in the USA.

43. *An Attendant to be invariably positioned in each FC Coach* – According to the extant directives [Railway Board's letter No. 67-TG1/146 dated 25-4-1967], excepting in the case of vestibuled trains, an Attendant is to be posted in *each* First Class Corridor-type Coach for the convenience of passengers therein. As compliance with this policy would have [para 36] in all probability averted this disaster, it is strongly recommended that the deployment of an Attendant in each and every First Class Coach shall be regarded as a mandatory essential and that the Central Railway should urgently take suitable steps to ensure the same.

Railway Boards Comments on Various Paras of the Report

Para 42 (a) & (b): The following fire preventive measures, as recommended by RDSO, have been implemented by the Railway Administration:

(i) Replacement of combustible ceiling material by lumpet asbestos sheets.

(ii) Application of fire resistant paint over wooden batter troughing.

(iii) Metallising the fitting of the coaches except the seats and berths.

The question of finding suitable fire resistant material for interior furnishing of the coaches is receiving attention of the RDSO. As for correspondence resting with Commission of Railway Safety's letter No. RS. 23-T(3)/76, dated 28-2-1980, attention is invited to RDSO's letter No. MC/CB/Cushion, dated 27-4-1981, wherefrom it would be seen that the RDSO is in touch with M/s. Craftex Mills, Philadelphia (U.S.A.) for obtaining relevant information on the fire resistant material, the Commission had referred to.

Para 43: As advised by the Railway Administration, an attendant is provided in each of the first class coaches on Qutab Express with effect from 1-8-81. Necessary instructions are being issued to the Railways to ensure compliance of the directive contained in Board's letter No. 67/TG-I/146, dated 25-4-1967.

RAILWAY ACCIDENT INVESTIGATION REPORT ON COLLISION OF NO. E-3 DOWN EMU 'MADRAS CENTRAL-GUMMIDIPUNDI PASSENGER' TRAIN WITH A P.T.C. BUS NO. TMN 1607 AT MANNED LEVEL CROSSING NO. 10 AT KM. 13/2 BETWEEN TIRUVOTTIYUR AND ENNORE STATIONS MADRAS-GUDUR BROAD GAUGE DOUBLE LINE SECTION OF SOUTHERN RAILWAY ON OCTOBER 17, 1980 — REPORT[1]

One Man Commission Shri B.P. Sastry

Appointment

The Commission was appointed under Ministry of Tourism and Civil Aviation (Commission of Railway Safety) in Accordance with Rule 4 of the Statutory Investigation into Railway Accidents Rules 1973 Vide its Notification No. RS. 13-T(8)/71 dated April 19, 1973 on October 17, 1980.

Terms of Reference

To enquire into the Collision of No. E-3 Down EMU 'Madras Central-Gummidipundi Passenger Train with a P.T.C. Bus No. TMN/1607 at Manned level crossing No. 10 at km. 13/2 between Tiruvottiyur and Ennore Stations Madras-Gudur Broad Gauge Double Line Section of Southern Railway on October 17, 1980.

Contents

Summary; Inspection and Inquiry; Relief Measures; The Train; Local

1. Delhi, Controller of Publications, 1983, 17 p.

Features; Summary of Evidence; Observation and Tests; Discussion; Conclusions; Remarks and Recommendations; Railway Board's Comment on Various Paras of the Report.

Conclusions

Cause of the Accident

On a careful consideration of the factual, material and circumstantial evidence at my disposal, I have come to the conclusion that the collision which occurred on the morning of 17th October 1980 between E-3 Down Electric Multiple Unit "Madras-Gummidipundi Suburban Passenger" train and Pallavan Transport Corporation Bus No. TMN 1607 at level crossing No. at Km. 13.20 between Tiruvottiyur and Ennore stations on Madras-Gudur Broad Gauge double line section of Southern Railway was caused on account of the road vehicle infringing the path of the Suburban train while it was on run on clear signals between Automatic Signal No. 120 and Home Signal No. 1 of Ennore station.

Responsibility

I hold the following persons responsible for the accident:

- *(i)* Shri Dorairaj, Gangman, who was on duty as a Gateman at the time of the Occurrence.
- *(ii)* Late Shri Raman Nair, Driver of Bus No. TMN 1607.
- *(iii)* Certain other Railway Officials who had by their acts of omission and commission allowed the functioning of the level crossing became more and more vulnerable to accidents.

Shri Dorairaj was appointed to casual Railway service as a Gangman on 1-9-1973. On the date of occurrence he was working as a substitute Gateman at level crossing No. 10 under the instructions of his Gangmate. The extenuating circumstances under which he was functioning on the date of occurrence will no doubt be taken into consideration by the Railway Administration while quantifying his responsibility for the collision.

Southern Railway Administration may identify and determine the individual share of responsibility of each of the officials coming under

8.2.1 (*iii*) above on the basis of their respective functions and the degree of failure in discharging those functions.

Relief Arrangements

I am satisfied that the injured had received prompt medical attention from the public of the locality who had taken the initiative to shift them to the nearest Government Hospital expeditiously and from the Hospital Authorities on their being admitted as patients.

Recommendations

9.1. While interlocking of the level crossing near Ennore with signals (which has since been completed) considerably improves safety to road and rail traffic, it is likely to aggravate detentions to road vehicles at the crossing. Crossing. The ultimate solution to this problem will, therefore, be replacement of the crossing by a road-under-bridge. The Railway Administration appears to have initiated some action in this regard. In view of the rapidly increasing road traffic at the level crossing, it is recommended that early steps may be taken by the Railway Administration in co-ordination with the State Government to get the proposal finalised and the work executed.

9.2. From what has been brought out in paras 7.5 and 7.6 of the Report, it appears that even important safety instructions issued by a higher authority are viewed in a rather routine manner by certain Railway Officials. Southern Railway Administration may consider measures which would promote respect for such instructions by all Officials connected with safety.

9.3. A review of the present policy and practice in the matter of posting of officers and Inspectors for posts connected with safety appears called for (paras 7.7.2, 7.7.3 and 7.7.4). Southern Railway Administration may consider measures which would keep up the morale of these Officials at a reasonable level and ensure reasonable tenures for them once they are posted to the Safety Branch. Railway Board may consider issuing suitable guidelines to the Railways in this respect.

9.4. A suitable machinery which would enable the safety Officers on the Divisions and at Headquarters of the Railways to keep track of implementation of important safety recommendations made by Departmental Enquiry Committees or Commission of Railway Safety and accepted by the competent Authority is recommended.

9.5 An urgent review of safety aids required to be provided at manned level crossings on the basis of the guidelines contained in Railway Board's No. 77/W3/SG/LX/2 dated 16-3-1979 and preparation of a priority plan of action on the Railway is recommended (para 7.6.1). The position is not very different on South Central Railway. Railway Board may consider suitably advising South Central Railway Administration and other Railway Administrations which may be in a similar position. Railway Board may also consider how quickly funds for execution of such works could be made available to meet the requirements of Railways on a programmed basis.

9.6. Railway Board in their letter No. 63/W3/SG/88 datec 16-11-1970 advised the Railways that the approach operated warnin; bell cannot ensure the standard of safety desired, particularly at bus; level crossing gates. Experience has shown that the bell arrangemer itself is not a very reliable arrangement. Several witnesses wh deposed before me have also given expression to this besides my ow observations while I was at this and some other level crossings. I particular, the bell arrangement for non-interlocked level crossing may even mislead the Gateman thus endangering safety. It recommended that bell warning as a safety aid to non-interlocked lev crossings may be discontinued.

Railway Board's Comments on Various Paras of the Report

Para 9.1: Construction of Road Over/Under-bridges in replaceme of existing level crossings is undertaken on cost-sharing basis with tl State Government/Local Authority. Proposals for such schemes ha to be sponsored by the State Government/Local Authority togeth with an undertaking to bear their share of the cost as per extant rule No proposal for construction of a Road-over-bridge in replacement existing level crossing at Km. 13/2 between Tiruvottiyur and Ennoi stations on Madras-Gudur section of Southern Railway has so far bee received from the State Government/Local Authority.

However, in view of increasing traffic at this level crossing Southern Railway are processing the proposal for replacement of thi level crossing with a road over-bridge. The State Government has alsc been requested to initiate necessary proposal in the matter.

Para 9.2: Commissioner of Railway Safety has apparently based his recommendation on the fact that the Railway had not complied with the provisions of Railway Board's letter No. 77/W-3/SG/LX/2 dated 16-3-79, referred to in para 7.6.1 of the CRS's report. While issuing these instructions, the Board were very clear in their mind that it would not be possible for the Railways to introduce all these desirable safety features in the immediate future. The idea behind issuing such comprehensive instructions, was to enable the Railways to act in a planned manner so that over a period of time all the level crossings could be provided with necessary facilities. In the absence of such detailed guidelines, the provision of safety equipments/devices at the level crossings, was not being done in a planned manner resulting in adhocism.

In view of the financial constraints, it is not possible to provide all the facilities at all the level crossings envisaged in the above referred Railway Board's letter within a short time. All the Railways have been repeatedly reminded to start planning for the provision of these safety devices at the level crossings in a phased manner. However, as desired by CRS, necessary instructions have been reiterated to the Zonal Railway (Copy enclosed).

Para 9.3: In pursuance of the recommendations made by the Railway Accidents Enquiry Committee (1978) in part-II of their report, the Board have approved of a minimum tenure of 2 years to the persons posted in the safety Organisation. Necessary instructions, in this regard, are being issued separately.

Para 9.4: Necessary instructions have since been issued (copy enclosed for ready reference).

Para 9.5: Guidelines for the provision of safety aids at manned level crossings have been given to the Railways vide Board's circular letter No. 77/W-C/SG/LX/2 dated 16-3-79, superseding all earlier instructions on the subject. Although it is very much desirable for the Railways to implement these instructions expeditiously, nonetheless due to financial stringencies the implementation has necessarily to be done on a programmed basis.

Para 9.6: Accepted. Instructions have been issued to Railways that provision of Warning Bells at non-interlocked level crossing gates may be discontinued.

RAILWAY ACCIDENT INVESTIGATION REPORT ON COLLISION OF NO. 6 UP PUNJAB MAIL WITH STATIONERY GOODS TRAIN NO. 747 DOWN IN ITARSI STATION YARD ON CENTRAL RAILWAY ON OCTOBER 20, 1980 — REPORT[1]

One Man Commission Shri N.P. Vithal

Appointment

The Commission was appointed under Ministry of Tourism and Civil Aviation (Commission of Railway Safety) in accordance with Rule of the Statutory Investigation into Railway Accidents Rules 1973 Vide its Notification No. RS.13-T(8)/71 dated April 19, 1973 on October 20, 1980.

Terms of Reference

"To enquire into the Collision of No. 6 Up Punjab Mail with Stationery Goods Train No. 747 Down in Itarsi Station Yard on Central Railway on October 20, 1980".

Contents

Summary; Inspection and Inquiry; Relief Measures; Composition of Trains and Damage; Local Features; Summary of Evidence; Tests and Observation; Discussion; Conclusions; Remarks and Recommendations; Annexure I; Railway Board Views on the Recommendation.

Conclusions

65. (a) Upon full consideration of the factual, material and cir-

1. Delhi, Controller of Publications, 1986, 41 p.

cumstantial evidence at my disposal, I conclude that the head-on collision of 6 Up Punjab Main with a stationary Goods Train near Itarsi 'B' Cabin on the Central Railway's Bhusaval Division at 22.27 hours on 20-10-1980 was the result of 6 Up's Driver passing an un-prewarned MACL Signal No. S-7B at Danger. I also conclude that the said Driver was indeed a victim of a combination of several adverse circumstances, some of which had sorely handicapped his sense of judgement and, but for the simultaneous co-existence of which, this accident would not have happened.

(b) This accident is accordingly classified under the category "Failure of Railway Staff".

66. *Responsibility*

(a) Individual responsibility as such for this collision can only devolve on Shri G.H. Patil, the Driver of 6 Up, whose bio-data has been given in para 42(d). Nevertheless, for reasons brought out in para 63(c), I cannot with logic hold him guilty of negligence or culpable for this freakish accident which had in effect resulted from the cumulative effect of, besides the unsafe design and installation of the Signalling System that left MACL Signal No. S-7B un-prewarned, also a variety of human failures on the part of several others.

(b) And, for the same reasons, I do not hold Shri Gurunath Seetharam, the Assistant Driver of 6 Up, culpable for this accident.

(c) For the said unsafe design/installation of the Signaling System at 'B' Cabin, whereas the Railway's Signal & Telecommunication Department has to shoulder the responsibility, no individual official is held blame-worthy.

(d) For reasons elucidated in para 63(b), I do not also hold any single individual responsible for the various failures of the human element.

(e) Infractions relating to what has been brought out in para 62(e), etc., have been separately referred to the Railway Administration for appropriate action.

67. *Relief Measures*

With reference to para 64(a), I was entirely satisfied with the quality of medical attention provided to the injured.

Recommendations

68. *Development of measures to reduce the range of visibility of MACL Signals*

As it is eminently desirable to eliminate the possibility of any confusion likely to be caused to the Driver through sighting too many signals within the field of his vision, it is recommended that the Railway Board may direct the RDSO to develop suitable measures aimed at curtailing the visibility of MACL Signals to about 500m. or thereabouts, such as, tilting the 'signal unit' slightly downwards and lengthening the hood, etc.

69. *Pre-warning of MACL Stop Signals*

In an age characterised by the direction of inputs of technological growth towards providing an improved information system for Drivers, it is only proper that the Railway should, hereafter at least, ensure strict and unexceptional compliance with SEM para 119(c)(i) in this respect, even if the introduction of Colour Light Signals has to be progressively "phased" in the case of large yards like Itarsi. Whereas it is understood that this proviso will be met when the new route-relay-interlocking installation of the Itarsi Central Cabin is commissioned, it is suggested that the Railway should review the situation obtaining at present in the various other large marshalling yards so as to check up whether or not the un-prewarned condition of the said Signal No. S-7B was an isolated instance and take such appropriate action as necessary to comply with the relevant SEM stipulation.

70. *Design of a proper syllabus and suitable modalities for training CASMs in charge of 'Panel' working*

(a) At present, it is largely left to the Chief Signal Inspector's own initiative to devise his own methodology for training CASMs responsible for operating route-relay-interlocking 'panels'. While on the one hand the easy push-button operation does seem, prima facie, elementary to master, there is no denying the fact that such installations are conceptually extremely sophisticated, requiring a thorough grasp of the various intricacies involved. It is accordingly recommended that the Railway should standardise the syllabus as well as modalities for imparting training to such CASMs and also evolve an exhaustive catechism to enable the extensive quizzing to CASMs as to their proficiency.

(b) It is also recommended that CASMs – particularly those with a short service and hence limited experience – be deputed to undergo an institutionalised short-duration training programme on panel working at the Zonal Training School, in order that they are fully equipped with all the requisite knowhow as also the basic background that is so vital for gaining indepth appreciation of the ensuing on-the-job training. It is further recommended that, as a pre-requisite to the issue of the Competency Certificate, *such* CASMs shall be re-tested on their knowledgeability in the General and Subsidiary Rules in respect of train passing duties. With some advance planning, it should be quite easy to fulfil these requirements.

71. *Station Working Orders of not only 'B' Cabin but also 'A' and 'C' Cabins to prohibit hazardous cross movements*

(a) In the interest of safety, it becomes essential to display prudence and caution by inserting suitable instructions in the Station Working Orders for these Cabins prohibiting any cross movement across/over the Main Lines in the face of 'line clear' granted for a through train, in order to cater to the possibility of this latter train overshooting a Signal at 'Danger'.

(b) Similarly, in the event that such 'cross-movement becomes inescapable, suitable instructions should also be incorporated in the Station Working Orders to ensure that the said through train is stopped, rather than take the risk of allowing it to come up to the last possible Stop Signal on the run-through line, at a safe margin in rear, with any further movement enabled by the use of 'Calling-on' Signal. Since the Main Line trains will have to stop anyhow, it would be pertinent to note in this context that the wording of SR 42-1, "If, however, Calling-on Signal has been taken 'Off' before the train has arrived at that Signal –", would facilitate the use of a Calling-on-Signal without loss of time, even where the CASM positioned in a large RRI Cabin has no direct view of the entire yard.

(c) Whenever an otherwise run-through train has to be stopped on the Main Line thus, it is further recommended that the Station Working Orders should expressly stipulate that, wherever practicable, the farther Signals applicable to the relevant Main Line shall not be taken 'Off' unless and until the Stop Signal immediately ahead of the stopped train is itself taken 'Off'.

72. *Cabins to be constructed invariably at a raised elevation and also to provide the maximum visibility of the yard from within*

In this case, the Relay Room could have been positioned at the ground floor level with the Cabin located above, which is almost a standard practice all over. It is recommended that the construction of future Cabins should invariably be so planned as to provide the Panel Room at the highest possible elevation that may be commensurate with the actual requirements. Such Cabins should also provide for the widest possible range of over-view of the yard to enable the CASM to profit by using his perceptive knowledge of the movements taking place to supplement the information already indicated on the Panel. To the extent possible, it is desirable that this facility be provided via all-round glazing which obviates a need for the CASM to go outside the Panel Room for instance, he would have to, if instead a balcony provided skirting around it.

73. *Positive steps to familiarise Drivers with a changes made in the Signalling*

Drivers, who are required to be knowledgeable about the section ahead and who must implicitly obey Signals at all times, have the right to be explained unambiguously about any Signalling changes that a contemplated/installed. The Administration should thus regard it as one of its sacred duties to educate the loco crew in simple and lucid terms regarding a change(s) in the existing signalling lay-out. It accordingly recommended that the Railway should quickly evolve suitable procedures to fulfil this requirement and identify, from amongst the existing categories of personnel, upon whom this responsibility would devolve, as also those whose duty it will be to exercise a check on the task as performed.

74. *Exercise of due care in imposing speed restrictions*

There is no gain-saying the fact that any and every speed-restriction per se is counter-productive to train-running. Hence, any overly restrictive speed restriction imposed merely for the sake of a formality, would only serve in the end as a provocation for the Drivers to disregard it, particularly when the accent is rightly on punctuality, higher average speeds, etc. As the development of such an anamolous situation is against the interests of safety, it is recommended that any speed restriction on account of change(s) in the signalling should hereafter be imposed only with due care aforethought, depending upon the needs of the actual circumstances obtaining; necessary instructions may be issued to all concerned.

75. *Use of non-touch-based equipment in Breakdown operations*

It is lamentable enough to incur a serious accident but it would appear unforgiveable that the pathos of the situation should be aggravated by further damage through fire erupting during breakdown operations. The present-day technology has already made available, for example, at the airports in India, miniature high-power cutting tools capable of attaining very high speeds in wreckage clearance operations. It is, therefore, recommended that the Indian Railways should likewise procure similar light-weight, high-speed non-torch-based equipment for use at all depots meant to handle rescue operations.

Railway Board's Views on the Recommendation

Para 65: The cause of the accident as given by CRS is prima facie accepted. It is mentioned however that the accident resulted directly from the failure of the Driver to obey a signal and in his passing it in the 'On' position. It is also mentioned that pre-warning of signal No. S-7B of 'B' Cabin which the Driver of 6 Up passed at danger was not a codal necessity, as has already been pointed by the Railway.

Para 66: It is noted that CCRS considers the Driver of 6 Up responsible for causing the accident and it is prima facie accepted. Regarding provision of signals, signal No. 23-C preceding signal No. 7-B was a two aspect signal. On passing the signal No. 23-C, the Driver was expected to necessarily keep a look out for the next signal which in this case was signal No. 7-B presuming it to be at danger unless seen by him otherwise. The Driver was obviously still travelling in two aspect signalling territory and considering the layout and scheme of working in the yard, it was not a codal necessity to pre-warn this signal. The signalling arrangement provided were quite adequate from safety point of view and hence there is no question of Signal &

Telecommunication department of the Railway shouldering the responsibility.

Para 68: Development of measures to reduce the range of visibility of MACL signals

The railway is already aware of this problem. Due to inherent feature of this system there is a wide variation in the range of visibility of Colour Light Signals at night and during the day. Any attempt to restrict the visibility at night affects the range of visibility during the day also. Knowledge of the road for the drivers is therefore an essential requirement.

Para 69: Pre-Warning of MACL stop signals

As indicated against views in para No. 66(C) it would not be correct to interpret as a case of unprewarned stop signal in multiple aspect signalling territory. There is, therefore, no need to issue any instructions from the Board arising out of this.

Para 70(a): Design of proper syllabus for training CASMs

The Railway has been asked to standardise the syllabus and modalities for imparting training to staff.

Para 70(b): Panel training

The Railway Administration has advised that panel training is to be included as a part of initial training of freshly recruited Cabin ASMs/ASMs at zonal training school at Bhusaval. As far as training in the in-service Cabin ASMs on panel is concerned, the same is being organised by the Railway Administration on the Division. In addition, the refresher course is also being modified to include panel training.

Other Railways are also being suitably advised, as suggested by CCRS

Para 71(a) & (b): Station working orders of not only B Cabin but also A & C Cabins to prevent hazardous cross movement

The Railway Administration has accepted the recommendations and incorporated necessary provision in the station working order of Itarsi station. This has been noted by CCRS. Instructions are being issued to other Railways to take similar action.

Para 71(c): Aspect of signal ahead

CCRS has appreciated the difficulty in implementing CRS's recommendations in this respect. However, as desired by him necessary directives are being issued to Railways that in case any signal is put back to 'On' in an emergency the signals ahead should also be put back to 'On' immediately thereafter.

Para 72: Cabins to be constructed at raised elevation to provide maximum visibility

The Railway Administration has accepted the recommendations for implementation in future cases. Other Railways have also been advised in this regard under Board's letter No. 83/WDO/EV/1 dated 28-12-83 (copy enclosed).

Para 73: Positive steps to familiarise drivers with any changes made in the signalling

The recommendations that the drivers should be acquainted with any changes made in the signalling is being implemented by the Railway Administration. CCRS has noted this. Other railways are also being advised in the matter.

Para 74: Exercise of due care in imposing speed restriction

Speed restrictions are imposed where it is inescapable for safety running of trains. The speed restriction under consideration was imposed by the Railway Administration on account of changes in Signalling. The restriction was lifted when no longer required and was not current at the time of the accident "but wrongly issued". CCRS has noted this.

Para 75: Use of non-torch based equipment in breakdown portions

The Railway Administration has advised that cold cutting equipment has since been provided in all the A class breakdown trains on Central

Railway. It has been noted by CCRS. Other railways have been asked to do likewise as desired.

Para 76: CCRS's additional remarks: Check on repeated contravention of speed restriction

Instructions have been issued to intensity supervision to ensure safe running of trains including implementation of speed restrictions, etc.

18

COMMITTEE ON CONSUMER PRICE INDEX NUMBERS, 1980 – REPORT[1]

Chairman Dr. K.C. Seal
Members Shri Mahfooz Ahmed; Shri A.V.R. Chari; Shri H. Pais.
M. Secy. Shri R.S. Deshpande.

Appointment

The present series of the Consumer Price Index Numbers for Industrial Workers are compiled by the Labour Bureau on base 1960=100 and are based on the Family Budget Enquiries conducted in 1958-59. In order to ascertain the shifts in the consumption pattern of the working class, the Labour Bureau to undertake a Fresh Family Budget survey during 1980-81. The Government of India in the Ministry of Labour Constituted the Committee on Consumer Price Index Numbers Vide its Resolution No. Y-16013/8/80-LB, dated November 18, 1980.

Terms of Reference

"To go into the question of preparation of a new series of Consumer Price Index numbers compiled by Labour Bureau with 1980-81 as the base year and suggest how the new series of Index Numbers may be compiled".

Contents

Introduction; Background; Family Income and Expenditure Survey 1981-82; Compilation of the New Series of Consumer Price Index Numbers; Price Collection System; Summary of Main Recommendations; Acknowledgement.

1. New Delhi, Ministry of Labour, 1981, 93 p.

Recommendations

Conduct of Family Income and Expenditure Survey

6.1 The Committee endorses the decision of the Technical Advisory Committee on Statistics of Price and Cost of Living (TACSPCL) on various technical aspects of the family income and expenditure survey 1981-82 and recommends that Labour Bureau should continue with the Survey as directed by the (TACSPCL). (Para 3.6)

Off Take from Fair Price Shop

6.2 The Committee recommends that off-take rather than admissible quantity should be the basis of weighting the price in the fair price shop. (Para 4.6)

6.3 According to one member of the Committee (Dr. Mahfooz Ahmed), the average quantity available per unit of consumption in the fair price shop should form the weight for the price in the fair price shop. According to him, the industrial workers' actual off-take is unlikely to be much different from the amount actually available from the fair price shop and that conducting of off-take Survey in 70 Centres will, besides, posing conceptual and practical problems, involve heavy manpower and financial resources; it may also delay the compilation of the index. (Para 4.8).

6.4 Other four members of the Committee felt that instead of relaying on such a priori assumption, Labour Bureau should collect actual off-take data from samples of families selected for half-yearly house rent surveys for weighting the price in fair price shop. They feel that it would be appropriate to collect the actual off-take data through regular off-take survey as is being done in the case of CPI for urban non-manual employees. The extra expenditure on conducting the off-take surveys would be marginal as the Staff of Labour Bureau engaged in the half-yearly house rent survey would be utilised for the survey. (Para 4.9)

6.5 Till a final view is taken on the feasibility of the two approaches, or for any reason if the measurement of average monthly off-take on the lines suggested above is not possible, the existing procedure based on the quantity admissible to the ration card holders may be continued. (Para 4.10)

Price Index for Cereals in Statutory Rationing Area

6.6 The Committee recommends that black market price in the statutory rationing area should not be utilised for compilation of the CPI numbers. (Para 4.13)

6.7 The existing practice of "corrective action" should continue except that for measuring the shortfall from the quantity of consumption in the base year, the off-take from the ration shop should be estimated on the lines suggested in paragraphs 4.8 to 4.10. (Para 4.14)

Price Index for Sugar

6.8 The weight to be assigned to the ration price of sugar should be based on admissible quantity as at present the actual off-take is equal to the admissible quantity (Para 4.15).

6.9 If in future actual off-take in a month is less than the admissible quantity the weight assigned to the ration price should be based on the actual off-take or availability (Para 4.15).

6.10 In the tea gardens of Assam, there are no fair price shops. If the plantation owners make arrangements for the distribution of levy sugar to their workers, quantity sold through such arrangements should be taken for assigning weight to the controlled price. If no such arrangements exist, the open market price should be used. (Para 4.16)

6.11 If the admissible quantity of sugar is higher than the base year consumption the entire weight for sugar should be assigned to the quantity admissible in the fair price shops. (Para 4.17)

House Rent Index

6.12 Uniform method should be followed in calculating House Rent Index for all the centres. (Para 4.21)

6.13 Rent for rent-free houses should be treated as zero. In the calculation of the overall average rent index for the centre, the zero rent for rent-free houses should be weighted by the proportion of the index population residing in rent free houses. (Para 4.22)

6.14 For rented houses the present practice of constructing the rent index on the basis of six-monthly house rent survey should continue. This component of the rent index should be weighted with the proportion of the index population residing in rented houses. (Para 4.23)

6.15 The rent index for owner-occupied houses should be based on rent paid for similar rented accommodation in the same building or nearly locality. If it is not possible to collect data on comparable rent, the house rent index for owner-occupied houses should be taken to be the same as that of the rented houses. (Para 4.24)

6.16 The data on proportion of the index population residing in rent-free, rented and owner-occupied houses should be collected every six months by undertaking a special survey by the Labour Bureau. (Para 4.25)

6.17 One member of the Committee (Dr. Mahfooz Ahmed) felt that inclusion of new houses in the computation of CPI is tantamount to changing the base year consumption pattern and thus will violate the fixed basket principle of construction CPI. The solution to the problem of new houses, like many other items included in the consumption basket where similar situation arises, lies in revising the base of the index at shorter intervals. He, therefore, recommended that no account should be taken of new houses in the estimation of the average house rent index for the Centre. (Para 4.27)

6.18 Other four members feel that the fixed basket theory does not hold good for the house rent index as the quality of existing houses changes with age, even if repairs and maintenance are undertaken at regular intervals. The present method of determining the changes in the average house rent would be adequate if proportions of families residing in new houses is negligible. If new colonies come up and a large number of working class families start residing in them, it would be appropriate to find out average rent paid by them in the newly constructed colonies. They, therefore, suggested that the rent for new houses should be combined with the rent for old houses to determine the overall average of house rent for the compilation of the house rent index. The relative proportions of the index population residing in new and old houses should form the basis for weighting the two components of the index. All the centres should be covered in batches in the course of the next five years by the annual special house rent surveys to determine the average house rent prevailing in newly constructed houses (Para 4.28).

6.19 While compiling the house rent index for houses whose rent is subject to rent control regulations, rent for such houses should include both the rent paid as well as expenditure incurred by the worker on repairs and maintenance. (Para 4.29)

Adjusting the Index for Quality Changes

6.20 The present practice of constructing the index of rationed commodities, i.e., without taking into account the quality difference may be continued. (Para 4.30)

6.21 When an item is completely changed qualitatively or in terms of major characteristics, the new items should be introduced in the index after splicing its price. If this is not possible, the weight for such items may be distributed over other constituents included in the items basket. (Para 4.31)

Clothing

6.22 (i) In centres where well-known textile mills have opened their retail shops, the price index for clothing may be compiled on the basis of the prices collected from these shops. Prices of handloom products should be collected from Handloom Co-operatives or other shops where handloom products are sold, whenever difficulty is faced in pricing a clothing item by the price collector, price supervisor should personally visit the market and sent his report to the Labour Bureau. (Paras 4.34 to 4.36)

(ii) In view of the difficulties in measuring the price change for readymade garments, the weights for the readymade garments in the index may be appropriately distributed to the respective items under clothing and stitching charges under the miscellaneous group. (Para 4.37)

Tobacco and Liquor

6.23 Tobacco and liquor should continue to figure in the CPI numbers in case they are consumed by the index population. If prohibition is introduced during the life-time of the CPI series liquor should be excluded from the index and prices of any illegal sale should not be considered. If prohibition is lifted, liquor should be re-introduced in the index. Some members felt that as CPI is used for Dearness Allowance adjustment, users of the index may negotiate the question of what should constitute the item basket and the extent of compensation in the DA adjustment in respect of items included in the item basket. (Para 4.39)

Prepared Foods

6.24 It would not be possible to make adjustments for quality changes in prepared foods. If the price of the prepared foods is based on some quantitative measure, the index should take into account the change in the quantity. In case the price is not charged on the basis of quantity, the weight of the item should be distributed pro-rata to all the constituent items or all the items in the Food Group. (Para 4.41)

Free Primary and Secondary Education

6.25 Separate information should be collected for expenditure on primary and secondary education during the FIES and separate price indices should be compiled for primary and secondary education. While compiling price index of primary education the index should be calculated by using proportion of families obtaining free education on the one hand and those who are spending on primary education the other. Similar procedure should be adopted for compiling the index for secondary education if it is available free for certain sections of the index population. Changes in the expenditure on primary and secondary education should be ascertained by means of a sample survey to be conducted on an interval of about 12 months. In case any new concessions are announced for universal application, the weights for primary and secondary education should be revised by carrying out a fresh survey. (Paras 4.43 to 4.46)

Concessional and Free Items

6.26 (i) In the plantation centres concessional prices at which certain items are sold to the index population should be treated in the same manner as the prices in the fair price shops. If in certain centres plantation workers are not supplied foodgrains at concessional prices open market prices should be taken in proper conjunction for index compilation. Firewood supplied free or at concessional rates by employers should be treated in the same manner as free education. The average price paid for firewood should be calculated by weighting with the index population who receive free supply and these who purchase at the open market price. Treatment of other items like blankets, rubber chappals and umbrellas which are provided by certain employers free on at concessional prices should be similar to that of firewood. (Paras

4.48 to 4.52)

(ii) The procedure followed for free primary and secondary education should be followed for index compilation in respect of free medicines and health facilities. (Para 4.53)

Durable Items

6.27 Expenditure on consumer durables should be included in the weighting diagram of the index; the weight to be assigned to them should be based on actual expenditure reported in FIES. Where durable goods are purchased on instalment basis, expenditure incurred during the period of FIES only should be taken for assigning weight to them. Cost incurred on maintenance of durable goods should be included in the index compilation. (Paras 4.54 and 4.55)

Doctor's Fee and Medicine

6.28 The expenditure actually incurred by the workers including contribution to the E.S.I., as well as private doctor's fee and medicine should be taken under the head "medical care". The relative weight of the two items should be determined on the basis of the actual expenditure reported during the FIES. The relative proportion of families, incurring these expenditures, should be ascertained by periodical surveys, say once in three years, and revised, if necessary. (Para 4.56)

Suburban Railway Fares

6.29 Fares for both long distances and short distances should be taken into account for index compilation. In addition to suburban train fares, for Buses should also be taken into account in proper conjunction. (Para 4.57)

Train Fare in Calcutta

6.30 The information collected in the FIES on expenditure on tram fare should be utilised for deciding the class of tram fares to be taken for compilation of the index for the Calcutta Centre. When the underground railway in Calcutta starts operation, the underground railway fare should be taken into account in combination with the tram fare for index compilation. (Para 4.58 and 4.59)

Cinema Ticket

6.31 Information should be collected in the FIES on the class of Cinema ticket purchased by the workers and this information should be utilised in deciding the class of cinema ticket to be selected for index compilation. (Para 4.60)

Price Collection System

6.32 Labour Bureau should have a second look at the markets and shops selected for the new series of CPI numbers and see that as far as possible markets and shops which are popular among the working class families are selected. (Para 5.7)

6.33 With the same objective in view, the Labour Bureau may also have a second look at the markets which are common for the 1960 series and new series. (Para 5.8)

6.34 The Committee recommends that the visit of the price collector to each shop every week is absolutely necessary to ensure that prices prevailing in two selected shops are correctly recorded in the price schedules. [Para 5.14(i)]

6.35 The State Governments should rotate price collectors after an interval of one year or so. [Para 5.14(ii)]

6.36 The Labour Bureau should take up with the State Governments the question of allowing the price supervisors more time to visit each market at least once a month. [Para 5.14(iii)]

6.37 As far as possible senior officers in the State Governments should not entrusted with the work of the price supervision. [Para 5.14 (iii)]

6.38 Price collectors and price supervisors should hold weekly meetings to scrutinise price data collected for the previous week for checking on inter-shop and inter-market variations in prices. [Para 5.14(iii)]

6.39 In case of doubts price supervisors may personally visit the shops before carrying out correction in prices, if required. [Para 5.14(ii)]

6.40 Ministry of Labour may take early steps to increase honorarium payable to price collectors and price supervisors. The increase in the honorarium should be commensurate with the increase in their work and should serve as sufficient incentive for performing the extra work. [Para 5.14(iv)]

6.41 The Regional offices of the Labour Bureau should be strengthened by opening at least one Sub-Regional Office under each Regional Office. (Para 5.18)

6.42 The Staff of the Labour Bureau at the Headquarters should also be suitably augmented. (Para 5.18)

6.43 The Labour Bureau may conduct training classes at their regional officer or at Simla for Price Collectors and Price Supervisors. (Para 5.19)

6.44 The present system of employing part time price collectors and price supervisors wherever it exists may continue. (Para 5.20)

6.45 The existing level of informal consultations with the user interests which has proved adequate should continue. (Para 5.22)

6.46 The Labour Bureau should give maximum publicity to price information by displaying price quotations at all centres for verification by the interested parties. The price schedules should invariably be displayed at Labour Commissioners Offices and doubts and reservations expressed by the trade unions or employers should be promptly attended to. (Para 5.23)

6.47 The State level Committees on the Maharashtra pattern should be set up in each State to scrutinise and supervise the price data for the all-India series of the Consumer Price Index numbers compiled by the Labour Bureau as well as the State series. The Labour Bureau should consult the State level committees not only in regard to the price data but also in other matters relating to the central indices. The State-level committee should complete the scrutiny of the price data within the time-limit prescribed by the Labour Bureau. (Para 5.26)

6.48 The representatives of the State-level Committees, should be associated with discussions in the TACSPCL. (Para 5.29)

WORKING GROUP ON THE FINANCIAL RESOURCES SET UP BY THE APEX COMMITTEE ON INTERNATIONAL DRINKING WATER SUPPLY AND SANITATION DECADE 1981-90, 1980 – REPORT[1]

Chairman Shri Baldev Singh

Members Representative of the Health & Family Welfare Ministry; Representative of Department of Expenditure, Ministry of Finance; Representative of Department of Economic Affairs, Ministry of Finance; Representative of the Ministry of Rural Reconstruction, Finance or Planning Secretary, Government of Maharashtra, Finance of Planning Secretary, Government of West Bengal; Finance or Planning Secretary, Government of Punjab; Secretary, Panchayat Raj Department, Government of Andhra Pradesh.

M. Secy. Shri V. Venugopalan.

Appointment

The Apex Committee on the International Drinking Water Supply and Sanitation Decade set up a Group on the Financial Resources Vide Ministry of Works & Housing, Government of India's No. M-13014/9/79-PHE dated December 22, 1980.

Terms of Reference

To assess the resources available for implementation of the International Drinking Water Supply and Sanitation Decade Programme in the country during the Sixth Plan period and to estimate the resources ex-

1. New Delhi, Ministry of Works & Housing, 1982, 22 p.

pected to be available during the remaining period of the Decade from all resources including:

(i) Related Programme of the Centre and the State (including U.Ts);
(ii) Expected and possible resources which could be generated by local bodies through optimum exercise of their existing powers;
(iii) External Assistance-the possibility of treating such assistance as total additionality to plan resources should also be explored; and
(iv) Loans through institutions like LIC, HUDCO, Commercial Banks, etc.

Contents

Introduction; Constitution and Membership; Terms of Reference; Cooption of Members; Present and Proposed Levels of Coverage; Need for Higher Plan Allocations and Revising Priorities and Allocations in M.N.P.; Suggestions for the States-States to take innovative Measures; Resources from Local Bodies and Fixing Economic Water Rates; Special Purposeless; Financing Pattern in Urban Schemes, Financial Pattern of Rural Schemes; More Economic Options; Drinking Water Supply Schemes as an integral Schemes through Employment Programme; External Assistance; Loans through Life Insurance Corporation; Income Tax Relief; Formation of a New Financing Institution; Conclusion; Recommendation; Annexures from I to 4.

Recommendations

13.1 The Plan out lays for the water supply and sanitation sector may be stepped up from 4 per cent in the Sixth Five Year Plan to a minimum of 6 per cent of the total plan outlay during the Seventh and Eighth Five Year Plans.

13.2 The Planning Commission may be requested to re-allocate the priorities of minimum Needs Programme in various sectors and upgrade Water Supply and Sanitation Sector so that more funds are made available henceforth, particularly during the Decade period. Two-thirds of the additional outlays may be provided in the Central Sector as an augmentation of the Accelerated Rural Water Supply programme.

13.3. The State Governments may be urged to see that water rates are so fixed that they ensure repayment of loans with interest as well as recovery of operation and maintenance cost and provision for building up of a reserve fund. Surpluses from urban water schemes or from supplies made for industrial and commercial purposes should be utilised as cross subsidy to sewerage schemes and rural water supply schemes.

13.4. Active participation of the urban local bodies should be secured. A minimum contribution of 10 to 25 per cent of capital cost may be taken from the urban local bodies, depending on the size of the local body and its resources.

13.5. In the case of Rural Water Supply Schemes, the State Governments should stipulate a minimum contribution by the people/Gram Panchayats amounting to 10 per cent of the cost of the scheme. This contribution could be substantially raised in suitable cases depending upon the people's response and the resources of the Gram Panchayat concerned.

13.6. The State Governments should try innovative methods of raising resources for water supply and sewerage schemes during the Decade Programme. They should consider imposing of a special purpose cess as a surcharge on selected taxes like land revenue, sales-tax, passenger tax, motor vehicle tax, etc., which should be exclusively utilised for water supply and sanitation schemes.

13.7. All major and medium irrigation projects should include drinking water supply requirements of the areas served by them, as an integral part of the projects. Where the requirement of water is small for rural communities, it should be provided free of cost. In other cases costs could be suitably apportioned. Except in the case of very large urban projects, the charges of water supplied for drinking purposes should not exceed the rates at which water is supplied for irrigation.

13.8. Wherever feasible, water supply schemes may be taken up under the Employment Guarantee Scheme and the NREP.

13.9. The State Governments may be asked to prepare a shelf of projects which can be posed to external agencies for provision of credit assistance during the decade programme. Funds passed on to the States from external sources may be exclusively used for the earmarked sectors.

13.10. The L.I.C. should be persuaded to earmark at least 8 per cent of their investible funds for water supply and sanitation sector in comparison to the current amount of 6 to 7 per cent.

13.11. Secretary, Ministry of Works and Housing, should be included as a Member of the "prescribed authority" in the rules called the "Income Tax (Fourth Amendment) Rules, 1977". Water Supply and Sewerage Boards may be included in the list of "approved association/institution" for undertaking water supply and sanitation schemes in rural areas to enable them to get the benefit of exemption of income-tax under Section 35 CC and 35 CCA.

13.12. A National level refinancing/financing institution should be set up on the lines of HUDCO or REC to serve as the Central agency for the flow and regulation of credit to the water supply and sanitation sectors. The new institution should be empowered to raise loans from the LIC, GIC and financial institutions, commercial banks and raise funds from open markets by issue of debentures, etc.

13.13. Data may be collected regarding utilisation of advance plan assistance given in drought affected areas and its utilisation for water supply schemes to assess the benefit to this sector accruing from this source.

...

20

WORKING GROUP ON THE MATERIALS AND EQUIPMENT SET UP BY THE APEX COMMITTEE ON INTERNATIONAL DRINKING WATER SUPPLY AND SANITATION DECADE 1981-90, 1980 – REPORT[1]

Chairman Shri B.R.R Iyengar

Members Shri V.R. Iyer; Shri V. Venugopalan; Shri M.M. Datta; Shri O.P. Ratra; Shri A.N. Rajagopalan; Shri S.C. Ray, Shri S.K. Ray; Shri S.V. Sundaram; Shri M. Sundara Raman; Shri Mathew John; Shri N.K. Chakrabarti; Shri R. Krishnaswamy; Shri S.P. Rajvanshi; Shri P. Arunachalam.

M. Secy. Shri T.G. Sankaran.

Appointment

The Apex Committee on the International Drinking Water Supply and Sanitation Decade set up a Working Group on Materials and Equipment Vide Ministry of Works & Housing, Government of India's No. M-13014/9/79-PHE dated December 22, 1980.

Terms of Reference

(a) To assess the total requirements and Materials and equipment, including steel, cement pipes, pumps, motors, Vehicles, Chemicals as well as the position of availability of power for the International Drinking Water Supply and Sanitation Decade Programme in the country.

(b) To report on how the requirements could be met from the indigenous or external sources keeping in view, *inter alia*, the existing capacity, production and possibilities of increasing production.

1. New Delhi, Ministry of Works and Housing, 1982, 94 p.

Contents

Introduction; Constitution of the Working Group; Terms of Reference; Working Group's Programme of Work; Assessment of the Total Requirement of Materials and Equipment – General, Materials, Pipes, Plastics, Asbestos Cement (AC), Galvanized Iron (GI); Stoneware, Cast Iron (CI) Reinforced Cement Concrete (RCC), Steel, Pre-Stressed Concrete (PSC), Mild Steel Bars; Mild Steel Plates, Cement, Chemicals, Alum and other coagulating materials, Chlorine, Bleaching Powder, Lime, Equipment, Pumps; Electric Pumps – Bore Hole, Vertical, Horizontal, Deepwell Handpumps, Vehicles; Energy Requirements – Electric Power, Petrol Diesel and Lubricating Oil; Transportation; Actions Taken; Recommendations; Appendices I to XXXXI.

Recommendations

8.1 *Pipes*

Noting the fact that the assessment reports of the various types of pipes required during the first four years (1981-85) and the subsequent six years (1985-91) of the Decade have been received by the Ministry of Industry (Department of Industrial Development) the Working Group recommends that all-out efforts should be made to make available the required quantities of pipes through indigenous sources.

(a) *Plastic Pipes* – It is suggested to the Government that they may review the import duty levied on imported resin and also the excuse duty on the indigenous resin so that the finished plastic pipe product would become still cheaper which is essential for the implementation of the rural water supply schemes.

(b) *A.C. Pressure Pipes* – The Panel for Asbestos Products is under reconstitution and would soon go into the requirement of A.C. Products for various uses. Cement and asbestos fibres are the two basic raw materials for making AC pressure pipes and since cement is already in short supply in the country and the entire asbestos fibre is being imported, it is felt that the above Panel may be asked to look into the requirement of AC pressure pipes for the Decade Programme and make available the necessary raw materials to the concerned industries for the manufacture of these pipes.

(c) *G.I. Pipes* – The procurement of raw materials for the manufacture of GI pipes is a problem. It is suggested that the Ministry of Industry may look into this and take remedial measures in order to meet the requirement of GI pipes for the Decade Programme.

(d) *Stoneware Pipes* – DGS&D may be requested to finalise the rate contract for this item. Any state experiencing difficulty in the procurement of stoneware pipes may be requested to contact DGS&D furnishing the particulars of orders placed, the quantities required and other relevant details so that DGS&D may look into the case and do the needful.

(e) *C.I. Pipes* – The Working Group noted that there is shortage of CI pipes in the country which has affected the Water Supply and Sanitation Programme. This is due to several factors like:

– shortage of raw materials
– shortage of power
– industrial relations problem
– non-availability of wagons, etc.

Since the shortage is very acute in the smaller sizes, the Ministry of Works and Housing have already issued a circular to all the State Governments urging them to use alternative pipe materials to overcome this shortage to a certain extent. The response from the State governments is very encouraging. Keeping in view the above, the following recommendations are made:

(i) At present the CI pipes are manufactured up to the size of 750 mm dia. Keeping this in view, it is felt that the concerned state governments who want to use these pipes above this size may be requested to use the alternative pipes like RCC/pre-stressed concrete pipes, etc.

(ii) Regarding the sick unit M/s. Shakti Pipes, M/s. Shakti Sugars, another industry in the same group, has approached the Industrial Credit and Investment Corporation of India, Bombay to take over the film and revive the factory. If this is not feasible, the Tamil Nadu Government who have advanced a large sum of money to the defunct firm may be requested to take over the factory and run it themselves. Similarly, efforts should be made to revive some of the sick plants in the CI pipe sector.

(iii) One of the important raw materials used is pig iron. Government may explore the possibility of reducing the customs duty on pig iron imported so that the price of the finished product could be within the range of rate contract entered into with DGS&D. Similarly, the industry should also be made available the hard B.P. coke and also ferro-silicon. Export of ferro-silicon should be reviewed so that the quantity required for the manufacture of CI pipes to meet the demand of the Decade is available to the industries.

(iv) At present CI pipes manufacturers import moulds for the manufacture of spun pipes. Efforts should be made to get them manufactured through Heavy Engineering Corporation, Ranchi so that the dependence on import could be reduced and at the same time to save the valuable foreign exchange.

(f) *Ductile Iron Pipes* – Ductile iron pipes are lighter and economical in comparison and also have longer life. Efforts should be made to encourage the industries to manufacture these pipes.

If all the above efforts fail to meet the requirement of pipes then there is no other alternative than to import these pipes from abroad. This should be resorted to as a last measure.

8.2 *Handpumps* – (a) Indian Standards Institution has prepared specification for deepwell handpumps called "India Mark II" and the specification number is IS: 9301-1979. Recently, they have revised this specification. All the pump manufacturers should be asked to follow this specification and get ISI marking. The State Governments should be asked to purchase only those pumps which conform to ISI specification and also have ISI marking.

(b) It is expected that the demand is to go up in the years to come. At present, the purchases are made by the State Government at different prices and the quality of pumps is also not uniform. In order to overcome this, it is suggested that the rate contract for the supply of these pumps may be concluded by DGS&D. This will prevent sub-standard pumps being purchased at cheaper prices.

8.3 *Cement* – Cement is in short supply, at present, in the country. The Working Group noted that the Working Group on Cement Industry appointed by the Planning Commission in their report has stated that the industry would reach a stage of self-sufficiency by 1984-85. However, if the production of cement is not sufficient to meet the demand (including Water Supply and Sanitation Sector also), advance planning for import of cement should be made by the Ministry of Industry, Deptt. of Industrial Development. While allocating the cement to the various State Government/U.T. Administrations, the cement required for Water Supply and Sanitation Sector may also be earmarked.

8.4 *Vehicles* – (a) The Ministry of Industry (Deptt. of Industrial Development) have written to the manufacturers (numbering about 13) regarding the requirement of trucks of various types. However, to enable the manufacturers to supply the right type of vehicles, it is suggested that the State Governments while placing orders should furnish the following particulars:

(i) complete specifications
(ii) models
(iii) types
(iv) any other relevant detail.

(b) If the procurement is desired to be done through DGS&D, formal indents completed in all respects should be sent to DGS&D. This will enable DGS&D to find out whether their requirements can be met from indigenous sources or have to be imported.

8.5 *Energy*

(i) *Power* – The statements indicating the requirement of various State Government/U.T. Administrations for electric power for Water Supply and Sanitation Sector have already been forwarded to the Ministry of Energy. It is also suggested that the State Governments may be advised to approach the electricity boards in their States indicating the requirements so that the Board may take necessary action in this behalf.

(ii) *Petrol, Diesel and Lubricating Oil* – The requirement of the various States have been forwarded to the Ministry of Petroleum, Chemicals and Fertilizers. This Ministry may be advised to take into consideration the requirement of Water Supply and Sanitation Sector also while importing these items. They may also earmark the quantity to be given to this Sector while allocating these items to the States from time to time.

8.6 *Drilling Rigs* – In view of the terms of reference, it was not possible for the Working Group to go into the requirements of rigs. Besides, since India is a very vast country and various types of rigs would be needed to suit the local conditions, the specifications for the same would not be the same. Different types of rigs have to be operated in different terrain and specifications for these would vary very much. Therefore, it was not possible for the Group to assess the requirement of rigs and also draw up specifications for the same in view of the short time available to the Group. Therefore, it is suggested that a small Committee may be appointed by the Central Government consisting of representatives from the Central Government Departments (including, DGS&D) and some of the State Governments to look into this question and draw up suitable specifications for the rigs to be procured for the Decade Programme.

8.7 During the deliberations, certain new ideas came up and it would be worthwhile to carry out research and development before they could be translated into action. The following items are suggested:

(i) *Polymers* – for treatment of water which would reduce chemicals to be used for the same resulting in greater economy.

(ii) *Rejuvenating the old pipes* – The replacement of existing pipes with new ones is a costly proposition. There are methods employed in foreign countries by which the old pipes are rejuvenated and reused even without removing them from the ground.

(iii) *Use of fibre glass materials* for the manufacture of water closets, manholes chamber; etc.

(iv) *Development of variable speed motors* to deal with variable flow rates of water.

Reference may be made to research institutions like National Environmental Engineering Research Institute, Nagpur to carry out the research and development and based on their findings field applications may be thought of.

8.8 *Transportation* – The Working Group recommends that State Governments/Union Territory Administrations may be requested to intimate the overall requirement of wagons for the first four years and the subsequent six years of the Decade Programme to the Traffic Transportation Directorate of the Railway Board in advance commensurate with the stock of materials ready for despatch to make suitable arrangements so that highest priority for transportation of pipes and other essential items required for water supply and sanitation sector could be given.

8.9 *Rate Contract* – The Working Group recommends that the DGS&D should explore the possibility of evolving a system of running contract instead of rate contract with regard to materials and equipment required for the Decade Programme.

8.10 *General* – The Working Group felt that it is very essential to have Nodal Bodies both at the Central and State levels for making available equipment and materials required for the Decade and also to do necessary monitoring work.

21

WORKING GROUP ON THE PROGRAMMES AND MANPOWER SET UP BY THE APEX COMMITTEE ON INTERNATIONAL DRINKING WATER SUPPLY AND SANITATION DECADE 1981-90, 1980 — REPORT[1]

Chairman Shri P.K. Chatterjee

Members Representative of the M/o Labour; Representative of the M/o Rural Reconstruction; Representative of the Central Ground Water Board; Dy. Director General, Ministry of Health & Family Welfare; Representative of the Central Board for Prevention and Control of Water Pollution; Director, All India Institute of Hygiene and Public Health; Representative of the Government of U.P.; Representative of the Government of Karnataka; Representative of the Government of Gujarat; Representative of the Government of M.P.

M. Secy. Shri V.A. Anandadoss.

Appointment

The Apex Committee on the International Drinking Water Supply and Sanitation Decade set up a Working Group on the Programmes and Manpower vide Ministry of Works & Housing, Government of India's No. M-13014/9/79-PHE dated December 22, 1980.

Terms of Reference

(a) To draw up realistic programmes in connection with the International Water Supply and Sanitation Decade in the country and recommend their phasing according to the National Plans taking into

1. New Delhi, Ministry of Works and Housing, 1982, 52 p.

account also the plans and programmes in the Irrigation (including minor irrigation) and Ground Water Development Sectors. The Working Group may also suggest how to dovetail related programmes of other ministries and organisations into the Decade programmes.

(b) To indicate the role of local bodies in the Decade Programme, particularly their involvement in the operation and maintenance of projects and possibility of their contributing to capital works.

(c) To assess the manpower requirement for the Decade Programme including those for design, administration operation and maintenance.

(d) To report on the training requirement of the various categories of personnel involved in the programmes and to recommend measures for meeting the training needs from indigenous or external sources.

Contents

Introduction; Constitution of the Working Groups; Terms of Reference; Meetings of Working Group; Achievements in the Sector; Programmes and Phasing; Factors of Programming for the Decade; Physical and Financial Achievements and Targets; Norms Distortion; Urban Water Supply; Operation and Maintenance; Urban Sanitation; Rural Sanitation; Phasing and Programme; District-Level Coordination; Dovetailing other Sectors Programmes; Irrigation Schemes; Construction of Water Supply Schemes by other Public Agencies; Coordination with Ministry of Rural Reconstruction; Coordination with the Programme of the Health-for-all by 2000A.D.; Coordination with Ground Water Boards; Role of Local Bodies; Support Programmes; Health Education; Health Education/Community Participation (WHO & UNICEF Mission); Manpower Development, General, Present Status and Future Requirements; Strategies to Develop Engineering Manpower for the Sector; Methodologies to Develop Manpower required in the Technicians/Craftsmen/Skilled worker Cadres; In-house Expertise, Consultancy; Inservice Training; Training at Undergraduate Level; Training at Post-Graduate Level; PHE Training Programmes under the Ministry of Works and Housing; P.G. Course; Short-Term Course; Refresher Course; State-Level Courses; Rigs Training Programme; Course on Project Formulation and Appraisal; Seminars; Meetings of Chief Engineers and Senior Engineers; PHE Cadre — Urban and Rural; Exposing non-officials for Training; Bureaucratic Delay; Continuity in Administration; Research and Development of

Appropriate Technology; Exchange Programme — Training (Internal and Foreign); Management Information System; Information System (Data Bank); Documentation; Recommendations; Programme; Manpower; Appendices from 1 to 14.

Recommendations

The Working Group after considering all relevant aspects make the following Recommendations:

I. Programme

1. The Decade programme may be divided into two phases—Phase-I covering the remaining 4 years of the 6th Plan, i.e., from 1981-82 to 1984-85 and Phase-II the remaining 6 years of the Decade, i.e., 1985-86 to 1990-91. In Phase-I of the programme the population coverage that can be aimed at, with the outlays provided, will be 93 per cent in urban and 52 per cent in rural communities in respect of water supply and that in respect of sanitation will be 39.3 per cent in case of urban and a meagre 1.5 per cent in rural communities. The target to be achieved in the second phase would be 7 per cent in urban water supply, 48 per cent in rural water supply, 40.7 per cent in urban sanitation and 23.5 per cent in rural sanitation.

In order to achieve the desired targets, the States lagging behind should be given due consideration while allocating funds for their water supply and sanitation plans.

2. To make the programme realistic, the following guidelines may be adopted:

(a) In urban communities the levels of service should be about 140 lpcd on an average; and
(b) In urban fringe areas standposts will be provided for economically weaker sections.

The following priorities may be kept in view by all State Governments and Union Territories in drawing up and implementing the Decade programme:

(a) Safe drinking water to problem villages;
(b) Safe drinking water to uncovered towns or uncovered urban

areas;

(c) Rehabilitation of old urban water supply systems;
(d) Low cost sanitation to towns other than Class I cities;
(e) Safe water supply to non-problem villages;
(f) Augmentation of urban water supply systems;
(g) Sewerage facilities to Class-I cities lacking them at present; and
(h) Sanitation in rural areas.

3. State Governments and Union Territories may allocate additional finances and other resources to the Decade Programme. The progress of the Decade Programme may be frequently monitored by the state level Apex and Action Committees,

(i) The total number of problem village numbering about 2.31 lakhs as on 1-4-80 may be accepted as the target coverage under the State Sector minimum needs programme and the Central Sector accelerated rural water supply programme during the Sixth Five Year Plan;
(ii) In the implementation of the rural water supply programme the needs of the scheduled castes and scheduled tribes may be given high priority. Every new source of drinking water in a village may be located in the scheduled castes habitation, open to all communities where it is logistically and technically not impossible to do so;
(iii) The following guidelines may be followed in the implementation of the rural water supply schemes in view of the limited resources available;

(a) According to Sixth Plan document about 57000 problem villages still remained to be covered as per the earlier list prepared in 1972. First priority may be accorded to these villages which have remained so far without water supply facilities;
(b) All villages which have sanitary dugwells as existing source of water supply should be identified and deleted from the list of problem villages already sent by the State Governments. Moreover, problem villages that have been provided with permanent safe water supply facilities under the advance plan assistance programme for natural calamities should also be deleted from the list. In all the remaining

problem villages first priority may be accorded to no source villages and at least one source of potable water should be available throughout the year in every problem village;

(c) Where the population of villages is more than 300, additional sources may be provided on the basis of one for 250-300 population. Additional source should be provided preferably in harijan bustees;

(d) For hard rock areas, tubewells with handpumps should be the first preference. Piped water supply schemes might be necessary in places where water is brackish or source of water is at a distance. However, piped water supply scheme or power pump should be the last alternative;

(e) Suitable engineering solutions may be worked out and most economical alternative may be adopted in the hilly areas, deserts and other strategic places. In hilly areas gravity flow or devices like hydraulic rams could be economical alternative; and

(f) Augmentation of rural water supply schemes should be avoided.

4. In the urban sanitation programme of the Decade, only the Class-I cities can at best be provided with a complete sewerage system. Even in these cities community toilets and public latrines with attendants will have to be provided to meet particular needs and circumstances. For other classes of towns, only low-cost sanitation, which provides for conversion of existing dry latrines and installation of sanitary latrines with cess pools, would be a viable solution. 100 per cent sewerage facilities will be provided in Class-I cities and the overall coverage in urban sanitation will be 80 per cent. For providing low cost sanitation, the towns should be selected on the basis of the following criteria:

(i) They should already have piped water supply;

(ii) They are not sewered and are not to be sewered in the next decade;

(iii) They represent varied socio-economic and geophysical conditions; and

(iv) Their local bodies are enthusiastic about the project and are financially sound so as to execute the projects expeditiously.

5. In the rural sanitation sub-sector, 25 per cent of the population may be provided with simple sanitary latrines. The Government may give a subsidy of Rs. 50 per capita, while the rest of the charges may be borne by the community by way of labour, locally available materials, etc.

6. In regard to operation and maintenance of the water supply schemes the emphasis should be on preventive, rather than corrective maintenance. While planning the schemes, the requirement of funds, personnel, etc., for efficient operation and maintenance of the schemes should also be planned and budgeted. There should be adequate water quality surveillance also. For the maintenance of handpumps in rural areas, the three-tier system adopted in Tamil Nadu could serve as a model to be followed by other States.

7. In the irrigation sector, major and minor irrigation projects, reservoirs, canal systems and tubewells are being constructed. The water supply schemes would advantageously be planned and implemented as a part of the Irrigation projects wherever feasible. Since the drinking water supply needs are small, a small portion of the irrigation water should be adequate for drinking purposes. The villages along irrigation canals should be provided with drinking water supply from these canals free of cost.

8. Under the National Rural Employment Programme durable assets such as drinking water wells can be constructed. State Governments may therefore take up the construction of drinking water wells also, by utilising the foodgrains and cash allocated for the NREP.

9. The content of the training programmes of all levels of health personnel should lay stress on the following aspects:

The Health Assistants, Health Workers and Community Health volunteers of the Environmental Sanitation Wing (Block) of the Primary Health Centres should be given practical training in assisting the construction of sanitary latrines and soak pits and to disinfect drinking water wells, etc. As a part of Health Education Programme these personnel should be given training to educate the people in the aspects of:–

(i) Need for safe water supply; chlorination of water supply;
(ii) Need for maintenance of wells and handpumps and preventing contamination of wells;
(iii) Need for personal hygiene;

(iv) Need for sanitary latrines and their maintenance; and

(v) Idea of the work done by other field agencies in rural development such as ICDS, IRD and Health.

10. Coordination of the activities of State PHE Deptts., and Central and State Ground Water Boards is essential. The services of the Ground Water Deptt. personnel such hydrogeologists and geophysicists may be utilised, where required for investigations.

11. In the efficient operation and maintenance of water supply and sanitation schemes, the local bodies should play a vital role directly as well as indirectly by educating the community to make proper use of the water and to reducing wastes. The local bodies should be closely involved in planning for:–

(i) selection of community representatives for training in maintenance and repair of handpumps and construction of sanitary latrines and soak pits; and

(ii) health education programmes and campaign for safe water supply and environmental sanitation.

The Block Coordination Committee, wherever existing, should try to arrange for procurement of materials at reasonable prices for the construction of latrines and soak pits, etc., and to seek voluntary labour for the construction of such latrines and soak pits, etc. They should also coordinate the water supply and sanitation schemes with other block level programmes and make efforts to lower costs by community contribution in the form of labour and materials, maintenance of sanitary wells, and reporting of malfunctioning systems.

12. An appropriate health education programme for training health workers, health educators and social scientists, should be initiated jointly by the Ministry of Works & Housing and the Ministry of Health as a support for the Decade programme. The possibility of full mobilisation of available funds with supplementation from agencies like UNICEF for the purpose may be exposed. The involvement of communities in the water supply and sanitation coverage programme is very much essential for the Decade. The types of organisations involved may range from elected bodies to committees especially appointed for the Decade or Health Committees and may also include local non-governmental organisations such as women's associations and youth organisations, etc. The UNICEF has evolved programmes for

community participation under public co-operation and had suggested local participation in assessment of needs/selection of sites, actual execution, maintenance cost recovered and adoption of preventive health care practices. The ICDS programme sponsored by the Ministry of Social Welfare seeks to provide health and nutrition and educational services to children based on *Anganwadi* workers. The three-tier maintenance system for the handpump envisaged that the local caretakers will look after health education and sanitation practices. The essential elements of the basic services approach are:–

(i) Building linkages between the beneficiaries, voluntary agencies and local bodies;
(ii) integrated delivery of all services through field workers under different programmes; and
(iii) monitoring benefits flowing of beneficiaries and not just execution of engineering schemes.

13. (i) It is desirable to involve training administration at the district level from the stage of Planning itself so that projects relevant to the needs of the people are drawn up and priorities fixed in consultation with district level administration.

(ii) Intersectoral coordination at district level itself is essential for effective planning, implementation and monitoring and also to maximise the benefits to the people from various schemes and also to avoid duplication of efforts.

(iii) Similarly the water supply inputs in various rural and urban development resources taken up by different State agencies need to be coordinated at the budgetary and secretariat level to maximise the input.

(iv) The norms specified by Government of India should be followed as far as possible in the case of planning and implementation of water supply and sanitation schemes and also in the manner of projecting contingencies and escalation and maintenance estimates.

(v) The dependence on outside consultants should be reduced by building up project planning and preparation cells in the PHE Deptts. of water supply and Sewerage Boards. The officials trained by Government of India and WHO Fellowships should be utilised to the full extent in the field of project appraisal, and financial analysis and monitoring. Foreign technical assistance could be used to train the trainers only.

(vi) The administrative process and procedures in the Government machinery should be streamlined and made flexible by adequate delegation of powers at various levels so as to minimise the delay in the planning and implementation of the decade programme.

(vii) It is desirable that one organisation at the State level be responsible for all water supply and sanitation activities for better implementation and control of Decade programme. There should be integrated administrative framework from the programme formulating stage to execution and maintenance. It would be advisable that the senior officials in charge of water supply and sanitation are not transferred frequently in the interest of continuity and efficiency.

(viii) The elected members of local bodies and non-officials who are responsible for overall functioning of the water supply and sanitation programmes in their purview should be exposed to training courses, seminars, etc.

(ix) The training facilities for the operation and maintenance personnel from grassroot level to higher level should include on-the-job training also with a mobile training team and kit with a vehicle so that more people could be trained at many places in a short period. These training unit should be established at least at the district level.

II. *Manpower*

14. Considering the potential for training of civil engineering graduates in various institutions in the country and the needs of the PHE departments, the existing facilities may not be adequate to provide all the manpower needed in the short-term but will be able to meet the requirements by the end of the Decade. Hence there may not be any need to increase the intake capacity of these institutions or create additional institutions.

However, a qualitative improvement is necessary which would equip the personnel with the necessary orientation in PH Engg. and the following strategies could be employed:–

(i) The Civil Engineering curriculum could be retailored to include a separate elective namely environmental engineering. The graduates with such electives could be given preference at the time of recruitment to the PHE Departments. The diploma course in civil engineering could also be remodelled to foster the specialisation of Environmental Engineering;

(ii) To attract graduates to this sector, the service conditions may be improved by giving incentives like special pay or higher pay, etc.

(iii) If there are not sufficient number of Senior Personnel such as hydrogeologists and geophysicists available, then they can be brought on deputation from Central and State Ground Water Boards to assist the PHE Departments.

(iv) The requirement of about 10000 Craftsmen/Skilled Workers for supervision to be directly deployed in the field in the PHE Deptts., every year can be met if 22 persons passing out of each of the 466 ITIs join the PHE Departments.

15. Public Health Engineering being a field of specialisation, it is very essential that a crash programme of existing on-the-job training be continued with increasing tempo during the decade period. The training programme should be for:–

(i) Planners and administrators to gain knowledge about relationship between service and health benefits and long range implication of technologies so that they can programme long term water supply and sanitation investments;

(ii) Engineers to update technical information on planning, design, implementation and operation and maintenance of water supply and sanitation projects; and

(iii) Subordinate Engineers, plant operators and other technicians, skilled workers and community workers to undertake necessary field work to oversee operation & maintenance and organise the community.

16. The training programme can be adopted in the following manners:–

(i) Training at undergraduate level;

(ii) Training at Post Graduate level; and

(iii) PHE training programme under the Ministry of Works & Housing and other programme of training.

17. The course content at the U.G. level should have some field orientation so as to equip the graduates to tackle the field problems confidently. For this it may be worthwhile to start a new branch of En-

vironmental Engineering having 4½ years duration. The first 2 years will be common for all the courses. The next two years will have syllabus with basic Civil Engineering with orientation in Environmental Engineering; a six month project covering the design and cost aspects of the water and waste water treatment plants which will give the necessary introductory exposure for the student to face any problem in the P.H. Engineering field.

18. To acquire the proficiency needed for middle and senior level positions in the departments, a post-graduate level training is of utmost necessity. In the P.G. course, the dissertation problem should be field oriented instead of being purely laboratory oriented and this can be achieved by deputing the students to industries and water and sewage treatment plants to obtain practical experience. According to the recommendations of the Review Committee on P.G. Education and Research in Engineering & Technology the admission to P.G. Programme should be through GATE (Graduate Aptitude Test in Engineering); 50 per cent seats should be reserved for sponsored candidates from industries and PHE Departments. All ME/M. Tech. programmes of Environmental Engineering should be of three semesters duration consisting of two semesters course work and one semester dissertation work.

19. The PHE training programme by the Ministry should be continued with increasing tempo and should incorporate the following:–

The restoration of the Central support of giving stipends to the sponsored candidates of PHE Deptts., is very much essential so as to upgrade the quality of personnel and to attract more sponsored candidates from PHE Departments which has been affected by the withdrawal of the stipend facilities. The stipend should be increased from Rs. 300 to Rs. 450 in as much as the Ministry of Education has already increased the scholarship from Rs. 400 to Rs. 600 per month.

20. It is necessary to introduce P.G. course in a few more institutions with an intake capacity of 20 trainees in each institution so as to cope up with the huge backlog of trained personnel requirements in PHE Deptts. It is also felt that the educational institutions to be identified for this purpose should already have the structural and professional framework for conducting the courses under the scheme of Ministry of Education. An initial grant of Rs. 2 lakhs should be given to the new institutions coming under this purview.

21. The short-term course available now in one institution should be extended to three more institutions so as to meet the training needs

of the subordinate engineers in the PHE Deptts. Stipends should be increased to Rs. 900 in place of existing Rs. 600 per course and the staff support should be increased to Rs. 30,000 from the existing Rs. 22,500.

22. It is very necessary that the levels of stipends for the refresher courses conducted by the Ministry of Works & Housing to provide opportunities to engineers and para engineering personnel should be enhanced in tune with the escalating costs in order to encourage the participation of engineers and para engineers.

23. There should be a three level training system at the State level for (i) training for Executive Engineers; (ii) training for Deputy and Asstt. Engineers; and (iii) training for operators and other technicians. Each State should set apart a well operated and maintained plant exclusively for purpose of training with infrastructural support like workshops, lecture halls, hostels, etc. The trainees should be awarded certificates of competence after the completion of their training in various levels giving incentives also.

24. The course on project formulation and appraisal which facilitates the training of middle level and senior level engineers should be continued due to its usefulness.

25. The Ministry of Works and Housing being the focal point should promote exchange of ideas between practising PH Engineers in matters relating to cost effective solutions and to keep abreast with latest technology.

26. Periodical meetings should be convened inviting Chief Engineers and Senior Engineers to have an opportunity to discuss and interact in matters relating to planning policy and technical matters. The representatives of other concerned Central and State agencies in areas like hydrogeology, rural development and health may be invited wherever necessary for better interaction.

27. In order to meet the challenging task of providing water supply to all the problem villages by 1985 and all the habitations by 1991, the existing fleet of rigs and personnel should be utilised to its maximum. Therefore the band of personnel like drillers, mechanics, equipment and maintenance staff, geologists and supervising staff should be trained by providing suitable training facilities. These facilities should be arranged at the Central level for inservice personnel with support from international agencies. The training facilities may be linked with regional workshops and test drilling operations.

28. It is necessary to establish one organisation at National level to supervise and guide research in the field of water supply and sanita-

tion. The existing academic and research institutions may be rearranged to take up research work in the sector. Operational and design manuals should also bc brought out and circulated to all concerned. CPHEEO could be the Central agency to coordinate the activities of research institutes and zonal laboratories and service departments.

29. An effective information and documentation system is essential for sound planning, management, implementation and operation and maintenance. Action must be taken to develop a suitable system at the State and National level. This may be linked with International Institutions to facilitate referencing and exchange of experience. Over a period, the entire system could be stored in computer for easy retrieval and updating.

22

RAILWAY ACCIDENT INVESTIGATION REPORT ON DERAILMENT OF No. 217 UP ARISKERE-HUBLI PASSENGER TRAIN AT KM 462/5-8 BETWEEN KUNDGOL AND HUBLI SINGLE METRE GAUGE SECTION OF MYSORE DIVISION ON SOUTHERN RAILWAY ON DECEMBER 29, 1980 — REPORT[1]

One Man Commission Shri B.P. Sastry

Appointment

The Commission was appointed under Ministry of Tourism and Civil Aviation (Commission of Railway Safety) in accordance with Rule 4 of the Statutory Investigation into Railway Accidents Rules 1973 vide its Notification No. RS. 13-T(8) 71 dated April 19, 1973 on December 29, 1980.

Terms of Reference

To enquire into the derailment of No. 217 Up Ariskere-Hubli Passenger train at Km 462/5-8 between Kundgol and Hubli Stations on Bangalore-Hubli single line Metre Gauge section of Mysore Division on Southern Railway on December 29, 1980.

Contents

Summary; Inspection and Inquiry; Relief Measures; The Train; Local Features; Summary of Evidence; Observation and Tests; Discussion; Conclusions; Remarks and Recommendations.

---

1. Delhi, Controller of Publications, 1985, 20 p.

Conclusion

Cause of Accident

Having carefully considered the factual, material and circumstantial evidence at my disposal, I have come to the conclusion that the derailment of No. 217 up Ariskere-Hubli Passenger train at Km 462/5-8 between Kundgol and Hubli Stations on Bangalore-Hubli single line Metre Gauge section of Mysore Division on Southern Railway on December 29, 1980 was brought about by the train having been driven at a speed far in excess of the stipulated speed combined with deficiencies in track structure.

Responsibility

I hold Shri P. Narayanaswamy, Driver of No. 217 Up Passenger, as being solely and directly responsible for the accident.

Shri P. Narayanaswamy, who entered railway service in 1945, was promoted as Driver/B on 10-12-1977 and later promoted as Driver 'A' in 1979. He was once earlier punished for causing the derailment of train No. 2925 Goods in Ariskere-Harihar section on 18-6-1970 due to overspeeding.

I do not consider that any individual official of the Civil Engineering Department of the Railway is responsible in causing or contributing to the accident. I however, hold that Department in general as being morally responsible for not raising up to the level of performance expected of it to strive to maintain a reasonably good track fit for operation of train at reasonable speed in a busy Main Line Section.

Relief Arrangements

I am satisfied with the relief arrangements made by the South Central Railway Administration in promptly moving their Medical team to the site of accident on receiving a request from the Southern Railway Administration and shifting the injured to the Railway Hospital.

Recommendations

9.1 The current practices and procedures of Southern Railway in the matter of monitoring of speeds of trains as an important tool for ensuring safety need a review. As the situation does not differ very much on other Railways, Railway Board may consider giving the Railway Administrations necessary guidelines in this regard.

9.2 Two important witnesses who deposed before me in the inquiry (a Senior Railway Official and a Senior Police Official) gave vent to the feeling that detection of criminals who steal railway materials and securing their conviction in a Court of Law are greatly handicapped by the current practice of selling railway materials to outsiders, which the criminals use as a cloak for defending themselves. The Railway Administration may consider ways and means for removing this handicap without which criminals cannot be successfully brought to book and thefts cannot be brought down.

Comments of the Railway Board on Various Paras of the Report

Para 7.3.6—Instructions have been given to the Railway to carry out thorough renewal of sleepers in this length as already sanctioned and to take up the subject of missing fittings with the State Government also vide letter No. 81-W6-PRA-1 dated 5-6-81.

Paras 7.9.1 and 7.9.2—Reply against para 7.3.6 covers.

Para 9.1—The speed recorders are fitted on Mail and Express locos while on other services there are no recorders. The speed recorders currently in use on steam locos in VDO type. In these speed recorders, only the maximum permissible speed, in case a driver exceeds the same, can be checked. It is not possible from the recorder to check the speeds that a particular driver has followed against restrictions imposed. This is so because the recording chart is very small and the timings cannot be accurately read against the speeds attained by the drivers. The railways are being asked to introduce the system of staff checks of speeds attained by drivers against restrictions through stop watch.

Para 9.2—The Scrap arisings are sold to public for only those items and quantities which are not required by Railways. Efforts are also made to sell to Government units and public sector undertakings. Since these materials are not required by Railways for any further use, their disposal for public purchasers in the private sector cannot be avoided under the existing practice.

23

THE COMMITTEE ON WIND ENGINEERING, 1980 — REPORT[1]

Chairman Prof. Jai Krishna

Members Dr. P.K. Das; Shri G. Raman; Shri G.C. Mathur; Dr. B. Venkateswarlu; Prof. G.N.V. Rao; Prof. Prem Krishna; Dr. N.C. Nigam; Prof. B. Basu.

M. Secy. Dr. D.K. Rakshit.

Appointment

The Indo-US workshop on Natural Disaster (Earthquake and Wind) Mitigation Research was sponsored by the Department of Science and Technology and was held from Dec. 13-16, 1978. One of the topics discussed related to Wind Effects on Structures. It was noted that due to extreme wind conditions, there is loss of life and property in India almost every year, but no coordinated research in the area of Wind Engineering has been formally organised, excepting for Aeronautical purposes. The workshop, therefore, identified the following projects for research and collaboration:

1. Measurement of Wind Speeds in Intense Tropical Storms.
   Design and development of rugged and reliable anemometer for measurement of high wind speeds, including setting up of an experimental network in the east coast of India for measuring basic parameters of extreme wind and correlation with mathematical models.
2. Risk Analysis and Preparation of Wind Zoning Maps.
   Risk analysis based on available wind data for the preparation of zoning maps and recommendations for codes and standards.
3. Experimental Study of Wind Effects on Structures.

---

1. New Delhi, Department, of Science and Technology, 1983, 89 p.

Study of wind effects on structures through instrumentation and observations on models and prototype structures.

In addition to the above, the workshop recommended, that there should be an exchange of research workers and literature between the two countries in the area of Wind Engineering. It was also recommended that a Committee at the national level be appointed in India to draw up plans for comprehensive research in this field. As a follow up of the above recommendation, a committee on Wind Engineering was constituted by the department of Science and Technology in 1980.

Terms of Reference

(i) To review present status of wind observation, their use in code provision for design of structures and to quantify losses involved at present.

(ii) To identify R&D programmes for the design and development of proper equipment to measure high wind and estimate wind force and equipment for observation of strain in existing structures due to wind force. Also the optimum number of equipment required under each category may be projected.

(iii) To identify research programmes for understanding the behaviour of tall structures, light bridges and roofs due to wind force including aspects involving resonance phenomena.

(iv) To suggest change in the code provision for making design of structures more efficient.

(v) To recommend measures for promoting education and engineering on wind engineering problems.

(vi) To Liaise with other national and international agencies dealing with wind engineering problems particularly on wind effect mitigation.

Contents

Summary and Recommendations; Background and Objectives; Analytical Work; Wind Zoning and Codal Provisions; Wind Data; Infrastructural Arrangements; Annexure: A1 to A8.

Recommendations

1. Since the present teaching of Wind Forces is based on rules and practices, formal arrangement for giving scientific education to engineers on wind effects on engineering structures be made since future industrialisation will mean more tall buildings and industrial structures besides power and communication systems and the need for safeguarding them against failure will be felt more and more. It is recommended that the Ministry of Education and UGC may be advised to take necessary steps to get an optional subject 'Wind and Its Effects on Structures' introduced in the engineering curricula of the leading institutions so that, in due course, trained manpower is available for observation, research and design purposes. Support may be provided for short courses, workshops/conferences to educate the people.

2. The present wind observations taken by the IMD consist of measurement of velocity at low heights (about 10m). There is a need to build observation towers and utilise existing tall towers, e.g., T.V. Towers, P&T Microwave and AIR towers, chimneys and buildings to obtain variations in wind along height, in various parts of the country. Four places namely, Madras, Balasore, New Delhi and Varabal were identified for intensive observation on various parameters of wind in the Ist phase of establishing observation stations. A small committee may be appointed to prepare a detailed plan for these stations taking into account, the existing facilities there, with I.M.D. as Convenor, and scientists from SERC Madras, Institute of Science, Bangalore and University of Roorkee as members.

The committee is confident that installation of Wind measuring Instruments in the TV towers will not vitiate the performance of the towers.

3. One of the most important parameters to be observed is the variation of wind with time on a continuously recording system. The instruments presently available are not suited to measure the extreme wind speed and acceleration, which materially affect the behaviour of the engineering structures. It is, therefore, recommended that suitable instruments be developed for the purpose. The broad specifications have been indicated by the committee. (Reference Annexure A_5 – Wind Data). The proposed instruments should be operative up to an altitude of 150m and wind velocity up to 300 kmph with wide range of recording frequencies. The Institute of Science, Bangalore and and University of Roorkee have acquired expertise in developing and

testing equipment of the type indicated above.

After the instruments have been developed, arrangements need be made to manufacture a good number of such instruments and install them at the predetermined locations. The routine maintenance, operation and data collection should be the responsibility of the IMD which is already maintaining a network of wind observing stations in the country for weather prediction purposes. However, the analysis of wind data collected at the above specified network of stations and their conversion to usable design information will primarily be carried out by the research workers of the institutions where research on the effect of wind forces on structures in being undertaken.

4. Since the ISI code on Wind forces is based on limited data, there is a need to collect more data and also organise research for determining wind coefficients for different kinds of engineering structures. The committee recommends that the ISI may update the present code as indicated by the above work from time to time. The Committee notes that ISI has taken up work in this direction.

5. In order to give adequate encouragement to research in the area of Wind Engineering, the wind tunnel facilities, namely, at the I.I.Sc. Bangalore and the University of Roorkee be augmented to provide for adequate range of wind speeds and instrumentation in order that the various types of Civil Engineering Structures can be tested. The wind tunnel project of IIT, Kanpur may be continued. Further, since it is expected that there will be a considerable demand on such facilities in future, the facilities provided should be well distributed from the regional point of view, and thus the setting up of a new wind tunnel facility at the I.I.T. Kharagpur is also recommended. Each of the organisations may submit projects and estimates for the consideration of the DST.

The Committee noted the on-going project of SERC, Madras on constructing a wind tunnel for cyclonic study. The Committee hopes that the funds required for it will be provided by the CSIR and has made no provision in the estimate submitted as part of this report.

As regards developing the right type of instruments for the wind tunnel the Committee recommended to import initially one or two suitable instruments from abroad and thereafter develop them in the country.

The Committee also felt that in the area of Wind Engineering, particularly as regards the wind tunnel design and instrumentation, much richer experience is available in countries such as USA, Canada,

Australia and Japan and interaction of the Indian Researchers with them can be most fruitful. It would be useful to send a small team of research workers to the above countries to study this type of research on Engineering Structures in that country to take advantage of the experience already gained by them.

6. In addition to the facilities mentioned in (5) above the Committee considered the necessity of creating a large scale multi-purpose facility for testing of Civil Engineering Structures on a large enough scale to model the Reynold number values that occur in the field, and for tests on Aircrafts or Atmospheric flight vehicles. The cost of setting up such a facility is estimated to be Rs. 10 crores and it is recommended that the DST may introduce the outlay of these funds in its future plans. For the present, it is necessary to concentrate on smaller tunnels to develop expertise and solve usual problems.

7. A standing committee may be appointed by the DST to plan and evaluate research projects on Wind Engineering and monitor the projects from time to time.

The composition of the Committee may be as follows:

1. An eminent engineer/scientist (Chairman)
2. Representative of IMD, ISI, NTPC, NBO and CPWD
3. Representatives of I & B, Education, Science and Technology
4. Representatives of University of Roorkee, IISc., Bangalore, IIT., Kharagpur and SERC., Madras.

The committee may set up a small committee to prepare specifications of the observation tower along with equipment required as a complete plan as mentioned in para 2 earlier.

Also in cases of wide-spread failure due to a wind storm, or, the failure of an important installation, a systematic study be carried out by a team of experts formed by the committee.

8. Damage documentation should be taken up on a comprehensive basis.

Based on work done in regard to common man's dwellings, the SERC Madras, may take up the task of preparing a monograph laying down specifications for the safe design of such dwellings.

IMD and SERC may arrange publication of relevant wind data of selected stations from different parts of the country every 3 months.

9. The actual requirements of funds will be known when different organisations submit detailed estimates for their part of work,

but approximate projections are indicated below for a 5 year period 1983-88:

Items			*Rupees in lakhs*
1.	Development and acquisition of instruments and sensors		25
2.	(a)	Strengthening of existing wind tunnel facilities at Bangalore, Roorkee and Kanpur	60
	(b)	Installation of a new wind tunnel at I.I.T., Kharagpur	40
3.	Cost of towers, instruments and their installation and maintenance		65
4.	Specific Research Projects		50
5.	Co-ordination activity		15
	Total for 5 Years		Rs. 255 lakhs

CHAIRMAN INDEX OF COMMITTEES & COMMISSIONS IN INDIA 1947-80 Volumes 1 to 18

APPENDIX

CONTENTS SURVEY OF COMMITTEES & COMMISSIONS IN INDIA 1947-80

Volumes 1 to 18

Bombay Jayanti Janata Express Train and a Tourist Bus No. 1755 at Unmanned Level Crossing at Km. 80/12-13 Between Alwaye and Angamali Stations of Southern Railway on May 9, 1979, v17B:p341

Accident Investigation Report on Derailment of 3 PN UP (Pathankot-Nagrota) Passenger Train at Km. 37/5-6 Between Talara and Jawanwala Shahr Stations on Pathankot Joginder Nagar Narrow Gauge Section in Firozepur Division of Northern Railway at About 20.30 Hours on May 12, 1979, v17B:p346

Accident Investigation Report on Collision of K 121 UP Howrah-Kharagpur Local with the Rear of 3 UP Howrah-Madras Mail at Km. 25/25-27 on the UP Line Between Bauria and Chengail Stations on Howrah-Kharagpur Electrified Triple Line Section in Kharagpur Division of South Eastern Railway at 21-04 Hours on May 18, 1979, v17B:p353

Accident Investigation Report on the Derailment of 26 Down Passenger Train at Km 146/3-5 at New Bongaigaon Station on Bongaigaon-Alipurduar Jn. M.G. Section of Alipurduar Division of Northeast Frontier Railway of About 05.45 Hours on June 11, 1979, v17B:p431

Accident Investigation Report on the Rear-End Collision Between No. 1 Down Bombay-Howrah Mail and No. Y-10 Down Goods Train at Km-806/4-5 Between Borkhedi and Butibori Stations on Wardha-Nagpur B-G Section of Central Railway on August 4, 1979 v17B:p516

Accident Investigation Report on Collision Between 34 Down Jammu Tawi Mail and Light Engine at Diwana Station on Northern Railway on August 15, 1979, v17B:p521

Accident Investigation Report on Collision Between No. 374 UP Delhi-Palwal Shuttle Train and UP Bajwa Special Goods Train at Faridabad Station of Central Railway on 5th October, 1979, v17B:p530

Accident Investigation Report on the Rear-End Collision Between Electric Multiple Unit Train No. E-65 and No. E-67 on the Down Suburban Line at Madras Egmore Station on Madras Beach-Tambaram Suburban Metre Gauge Section of Southern Railway on 26th October, 1979, v17B:p537

Accident Investigation Report on the Rear-End Collision Between C-35 and T-81 Down Suburban Local Train on the Down Suburban Line Between Matunga and Sion Stations on Bombay V.T. — Kalyan Electrified Section of Central Railway on November 14, 1979, v17B:p556

Accident Investigation Report on Collision of 26 Down Gauhati — Dhubri Passenger Train with 1 Down Avadh — Trihut Mail at Km 87/11-12 Between Pathshala and Sorupeta Stations on Bongaigaon — Changsari CTC Metre Gauge Section in Alipurduar Division of N.F. Railway on 23rd December, 1979, v17B:p582

Accident Investigation Report on Accident to 11 Down Barak Valley Express Train at Km 51.863 Between Dihakho and Mupa Stations on Lumding-Badarpur Single Line Metre Gauge Section in Lumding Division of Northeast Frontier Railway at 0.5.05 Hours on 20th March, 1980, v18A:p21

Accident Investigation Report on Occurrence of Casualties to 352 Down Gua-Kharagpur Passenger Train at Km. 264/4-8 Between Sini and Gomharria Stations on the Double Line Electrified Chakradharpur-Tatanagar Section in the Chakradharpur Division of S.E. Railway at About 17.25 Hours on April 13, 1980, v18A:p55

Accident Investigation Report on Derailment of No. 156 up Villupuram-Katpadi Passenger Train at Km 52/0-2 Between Tandarai and Velanandal Stations on the Villupuram-Katpadi Metre Gauge Single Line Section of Tiruchchirapalli Division

February 8, 1977, v15A:p23
Accident Investigation Report on Derailment of 104 Down Kathgodam-Bareilly Passenger in the Catch Siding at Haldwani Station of Izatnagar Division of North Eastern, Railway at About 05.12 Hours on 7th February, 1977, v15A:p32
Accident Investigation Report on Derailment of 387 Down Bhusawal-Allahabad Passenger Train at Majhgawan Station on Satna-Manikpur Section of Central Railway at 11.58 Hours on February 17, 1977, v15A:p52
Accident Investigation Report on Collision of BPQD Goods Train with the Rear of No. 76 UP Waltair-Kazipet Passenger Train on the UP Main Line of Kesamudram Station on Vijayawada-Kazipet BG Double Line Section of South Central Railway at About 22.10 Hours on 25th March 1977, v15A:p57
Accident Investigation Report on Collision of Motor Car No. USR 9063 and Passenger Train No. 131 UPA 'B' Class Level Crossing on the Lalkua Jn.-Kashipur Jn. Section of the Izzatnagar Division of North-Eastern Railway at 18.45 Hours on March 28, 1977, v15A:p63
Accident Investigation Report on the Derailment of No. 28 UP Mangalore-Madras West Coast Express Train at Sevur Station on the Jolarpettai-Madras Broad Gauge Double Line Section of Southern Railway at About 12.50 Hours on March 30, 1977, v15A:p67
Accident Investigation Report on Derailment of 367 UP Sealdah-Lalgola Passenger Train at Km. 52/27-53/11, In Madanpur Station, In Sealdah Division of Eastern Railway at About 13.26 Hours on April 20, 1977, v15A:p83
Accident Investigation Report on the Collision of No. 20 UP 'Trivandrum Central Madras/Central Mail' Train with Two Coupled Light Engines at Km. 117/4-5 in Tiruvalam Station Yard on the Jolarpettai-Madras Double Line Broad Gauge Section of Southern Railway at About 04.07 Hours on May 27, 1977, v15A:p169
Accident Investigation Report on Derailment of 2 DSU Passenger Train at Modinagar Station of Delhi Division of Northern Railway on 4th August, 1977, v15B:p715
Accident Investigation Report on Collision Between 103 UP Howrah-Amritsar Deluxe Express Train and UP CPC Special Goods Train at Naini Station on Allahabad Division of Northern Railway at 00.15 Hrs. on October 10, 1977, v15C:p785
Accident Investigation Report on Derailment of No. 107 Down 'Madras-Rameswaram Passenger' Train Between Paramakkudi and Pandikanmoi Stations on the Manamadurai-Rameswaram Single Metre Gauge Section of Southern Railway About 08.15 Hours on October 17, 1977, v15C:p838
Accident Investigation Report on the Collision of No. 385 Down Bhusaval-Nagpur Passenger Train with Coupled Light Engines of No. D-30 UP Goods Train on the Down Main Line of Akola Stations on the Bhusaval-Badnera Double Line Broad Gauge Section of Central Railway at About 22.15 Hours on November 9, 1977, v15C:p916
Accident Investigation Report on Derailment of No. 2 Down Ahmedabad-Delhi Mail at Km. 18/6.2 Between Ajarka and Bawal Stations on the Bandikui-Rewari Single Line Metre Gauge Section of Western Railway at About 05.18 Hours on November 23, 1977, v15D:p1200
Accident Investigation Report on Derailment of 662 Up Mixed Train between Sillipur and Birpur Stations on Sheopur Kalan Gwalior Narrow Gauge Section of Jhansi Division on Central Railway on 9th March, Railway, 1974, v12:p119
Accident Investigation Report on the Fire on 311 UP Sealdah-Samastipur Fast Passenger Between Rampur Dumra and Hatidih Link Cabin on Danapur Division of Eastern